How to Motivate Your Students to Love Learning

Steve M. Potter

Skaludy SP Press

Copyright ©2020 by Steve M. Potter

Design, photos, text, figures and editing by Steve M. Potter, except as noted. All rights reserved. Copying, digitizing, transmission or reproduction of any part of this publication, except brief quotations, are allowed only by written permission from the publisher.

Please send correspondence, typos, reports of piracy, and suggestions for the next edition to Skaludy Press: Motivate2LoveLearning@gmail.com. Web links mentioned in this book are listed at https://steveMpotter.tech.

ISBN: 978-1-8381728-0-0

Library of Congress Control Number: 2020917575

Version 1.1 11:32:39 AM Monday, December 14, 2020
Word count: 92,183

To the memory of Jerry Pine,
who taught me many valuable lessons
and devoted his life to improving teaching.

TABLE OF CONTENTS

List of Figures vii
Glossary ix
Part I: My Unconventional Background 1
   1. This Book is a Memoir and a How-To 3
   2. Why I Left Academia 9
   3. Courses I Taught 15
   4. Lessons I Learned 27
Part II: The Neurobiology of Learning 59
   5. Humans are Learning Machines 61
   6. What Motivates Students? 67
Part III: The Learning of Neurobiology 109
   7. Engaging Lectures 111
   8. Creative Extra Credit 141
   9. Clear Rules 149
   10. Wikipedia Writing and Other Authentic Projects 155
Part IV: More Real-World Teaching and Learning 175
   11. Lab Class Without a Cookbook 177
   12. Problem-Based Learning 193
Part V: Feedback for Continual Improvement 201
   13. Too much effort? 203
   14. How to Get Feedback 205
Part VI: Where Education is Headed 219
   15. Rants and Suggestions for Change 221
   16. Hope: Alternative Approaches to Teaching 231
   17. Conclusion 241
Things I Did Differently Than Most Professors 243
Take-home Messages 247
Epilogue 249
Recommended Reading, Watching and Listening 251
Acknowledgments 255
Index 259

LIST OF FIGURES

Figure 1. Ant-proof candy dish at the Atlanta Maker Faire 13
Figure 2. Neuroengineering is not hard to define................................19
Figure 3. Problem-Based Learning room 21
Figure 4. BME Gordon Prize winners 23
Figure 5. Mahogany bookcase I made in 8th grade............................31
Figure 6. Cassette rack from wood shop class 32
Figure 7. Circuit diagram for the Drop Saver 45
Figure 8. VW Baja bug and Rav4, set up for carrying hang gliders 50
Figure 9. Young Steven asking lots of questions 52
Figure 10. Prof. Scott E. Fraser and Prof. Jerome Pine 53
Figure 11. Fraser Lab 2-photon microscope 55
Figure 12. Custom multiphoton microscope at Georgia Tech 56
Figure 13. Yerkes-Dodson Curve...71
Figure 14. A learning curve 73
Figure 15. Robotron: 2084 video game 81
Figure 16. Hang gliding in California..83
Figure 17. Shallow and steep learning curves 88
Figure 18. Example of a mind map 105
Figure 19. Georgia Tech students walking for extra credit...............147
Figure 20. Two deaf people conversing 182
Figure 21. Students in Neuroengineering Fundamentals lab class 190
Figure 22. Problem-Based Learning rubric 197
Figure 23. Peer evaluation forms...212
Figure 24. Project-Based Learning works for oldsters, too 237
Figure 25. Potter Lab research group 257

Glossary

Active learning: Learn by doing something constructive, as opposed to passively sitting and listening to the instructor. Usually involves physical movement.

Agency: Refers to being in control and able to effect change — a bit more general than "Voice and Choice."

Axons: The long tendrils branching out of the cell body (soma) of a neuron. These are usually the output side of the brain cell, and carry electrical impulses from the soma to the synapse, where neurotransmitters are released onto the next neuron, a gland, or a muscle.

Cortex: The wrinkled outer part of the brain, which serves many functions including sensing, motor (movement), higher-level processing, and memory storage. Adj., *cortical;* pl., *cortices*.

Differentiated learning: Giving each student a learning experience tailored to their inclinations, abilities, level, and personality.

Dopaminergic reward system: Parts of the brain that either secrete or are responsive to the neurotransmitter, dopamine. Increases in dopamine secretion signal the expectation of a rewarding experience, while decreases happen when an expected reward fails to happen. These induce learning that reinforces rewarding behaviors.

Executive functions: the brain's capabilities relating to holding information in working memory, and using it to accomplish goal-driven behavior. These cognitive functions include planning, inhibition of inappropriate actions, and focusing of attention.

Extrinsic rewards: Tangible rewards, such as money, good grades, trophies or gold stars, given by teachers, parents and supervisors to motivate specific accomplishments or desired behaviors. Research has shown that these can be addictive and are subject to habituation, that is, larger and larger extrinsic rewards are needed to produce the same level of motivation.

Flipped classroom: A teaching format in which the students watch recorded lectures at home, and carry out homework-style lessons in class, while the teacher roves the classroom and gives individual attention to each student.

Interoception: Sensory input about one's own body state. This includes information about body position and movement, and "gut feelings" from the digestive tract or other internal organs.

Intrinsic rewards/motivation: Intangible benefits and positive feelings derived from certain behaviors or accomplishments thanks to the individual's own sense of purpose or interests. Built-in (intrinsic) psychological mechanisms automatically activate reward circuitry in the brain, reinforcing behaviors that are intrinsically rewarding.

Glossary

Learning Curve: A graph of performance on a task to be learned as a function of time (or trials). A "steep learning curve" means that the material was learned quickly. Something difficult to learn would gradually approach the top right of the graph with a long, shallow slope (see p. 88).

Maker Movement: Starting around 2005, makers of all types began to meet in makerspaces where they could share tools, experience, and ideas to work on self-directed projects. These often involve STEAM topics: Science, Technology, Engineering, Art, and Math. Makers also began to organize Maker Faires where they show off their work and attendees can participate in making and learning activities of all sorts.

Makerspace: A shared workshop with equipment and supplies for individuals, small groups or startup companies to build projects. Makerspace equipment typically includes laser cutters, 3D printers, sewing machines, soldering and electronics, and computers. It may also include woodworking, metalworking, casting and molding, or other specialized tools that would otherwise not be accessible to hobbyists. Many libraries and schools have recently set up makerspaces.

Mastery: To be really, really good at something, an aspirational goal of learning. This process usually takes many years, so the popular use of "mastery" in educational literature refers to attaining an *adequate level* of performance, after which a student may progress to the next learning task.

Meta-skills: Learning goals that are above and beyond the specific subject matter of a traditional class. These might include (among other things) social skills, self-control, attention control, communication skills, brainstorming, and critical thinking. Progressive teachers explicitly include meta-skills-building lessons in their curricula. The prefix "meta-" implies something that is a level more abstract or above the thing being discussed. Meta-skills are sometimes called "soft skills" in the teaching literature. I object to the term "non-cognitive skills" that is sometimes used in this context; these skills require cognition to learn and to practice.

MPLSM: Multiphoton laser-scanning microscope, a type of microscope that uses pulsed infrared light to image living specimens with 2-photon excited fluorescence. It was originally called TPLSM, or just 'two-photon microscopy' until researchers began to use more powerful lasers needed to get 3-photon excited fluorescence.

Neuron: One of the two main types of brain cells (the other type is the glia or glial cells). Neurons send electrical impulses down their axons that can be recorded with electrodes, such as micro-electrode arrays (MEAs) or electroencephalograms (EEGs). They also synthesize and release neurotransmitters and are connected to each other via synapses. Adj., neural.

Neurotransmitter: A chemical produced by brain cells (neurons) that is released at the synapse to cause a rapid change in a target cell, which may be another neuron, a glial cell, gland, or muscle. A neuromodulator is a similar chemical released by neurons, but usually has more diffuse and slower effects than a neurotransmitter, and may be transmitted via the bloodstream or by spreading through the extracellular fluid.

Glossary

Noradrenergic system: Cells in the nervous system that release and respond to the neurotransmitter norepinephrine (called noradrenalin outside the US). This neurotransmitter tends to be used under conditions of high excitement or peril, and aids in memory retention, sometimes causing post-traumatic stress disorder.

Opiate system: A set of peptide neuromodulators (called endorphins) and receptors that when activated, induce feelings of calm, analgesia or euphoria. Morphine, heroin and related drugs act on this system.

Parasympathetic Nervous System: The neural and hormone systems in the brain and body that evolved in all mammals to take care of many involuntary and housekeeping functions when the animal (or person) is at rest.

PBL: Originally, *Problem-Based Learning*, in which students work over days or weeks in small groups to "solve" open-ended problems set by the instructor. Inquiry is self-directed, with instructors serving as facilitators only, coaching on meta-skills. The abbreviation PBL has more recently come to stand for *Project-Based Learning*, which is much more varied and real-world oriented. Since I talk quite a bit about both of these approaches in this book, I will spell them out to avoid confusion. The history of the original PBL is described well on Wikipedia, https://en.wikipedia.org/wiki/Problem-based_learning as is the new PBL, https://en.wikipedia.org/wiki/Project-based_learning. (Web links mentioned in this book are hyperlinked for your convenience at https://steveMpotter.tech.)

Plasticity: The brain's ability to be molded by experience. All learning is thanks to the plasticity mechanisms of the nervous system.

PTSD: Post-Traumatic Stress Disorder. Psychological problems such as depression and chronic anxiety result from bad memories that got reinforced by being replayed too many times, due to the influence of the noradrenergic system in the brain.

Real World: The messy, exciting and uncontrolled place outside the classroom. I will capitalize it as a noun, and hyphenate it when used as an adjective, meaning, "related to the Real World." Real-world learning experiences are sometimes referred to by others as "authentic" but I feel this term is too vague or ambiguous.

Rubric: A detailed set of objective and specific criteria used in the grading of an assignment.

Scaffolding: Teaching students some crucial background information that they will need in order to be successful at doing a project (Noun, or gerund. Verb: to scaffold). The scaffolding may also take the form of readings or other media the teacher provides or points them to.

STEM: Curricula focusing on Science, Technology, Engineering and Math. Sometimes includes Art: STEAM, a very popular term at Maker Faires, which attract artistic makers and fans of steampunk aesthetics (a mix of futuristic sci-fi and Victorian industrial).

Stub: A very brief and incomplete Wikipedia article, usually marked with a request to expand the topic.

Glossary

Sympathetic Nervous System: A large set of neural and hormone circuits throughout the brain and body that evolved to help animals deal with potentially deadly situations by springing into quick action. Although it is often called the "fight or flight" system, the sympathetic nervous system is also activated by positive situations that are perceived as exciting, such as mating opportunities. In the modern world, the sympathetic nervous system may also be activated by scary but non-deadly situations, such as having to speak in public, or by chronic stress.

Synapse: The place where one neuron communicates with the next cell down the line, by releasing neurotransmitters. These are detected by receptors that cause a physiological change in the receiving cell. Each neuron usually has hundreds or thousands of synapses.

TA: A teaching assistant. In the context of a university, this is usually a PhD (grad) student who helps run a course for a professor.

Three Rs: An informal nickname for "Reading, Writing, and Arithmetic," the basics traditionally taught in grade school.

Toy project or problem: A project or problem assigned by the instructor with a clearly defined end-point and no effect on the Real World. These tend to be put on the shelf and forgotten once the semester is over, but sometimes can be useful (see p.198).

Unschooling: A style of home-schooling in which children choose their own learning activities and projects and learn through free-form play.

Voice and choice: Refers to letting students make key decisions in their learning process. Related to Agency.

Part I

My Unconventional Background

This is not your typical dry book about education science, but a personal narrative mixed with plenty of practical advice for teachers. In this first Part, you will come to know me and my unconventional teaching trajectory. I will briefly summarize the structure of the book, the courses I taught, and the main points of the book as a prelude of what is to come in the subsequent Parts. I will highlight aspects of my life that shaped my thinking and the way I teach. I will reveal how I came to appreciate hands-on experiences and Project-Based Learning in the Real World as being the most motivating and useful approaches to teaching and learning.

Chapter 1

This Book is a Memoir and a How-To

I believe that any student who is sufficiently motivated will love learning and consequently, will learn to excel. Many of the problems and difficulties that instructors of all types face are related to motivation, or a lack of it. I am a neuroscientist who has been teaching since 1986. I will use both my understanding of the brain and my teaching experience to unpack the complexities of motivation as they relate to teaching and learning. I tried many things to encourage my students to love learning, and some of them eventually became remarkably successful, as you will see from my students' comments included in this book.

This book is half memoir and half how-to. My personal stories will reveal how I developed my ideas about teaching and learning. Throughout the book, I will span levels from the philosophical, down to the nuts and bolts — how motivation works in the brain and how to implement highly motivating learning experiences in your classroom. I will reveal all of my "secrets" that powerfully motivated my students, hopefully in ways that will allow you to apply them incrementally to your teaching, and in ways that you and the administrators are comfortable with.

Whether in traditional schools, in experimental schools, or with homeschooling, quite a few teachers are trying out new ideas about how to teach, what to teach, and even why to teach. If you are one of those, or would like to become one, then you will find this book useful. Parents and school administrators may also find this book useful in pointing the way to advocate for changes in the way teaching is done in their schools.

I will relate how I came to realize that **real-world projects are the most effective teaching and learning experiences**. They are highly motivating because they create excitement and a love of learning in students. Although my teaching was at the university level, most of my approaches are relevant and applicable to learners of *all* ages, and can be put into practice by instructors of all types. Students of all ages love to come up with projects they care about, and that make a difference. When such projects are included as part of our regular school curriculum, students become motivated to dive into learning with great enthusiasm. Most importantly, they will be much better prepared to be effective, valuable, and motivated citizens of our rapidly changing world.

Fixing what's wrong with schooling does not have to occur by disruptive revolutions. You do not need to throw out everything you know about teaching and start with something completely unfamiliar and uncomfortable. I continually added to my toolbox of unconventional approaches to teaching, while making small tweaks to standard practices that ended up having a large payback in terms of motivating my students to love learning. I advocate an evolutionary, rather than revolutionary, approach to improving teaching methods.

It may be clear to those of you who took the standard path to becoming a teacher (getting an advanced degree and credentials in teaching) that I did not get the proper training. I will reveal my ignorance of certain pedagogical terminology or approaches that you will have learned in your teacher training. I am not a scientist who studies education, and will not present any statistics or controlled experiments about the approaches I am suggesting. I hope you will forgive me.

I have always been a rebel, forging my own path through life, often with little regard to what was expected from someone in my situation. I entered teaching "through the back door," kind of like I did with engineering: I was a professor in the Coulter Department of Biomedical Engineering (BME) at the Georgia Institute of Technology (Georgia Tech) and Emory University[1] for 13 years, yet I studied neither teaching nor engineering for my college degrees. I learned teaching and engineering *by doing*, while getting my undergraduate BA degree in biochemistry (University of California, San Diego 1987) and PhD in neurobiology (University of California, Irvine 1993). In many ways, I am a living example of the usefulness of Project-Based Learning. I am a champion for, and product of, unconventional interdisciplinary learning approaches.

---

1. My department is shared between these two Atlanta universities. My research lab and most of my teaching were at Georgia Tech, though I had many collaborators at Emory University.

Rather than thinking of my lack of teaching credentials as limiting, I think of it as liberating. My thought process was perhaps less constrained than most well-trained teachers. Like Gumby's train, I laid my tracks as I went along.[2] My unconventional teaching path led me eventually to win the top teaching award at the Georgia Institute of Technology[3] and then the top teaching award across all research universities in the University System of Georgia.[4]

It is important to realize that my evolutionary process of improving my teaching involved repeated trial and error. Hoping to spare you some of that pain, I will describe a few of my failures that I re-cast as learning experiences. One of the most important pieces of advice that I will keep repeating is to **solicit feedback continually about how things are going and continually try new things.** Experimentation is a way of life for me. If you really take that on board, you too are bound to succeed at motivating your students to love learning.

My scientific research career was dedicated to understanding how learning, memory, and information processing occur in living networks of brain cells.[5] Because of my love of brains and obsessive dedication to uncovering some of their mechanisms, I may have gained some new insights about learning processes in human brains. That said, my research approach was to use simple model systems (Petri dishes of rat brain cells instrumented with electrode arrays) that were probably not capable of much of the learning or cognition that we associate with human brains. Most of the useful insights about brains and learning that I mention in this book came from teaching neurobiology and neuroengineering courses to college students for many years.

Although this book is a how-to book for instructors, it is written as a collection of essays and personal experiences. These serve to illuminate my teaching principles and where they came from. I will describe my experiences in a framework that emphasizes what I think is **the single most important idea for successful learning: motivation**.

---

2. In case you are not familiar with Gumby and his train, see https://youtu.be/Qs7fpgq6LUY. Https://steveMpotter.tech has a table of the hyperlinks mentioned in this book. Bookmark it to avoid having to type URLs.
3. 2011 W. Howard Ector Outstanding Teacher Award.
4. 2013 Felton Jenkins, Jr. Hall of Fame Regents' Award of Excellence in Teaching, https://www.usg.edu/faculty_affairs/awards/2013_fiscal_year_regents_award_recipients
5. For those who are interested in the idea of connecting brains to computers, you can read about my research on my lab's web pages. All of our publications are available for downloading there. http://potterlab.gatech.edu

I am not only referring to students' motivation, but teachers' as well. Unmotivated students tend to sap motivation from their teachers. As with their students, when teachers can reframe their own shortcomings and failures in the classroom as learning experiences, it can be a powerful tool for improvement of teaching and learning. By implementing the ideas that I used to enhance my students' motivation, your motivation to be a transformative teacher will increase, too. Consequently, I predict that your students will notice your increased enthusiasm and become more enthusiastic, highly motivated learners.

If you are afraid it takes too much time or effort to improve your teaching, don't think of it as something extra, but a new way to do what you are already doing. You can spend less time drilling for tests, grading worksheets, or other old-school onerous tasks that don't contribute much to student motivation. Because you will be highly motivated and excited about new approaches to teaching, any extra effort will seem like fun.

The Structure and Formatting of This Book

After reading **Part I**, which provides key background for understanding the rest of the book, feel free to use the **Table of Contents** to jump around to the parts of this book that most interest you. There is a **Glossary** at the front that defines terminology that may be unfamiliar. Some passages are presented in shaded boxes. These are the sorts of things that might be relegated to an appendix of a technical book. They contain details that may be skipped or scrutinized, as desired. At the end, I have a list of **Recommended Reading, Watching, and Listening** resources that I have curated as being especially helpful for developing into a better teacher. The end also has my **Acknowledgments** and an **Index**. I use footnotes to call your attention to related information; I feel these interfere less with the flow of reading than flipping back and forth to endnotes. I put article and book titles *in italics* so they stand out, and article titles will also be in "*quotation marks*."

The rest of **Part I** explains more about my background and how this book came to be written. I briefly introduce three courses I taught, which will be described in detail in later chapters.

I let my students themselves make many of my important points. Throughout the book, I include their quotations. I put their words in italics, indented and with `"quotation marks"` to make it clear they are direct quotations, not paraphrasing or recollections. I selected these quotations from among many similar ones in my students' course evaluations and spontaneous written communications. They highlight aspects of my teaching that were successful and, in some cases, big failures. Anything in **boldface** is my own emphasis to draw your attention to important points or glossary entries. Since I was busy running my research lab while teaching, I did not have a chance to carry out proper scientific or statistical analyses regarding the outcomes of my teaching methods. However, I did collect an unusual amount of useful student feedback (see Chapter 14), so I rely on their written words to convince you that my approaches are worth trying.

In Part II, The Neurobiology of Learning, I connect my understanding of how the brain works with what I observed in my classes, in terms of learning and motivation. I mention six aspects of human psychology that I believe are most important for teachers to keep in mind if they wish to enhance motivation in their students.

Part III, The Learning of Neurobiology, details how I managed to create an engaging neurobiology lecture course by making lectures very discussion-oriented, and by incorporating real-world projects into the curriculum.

My other two classes are detailed in **Part IV, More Real-World Teaching and Learning.** There, I explain how creating a lab class that was more like a real research lab was highly motivating to students. I compare Project-Based Learning with Problem-Based Learning, as it was taught to first-year biomedical engineering majors at Georgia Tech.

Part V, Feedback for Continual Improvement, describes how I kept improving both my teaching, *and* the students' learning, by getting and responding to student feedback.

In **Part VI, Where Education is Headed,** I reiterate things that I feel need to change about education in the US (and elsewhere) and describe a few efforts and resources by other progressive teachers whose approaches align with the things I have said here. They provide abundant proof that schooling at all ages and in all contexts can be much better than it generally is now.

Chapter 2

Why I Left Academia[6]

At the end of 2015, I closed my lab, became an adjunct professor in BME, and essentially quit my dream job. It's true: I dreamed of being a scientist since age 5. I loved my colleagues at Georgia Tech. My department was ranked in the top three biomedical engineering programs in the country for several years by *US News and World Report*, eventually reaching #1 while I was there. My research was going very well and my lab's papers are cited by over 6,000 other peer-reviewed papers.[7]

You might well ask, "If you were so successful with teaching and research, why did you leave Georgia Tech?" The short answer is that I found myself being a manager running a small "startup" of about a dozen people, and I was not doing what I really love. I love inventing and making things, coding software, soldering electronics, aligning laser beams, and doing experiments. I love working with my hands. I did all those things for 8 years as a postdoc at the California Institute of Technology (Caltech) in Pasadena, California, the city where I grew up.

But soon after I moved to Atlanta and began as a professor at Georgia Tech in 2002,[8] I found I no longer had time for any of that. It was my grad

---

6. *Spoiler alert:* Not because I was burned out by teaching. I LOVE teaching.
7. Google Scholar's list of citations: https://scholar.google.com/citations?user=LrbKjQMAAAAJ&hl
8. My research lab was one of 7 professors' labs in the *Laboratory for Neuroengineering* at Georgia Tech, an unusually supportive and collaborative research environment. See http://neuro.gatech.edu

students who were in the lab doing the fun stuff, while I was stuck in my office writing grants and scientific papers, and attending too many committee meetings.

I took a sabbatical to explore the **Maker Movement** (defined in the next section) in 2014. My Maker Sabbatical was so exciting that I extended it another year. I went to Maker Faires, and toured and worked in **makerspaces** in Seattle, the San Francisco Bay Area, and all across Ireland. By the end of those two years, it was clear to me that I would be happier doing more making and less managing.

I loved the teaching part of being a professor, but it did consume a good fraction of my time and energy, and it was not something the university valued; most of the incentives at research universities like Georgia Tech are pushing professors to get more papers published and to win more grant money, not to become great teachers. "Publish or perish" still rules the day in academia. Professors are only expected to do the minimum amount of teaching necessary.

Although I had tenure, an NIH R01 research grant with over $1M left to spend, and a very good salary, I could not see a way out of the managing and grant-writing rat race if I stayed. So, after much soul-searching, I closed my lab and moved with my wife to Ireland (where she is from and which I had come to love) and became a freelancer. Now I lead a much more relaxed and enjoyable life, not managing anyone. I finally have time to write books! I stay involved with my scientific interests by consulting for AI companies and advising movie directors. I spend time doing my favorite thing — making. This includes woodworking, CAD (computer-aided design) and CAM (computer-aided manufacturing), electronics, programming, writing maker how-to guides, and leading maker workshops. I absolutely love hands-on teaching and learning, and I plan to keep doing it until I die.

Once I had committed to my decision to leave the Ivory Tower and become my own boss, a number of my colleagues admitted to me that they wished they could do the same. I think they could, but such a career change takes a leap of faith that things will work out, and causes much disruption. I don't recommend it for everyone. Spreading the process across my two-year sabbatical got my colleagues, grad students, and myself used to the idea that I was closing my lab and leaving them and academia.

The Maker Movement

Since this book is about motivation, I would like to share more about the Maker Movement, why I am so excited about it, and why every teacher should be as well.

2. Why I Left Academia

Although human beings have always been makers, the Maker Movement officially began in 2005, when Dale Dougherty created *Make:* magazine and organized the first *Maker Faire* in San Mateo, California. The idea was to highlight all the creative making going on at what he calls the "World's largest show-and-tell." Since then, Maker Faires have taken place at more and more places across the globe and attendance has grown exponentially. Also growing rapidly are the number and diversity of **makerspaces**, places where makers congregate to DIT (do-it-together, as opposed to DIY or do-it-yourself).

Because schools have been pressured to focus on standardized testing and college preparation since the inception of the No Child Left Behind (NCLB) Act of 2001, and because of growing liability concerns, they largely closed up their shop classes. I feel this is a terrible shame. Maker Movement to the rescue! The great majority of making exhibited at the Maker Faires took place outside of a school. There have always been creative and inventive individuals with workshops at home in their basements, studios, and garages. But in the last decade or so, there has been a boom in the creation of shared makerspaces, where those creative minds can come together and make stuff. Makers may work as a group on a big project. Or they may work as a team of one, but never alone in a makerspace. They benefit by pooling their resources to get and use equipment that most individuals could not afford. They boost their creativity and learning by sharing ideas with each other. Frequent informal instruction goes on between makers in makerspaces. Most makerspaces also hold more organized workshops for novices to learn new techniques, such as soldering, 3D printing, computer-aided design, woodworking, metalworking, fabrics and textiles, paper crafts, ceramics, computer and microprocessor programming, and many other things.

MIT professor Neil Gershenfeld also deserves credit for getting the Maker Movement rolling as far back as the late 90s, by creating the idea of a FabLab, a standardized makerspace that could be replicated and adapted to locations all over the world, including in impoverished or underdeveloped countries. FabLabs grew out of, and were refined by, his popular engineering class, "How to Make (almost) Anything." [9]

What I noticed at the makerspaces I visited and the Maker Faires I attended during my Maker Sabbatical was how much more excited and enthusiastic the school-age makers were in that context than they were in school. The good news is that the popularity of makerspaces has caused a

---

9. I highly recommend Neil Gershenfeld's seminal maker book, *Fab: The Coming Revolution on Your Desktop–from Personal Computers to Personal Fabrication* (2005) Basic Books.

rebirth of shop class, often in the school library, where students can once again work on extended projects building things of their own design.

Georgia Tech has a fantastic makerspace called the **Invention Studio**[10] that is completely run by the students. Any student who wants to learn how to use the Invention Studio's large collection of expensive equipment can visit and make whatever they want. One student became famous when he gave a graduation address[11] mentioning another student who was building his own Iron Man suit in the Invention Studio, repeating the catchphrase, "At Georgia Tech, you can DO that!"

The whole Invention Studio itself runs like a well-oiled machine, thanks to a set of rules and etiquette the students have developed and thanks to all the peer-to-peer instruction they carry out.[12] The students have won a tremendous amount of corporate support to buy the large and expensive making machines, because the sponsors know that graduates who have made things will be much more useful than those who just kept their noses in the textbooks. High-tech companies recruit heavily from those who use the Invention Studio. More and more of them expect to see a job-seeking graduate's portfolio of things they have made, in addition to their transcript and résumé.

Makerspaces, whether in schools, universities, or in random warehouse spaces or libraries around town, are highly motivating for young people because they allow them to transform their ideas into actual things they can be proud of. Makers learn specific skills related to the things they make, such as how to use a laser cutter, or how to wire up an Arduino-controlled robot. They are also learning **meta-skills,** such as how to take an idea from concept to design, how to work in groups, how to plan and complete a complex project, how to iterate and improve a design, how to source supplies, how to ask for help, how to deal with failure, and how to present their work to others. These are all things that are valued in the workplace.

Maker Faires

If you want to get ideas for how to transform your teaching in ways that will engage and motivate your students, go to a Maker Faire! There is probably one near you. At Maker Faires, there are few rules and creativity abounds. It is a giant show-and-tell, with robots, drones flying around, BIG metal sculptures shooting flames, steampunk costumes, 3D printers, art activity booths,

---

10. https://inventionstudio.gatech.edu/
11. https://youtu.be/U_U4BBjC8tk
12. Here is a detailed description by Craig Forest et al., *"The Invention Studio: A University Maker Space and Culture,"* (summer 2014) Adv. Eng. Education, v.4 n2 ASEE, https://eric.ed.gov/?id=EJ1076126

soldering and knitting classes, weird bicycles, human-powered carnival rides and concerts, and makers of all ages, genders, colors and types.

In 2012, the Atlanta Maker Faire took place on the Georgia Tech campus. I had a booth where I presented a computer keyboard I had made out of wood, with Scrabble tiles as the keys.[13] I also showed off another electronics/woodworking project of mine, the Magnetic Levitating Candy Dish. I had built that a couple years earlier as an ice-breaker for my office. It was a fun conversation starter, floating magically (magnetically) in mid air. When our building got an ant infestation, I discovered that my invention is completely ant-proof! Candy that I had stored in the cupboard was covered with ants. They had even found a way into my mini-fridge, but no ants could get to the sweets in my Levitating Candy Dish! (Fig. 1)

Figure 1. Ant-proof candy dish at the Atlanta Maker Faire, 2012. Photo by Máiréad Reid.

---

13. You can see a detailed Instructable of how I made it here: https://www.instructables.com/member/stevempotter/instructables/

I realized at the Maker Faire that these makers were My People. The excitement that I had found my tribe, and the enthusiasm I got from those who came by my booth, planted the idea in my head that I must take some time off and do a Maker Sabbatical. I wanted to learn more about this Maker Movement by immersing myself in it. Most universities have a sabbatical policy to refresh and de-stress their faculty every few years and allow them to do big projects in a new setting. Alas, Georgia Tech does not. Therefore, I just told my Department Chair I was going to take a year leave without pay for a Maker Sabbatical and that was that. He was very supportive, actually, and did pay me for part of Year 2 when I extended it.

Get yourself (and maybe your students!) to a Maker Faire and check it out. They often have a students-only day before they officially open to the general public. If you think that the subject you teach has nothing to do with making, think again. Making can be very broadly defined as creating something that wasn't there before. Although we think of making as being mostly the making of tangible things, the things could also be more intangible or ephemeral. Writing could be making a poem, book or blog. Choreography is making a dance. We make speeches, music, analogies. There is probably a good reason why "to make" and "to do" are both the same word in Spanish (*hacer*). To make things is what humans do. *Nosotros hacemos*. There are some truly amazing and creative ways teachers have incorporated making into their curriculum to help teach the required material, skills, and meta-skills. A good place to begin exploring the possibilities is at a Maker Faire.[14]

---

14. For a list of upcoming Maker Faires world-wide, see https://makerfaire.com/

CHAPTER 3

Courses I Taught

As a teaser, and to get you oriented to the scope of this book, I will briefly introduce three of the courses I taught at the Georgia Institute of Technology (Georgia Tech). Later in the book, I will explain in more detail the student-motivating features of these courses, including the most effective aspects of my unconventional real-world teaching style. Spoiler alert: real-world assignments and projects were more successful at making my students love learning than anything else I tried. Here and elsewhere, I will include comments my students made about my courses and me to suggest how they benefited or what they found motivating.

1. IntroNeuro

From 2005 to 2013, I taught Introduction to Neuroscience ("IntroNeuro" BMED/BIOL 4752) to Georgia Tech seniors majoring in Biomedical Engineering (BME) or Biology.[15] This became an increasingly popular elective course, with enrollment growing each year to over a hundred. In the end-of-semester online course surveys, anonymous students focused on these things as being important for their learning and enjoyment: my passion, caring, and fairness; how guest lecturers and I made the material interesting and

---

15. For the first couple of years, I co-taught it with my colleague and excellent mentor, Prof. Nael McCarty from Biology, who subsequently moved to Emory University.

relevant; and being challenged to think differently and invest in their own learning. These will be expanded in detail in subsequent chapters.

> *"This class was easily the best/my favorite in my time at Tech. Each lecture exposed the class to some interesting new idea about the brain, and I was constantly amazed by how complex — and how COOL — the human brain really is. All of the guest lecturers were fantastic. I expected at least a few to be boring or less animated, but they all offered an interesting perspective in an engaging form. Overall, a great course."* - anonymous IntroNeuro student

> *"I learned a lot more from this class than I thought was possible. Not only was the material presented in class very thorough, but a lot of the concepts we learned challenged the way I think about everyday things."* - anonymous IntroNeuro student

To gauge whether these positive experiences had lasting impact, I sent a survey to alumni several years after they graduated:

> *"BMED 4752 was my favorite class in my undergraduate education. The assignments were interesting, and I honestly looked forward to each and every class session. I appreciated all of the guest lecturers who talked about their areas of interest, as well as your lectures on neuroanatomy, neurology, and other concepts related to neuroscience....I remember the passion that you had for neuroscience, and the passion you had for getting us interested in the subject. It really carried through to the content of the course, and it made neuroscience more than something to learn for a grade. The way you taught that course, neuroscience became something worth learning about and investing in."* - alumna Audrey Southard

> *"Dr. Potter, my sole exposure to Neuroscience prior to graduate studies, was your course at Tech. The class sparked within me an interest in the field, which resulted in the research that I am currently a*

> part of today. Thank you for both your dedication and hard work." - alumnus Nishant Zachariah

To introduce you to my neuroscience course (detailed in **Part III**), here is my description from the IntroNeuro Syllabus:

> *Welcome to BMED/BIOL 4752, Introduction to Neuroscience! This course provides a broad overview of the field of neuroscience, and includes a number of Real World Assignments to get you involved and interested in your own personal way. Emphasis will be on in-class lectures; the textbook is not to be read in its entirety, but is to be used to reinforce and elaborate on things you learned in class. It is a very labor-intensive but really fun and rewarding class.*

In every way I could, I tried to tie the course to the **Real World** to grab the students' attention, ramp up their motivation to get involved in the course, and infect them with a lifelong interest in brains and the nervous system. One student wrote in an email to me after the semester,

> "...As time goes on, I love brains more and more and love learning about them. This course has made me want to change my goals significantly.... Now I'm in love with brains. I probably sound like a crazy person, but I seriously think about brains almost every second of the day." - Jessica Holcomb

A brains obsession is OK in my opinion! Unlike the objects of other more conventional obsessions, like pop stars or sports teams, brains are relevant to everything we do. It was not hard to connect my course's subject matter to the Real World. If you have a difficult time doing that with your course material, try harder! If you just can't, perhaps the topic is not actually useful or relevant once the course is over, and it is time to re-think the course. I will help you do that. I will give many examples of how I used real-world teaching and learning to motivate my students.

2. Neuroeng. Fun.

From 2004-2013 I taught a lab+lecture course, NeuroEngineering Fundamentals, abbreviated Neuroeng. Fun. (BMED 4400). As detailed in **Parts IV and V**, after a rocky start and many improvements based on student feedback, this course eventually became quite effective at getting students to work very hard and to learn much more than just neuroengineering:

> *"I LOVED this course. I will miss my weekly dose of neuroscience very much. Dr. Potter does a great job motivating students and testing us on what we learned." - anonymous NeuroEng. Fun. student*

What is Neuroengineering?

In case you are not familiar with the term, "neuroengineering" is anywhere that brains and technology meet.[16] Apparently, it is such a new field that Dictionary.com still (in 2020) thinks I was searching for "nonengineering" and the Oxford English Dictionary's only guess is "value engineering" (Fig. 2).

Neuroengineering has actually been around since prehistoric times. Stone-age people practiced trepanation, or grinding a hole in the skull to relieve intracranial pressure.[17] Ancient Egyptians used electric fish shock therapy to treat seizures and headaches.[18]

The phrase "neural engineering" is often considered as synonymous with "neuroengineering," but I only use the former when neural cells or brain tissue are being altered artificially, such as with genetic engineering.

---

16. See my TEDx talk in which I define and describe "neuroengineering" https://youtu.be/j4SSQcHt220
17. https://en.wikipedia.org/wiki/Trepanning
18. https://www.targethealth.com/post/pain-management-in-ancient-cultures

3. Courses I Taught

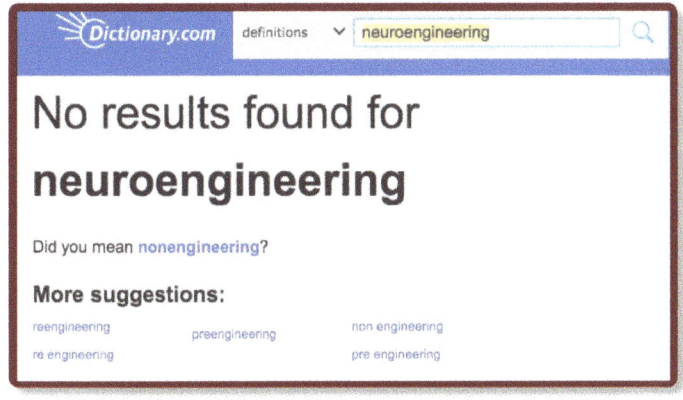
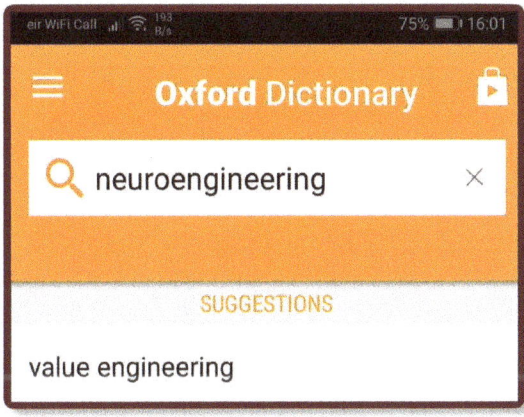

Figure 2. Neuroengineering is not hard to define. It is where technology meets brains.

This class was intended for Georgia Tech seniors majoring in Biomedical Engineering who had taken either my IntroNeuro class or another neurophysiology course.

Here is a brief introduction to this unusual course from my Neuroeng. Fun. syllabus:

> *This is a unique lab+lecture course that allows you to enhance your Problem-Based Learning skills by designing your own cutting-edge experiments with advanced ideas and equipment identical to those used in the Laboratory for Neuroengineering and elsewhere at Georgia Tech. The emphasis will be on teamwork, thinking, and self-directed inquiry. You will learn all about where brain tissue and technology meet. The course is*

designed to give you skills useful in the Real World, and it attempts to emulate the grad school experience.

Course Objectives:

- To become conversant in all of the fields where technology and neural tissue meet, in both clinical and basic-research settings.
- To hone self-directed inquiry skills through the design and execution of laboratory experiments.
- To build and work with actual neuroengineering research hardware and software.
- To learn to document lab work in an enduring, useful lab notebook.
- To learn to apply modeling and data analysis tools to real data obtained during lab.
- To hone group skills, working as small teams in and out of the lab.
- To learn practical neurophysiology.
- To develop an appreciation of neural dynamics, including sensory-motor integration and closed-loop feedback.

Note that many of these objectives are **meta-skills**, unrelated to the field of neuroengineering. I will detail this lab+lecture course and its motivating real-world aspects in Chapter 11.

3. Problem-Based Learning for BME first-years

Every year I was at Georgia Tech, I served as a Facilitator for the BME first-years' Problem-Based Learning class. While I was there, the course was referred to as "**PBL**." I will spell it out, to avoid confusion with Project-Based Learning. Each Facilitator (a professor or postdoc) was assigned two groups of 8 students. Each group met (with their Facilitators) for 90 minutes twice per week in a small room whose walls were made entirely of writable whiteboard.

3. Courses I Taught

Figure 3. Problem-Based Learning room at Georgia Tech. My Problem-Based Learning students are getting a lesson from their teammate. The Coulter Department of Biomedical Engineering at Georgia Tech has several of these dedicated Problem-Based Learning whiteboard rooms.

Students were given three 5-week problems per semester devised to be open-ended and difficult or impossible to "solve," such as "Research and propose a means to diagnose pancreatic cancer before it reaches Stage III." All the groups of Problem-Based Learning students (the entire incoming class of BME majors) tackled the same problem at the same time. In addition to the whiteboard room sessions, they met together in a big lecture hall one hour per week to hear a lecture about the problem topic from an invited expert, or about some crucial skill such as literature searching, from the course creator and administrator, Dr. Wendy Newstetter.[19]

One year early on there was an undergrad, John Brumfield, who had taken the initiative to get a research job in my lab, while at the same time taking the Problem-Based Learning class. As with all members of my research group, John attended and participated in our weekly lab meetings, and he became a valuable contributor to our research. Wendy related to me that he told her, "Dr. Potter runs his Problem-Based Learning sessions just like he runs his own weekly research group meetings." Apparently I had succeeded in recreating important aspects of working as a real-world research team in my Problem-Based Learning sessions.

In both contexts (the Problem-Based Learning whiteboard room and the lab conference room) I strived to make sure that everyone in the room paid

---

19. Wendy is the Director of Educational Research and Innovation for the College of Engineering. Dr. Barbara Fasse later was instrumental in helping to run the Problem-Based Learning courses along with Wendy. Barbara was Director of Learning Sciences Innovation and Research for BME. Our department had great forethought to hire these education science experts to set up and run problem-directed learning courses for undergrads.

attention and got involved. I helped the group answer the question, "Why are we doing this?" by calling their attention to important context. I helped them decide how to divide up and delegate tasks. I taught them to research the literature and to be skeptical scientists. I encouraged them to present all findings to the group, whether they be successful or seemingly "failures," so that all could learn. And through honest and constructive discussions, I helped them learn how best to work together as a team.

I was very fortunate to work in a supportive environment for innovation in teaching. My input was always welcomed by Wendy (and later, Dr. Barbara Fasse) to improve Problem-Based Learning, based on my facilitating experiences, and related experiences managing my research lab of about a dozen people. BME's trend-setting real-world teaching approaches won our department the Regents' Award for Excellence in Teaching in 2013,[20] a Georgia-wide competition. What's more, Wendy, and two other designers of our undergraduate program, Profs. Joe Le Doux and Paul Benkeser won the 2019 Gordon Prize for Innovation in Technology Education (Fig. 4).[21] Because of our ground-breaking approaches to teaching, the Georgia Tech/Emory BME department repeatedly ranked in the top three biomedical engineering undergrad programs at *US News & World Report*.[22] It was not always so rosy, though. I will detail the pluses and minuses of our Problem-Based Learning course in Chapter 12.

---

20. https://www.usg.edu/faculty_affairs/awards/ 2013_fiscal_year_regents_award_recipients
21. Here is an overview of my BME department's education innovations, including success stories from two alumni: https://www.youtube.com/watch?v=N8Fb3R90938
22. https://www.usnews.com/best-colleges/rankings/ engineering-doctorate-biological-biomedical

3. Courses I Taught

Figure 4. BME Gordon Prize winners. Founding Georgia Tech/Emory BME faculty members Paul Benkeser, Wendy Newstetter, and Joe Le Doux were awarded the 2019 Gordon Prize for Innovation in Technology Education from the National Academy of Engineering. The Gordon Prize medal comes with $500,000, "For fusing problem-driven engineering education with learning science principles to create a pioneering program that develops leaders in biomedical engineering." Screenshot from a video of the award ceremony by the NAE.

Overarching Theme: Real-World Curricula

You may not be particularly interested in the subject matter of my courses. They are not really important for the main points of this book. What are important are the meta-skills that can be learned by highly motivated students in any well-designed course. I chose to include many details about my courses in this book because they provide specific examples where I saw many highly motivated students exceed my, and their, expectations about what can be accomplished in one semester.

An alumnus said about my IntroNeuro course,

> *"The focus of the course is less on raw memorization of neuroscience principles and instead uses the*

23

> *general concept of neuroscience as a theme to engage students in 'real world' activities. The purpose of said real world assignments is to introduce students to the type of responsibilities they may be facing in the future. The real world assignment aspect of the course was one of the most valuable collections of activities I completed as an undergrad to prepare me for life as a graduate student." - alumnus Mike Weiler*

My guiding principle in developing my courses was always, **"Make it as real as possible."** I will give many specific examples of *how* I did that. But it is important to start out with *"Why?"* What is it about my real-world curricula that motivated my students and made them love learning?

Curricula that incorporate aspects of the Real World...

- prepare students for being active contributors in their jobs and to society after they graduate.
- give them **meta-skills**, such as inquiry, manners, writing, oral communication, skepticism, and many others.
- boost their confidence.
- ignite and maintain interest in the material.
- help make associations to aid memory retention.
- answer the question, "Why bother learning this?"
- improve the world with a permanent trace of their efforts.
- give them pride in what they accomplished.
- teach them what real research is like. (For my courses, that was scientific and engineering research.)
- provide intrinsic motivation.

I had long pondered the shortcomings of my own schooling. I sought to fix some of those problems by doing teaching differently than my less effective teachers did. I also took inspiration from the few good teachers and mentors I had, who gave me real-world experiences that have proven to be highly valuable to me throughout life. I will describe those in some detail. For better or worse, I never took any classes, courses or degrees in teaching, pedagogy, didactic theory, or education.[23] As with many other aspects of my life, I tended to ignore what my peers were doing and forged ahead with implementing my own ideas. Specifically, I strived to incorporate more of the Real World into my courses. I was very lucky to have a permissive environment at Georgia Tech (and Emory University, with which my Biomedical Engineering department is shared), and supportive Department Chairs. They allowed me to try out many unconventional things both in my research lab and in my classes.

I hope my unconventional trajectory as a teacher gives this book a fresh perspective, compared to other books on teaching and learning. Certainly, most of the practices I encourage are not yet mainstream, and will need more positive examples to become widely adopted. (I hope you will help with that!) Judging from other related books I have read, I think you will find this book to be more readable, with fewer specialized educational buzzwords and less jargon (I included a Glossary at the front, just in case). I will describe many specific, practical examples worth trying, in order to motivate your students.

There is clearly a wave of dissatisfaction breaking across the United States with how teaching is done at all levels. In K-12 schools, there is increasing damage and frustration being caused by standardized testing. The frustration of having to "teach to the test" is driving many instructors to try new approaches and revive old ones that may work better. I am sure we have hit upon some of the very same ideas independently. I will provide pointers to a few similar advances by others that I am aware of near the end of the book in **Chapter 16. Hope: Alternative Approaches to Teaching.**

Many (but not all) aspects of my real-world curriculum could be called Project-Based Learning. I am glad to see more and more examples of students taking on projects as part of their schooling, under the supervision of progressive teachers. I specifically promote projects that are not **toy projects**. Toy projects are safely sealed within the classroom walls. Toy projects, when finished, get put on the shelf or thrown away by the teacher or the student, and soon are forgotten. Students may have a hard time seeing the point of such a

---

23. Except for one quarter-long course I had to take to become an undergrad chemistry Teaching Assistant in 1986 at UCSD. This course merely focused on the nuts and bolts of our responsibilities as TAs, not how to teach. I am sad to admit that as a busy professor getting my research lab set up at Georgia Tech in 2002, I did not have time to read the helpful teaching guides I had received during the part of the New Faculty Orientation presented by Georgia Tech's *Center for Enhancement of Teaching and Learning* (CETL). Later on, when I was more deeply involved in teaching, I greatly benefited from CETL, and also gave CETL workshops about the material in this book, to my fellow faculty.

project. Although any project may be more fun than rote learning or a boring lecture, in my experience, toy projects are much less motivating than real-world projects. **When a project the student has helped to develop somehow improves the Real World, and leaves enduring public traces, it becomes the most powerful motivator I have seen.**

It is possible for Project-Based Learning to be a disaster. As one teacher I spoke with said to me, "If you think projects can be used to teach, I would like you to come to my classroom and show me how, because I just don't think most of my students could handle it. They don't have the attention span. Most are not smart enough." This teacher clearly does not share my growth mindset, that every student can excel with the right motivation. But she probably has a good point about attention spans. To stay focused and on-task is a key skill that many youngsters are lacking. They have been trained by TV, and by games and social media on their smartphones, laptops and tablets, to live a multi-tasking existence, continually interrupted by the next incoming distraction.

There are a number of reasons to be skeptical of Project-Based Learning. It can be organized poorly. Projects can be boring. They may not actually teach students anything. Unmotivated people on a project team may not pull their load. Projects can be rushed. Students may not have learned the needed background and may feel lost. Students may not be given the resources they need to do the project. Teachers may not give enough ongoing support to students, whether it is educational or emotional. Too many student-based decisions may make a poor project, just because of students' lack of experience. Students may get frustrated by failure.

These are all very valid concerns. I think they can all be addressed by designing the curriculum with care and, most importantly, by constantly monitoring how things are going by being observant and soliciting feedback, and constantly adjusting things as needed. **Part V** is dedicated to this approach.

As you read on, you will encounter many of my students' *and* my own projects and real-world activities, and what I learned from them.

Chapter 4

Lessons I Learned:

Experiences That Shaped My Approaches to Teaching

Art For Learning Creativity and Open-mindedness

Starting with crayon scribbling and finger painting, small children are all artists. I was very lucky that my mother (Mary Spears) was an artist who constantly encouraged my siblings and me to exercise our creative muscles. While we and other kids were doing fewer and fewer art projects in school as we got older, my siblings and I were doing all sorts of them at home. During my formative years (about age 4-10), Mom would bring home stuff to make candles one day, and then plaster casts another. We did macramé with string and weaving with yarn, pyrography with a wood burner. We made beautiful flowers by dipping wire shapes we made into clear colored liquid that dries into a transparent membrane. We made all sorts of Christmas decorations. We sandwiched autumn leaves in between wax paper and ironed them flat. And of course, we often did coloring, drawing and painting. Mom is to thank for my love of bright colors, and the colors I chose for this book.

I never became very good at any one artistic skill, but all this variety mixed with Mom's approach of giving practical advice by demonstration and encouragement, developed my meta-artistic skills. We learned how to think creatively, how to take risks, and how to refine something iteratively.

I picked up practical skills from both successes and failures, like how not to burn yourself while melting wax or soldering, and how not to cut your hand open while carving a block print. (I still have the scar to remind me to always cut away from my body parts.) We learned how to sketch, how to mix colors. Most of all, Mom taught us that any creative expression was OK. Artists can be as creative as they want. The creativity she had us practice came in handy with many other projects that may not have been considered art.

As a child, my sister Crista was the most entrepreneurial of Potter kids, selling elaborate papier mâché creations and books of drawings to family and friends. I still have a comic book I commissioned for her to draw for me at age 10, *Monster Comics*. We continued to make art as adults. Crista now makes a living selling her art, including useful and beautiful things she fashions out of driftwood.[24]

I included art in my scientific career. When I moved to Atlanta in 2002, we had recently established the field of *Embodied Cultured Networks* in my lab. We were the first ones ever to use a living network of brain cells in a Petri dish to control a robot.[25] I was approached by artists at the University of Western Australia to do an art-science collaboration. Most beginning scientists would regard getting involved in art as career suicide — I jumped at the chance. Our art-science projects with Guy Ben-Ary and Phil Gamblen at SymbioticA turned out to be among the most fruitful things my lab ever did. I participated in our art-science collaboration from a Big Picture perspective, cheering on my artist collaborators and grad students, and giving occasional aesthetic, scientific and philosophical input. We had living **neurons** in our lab remotely controlling a robotic arm that drew abstract renditions of gallery visitors, in *MEART, the Semi-Living Artist.*[26] My postdoc Tom DeMarse, and grad students Doug Bakkum and Riley Zeller-Townson, got to travel the world helping to set up the hybrid robot at various galleries and museums.

The second generation of MEART, called *Silent Barrage,* had a room full of drawing robots that the audience interacted with as they walked through

---

24. See Crista Smyth's driftwood handrails, drawer pulls and sculptures at http://NaturesHand.us/, and digital art at https://fineartamerica.com/profiles/crista-smyth.
25. Potter, S. M. (2002). "*Hybrots: Hybrid systems of cultured neurons+robots, for studying dynamic computation and learning,*" Simulation of Adaptive Behavior 7: Motor Control in Humans and Robots—On the interplay of real brains and artificial devices, Edinburgh, Scotland.
26. MEART stands for Multi-Electrode Array Art. The exhibit toured the globe, and was often featured in the media, including this documentary about our art-science project: https://www.artfilms.com.au/item/meart-the-semi-living

the exhibit. Viewers' movements would cause electrical stimuli to be delivered to the living neuronal network in my lab, which then triggered more robot movements. *Silent Barrage* was even more successful than *MEART* at inspiring many lay people to think deeply about neurobiology, the inevitable merging of brains and machines, and what is the minimum neural wetware needed to be creative.[27]

Now, in my freelance Maker lifestyle, I am getting to use my creative skills a lot more than I could as a professor, doing projects and teaching hands-on workshops that combine woodworking, computer-aided design, electronics and coding (Fig. 24, p. 237).[28] I don't think any of the few art classes I had in school did much to give me the confidence and skills to do this. It was mostly thanks to my Mom and things I did outside of school, propelled by a kid's natural motivation to create. There were a few notable exceptions, useful projects I did in school, as recounted below. All that art-making gave me many useful manual skills. But it also helped me see the art in everything, and the power of art to draw attention to things and to tell stories. It taught me always **to appreciate and encourage the creative efforts of my students**, even if they were not doing art.

Functional Art Projects in School and Out

Many of my ideas about teaching were inspired by how bad my own schooling was. I feel my schooling failed me by not encouraging me to do more projects in school and to learn from them. I recall doing only a few long projects in my whole time (13+10 years) in school. Many were prescribed by the instructor (like all my lab classes' projects) in cookbook style. I had a bit of choice about some of them, within narrow constraints, like my written term papers. I got to design a few school projects, and I loved doing them.

In 12 years of grade school I only did one science fair project, even though I LOVED science. That 8th-grade project I chose because I had already done it and loved it: to make an electric motor out of paperclips and wire. I had made one with my Dad about five years earlier as a home hobby project, not at all related to school. I learned it so well then that I was able to do it again entirely from memory. However, there really was no science in the paperclip motor project. I did not do any experiments with it or try to convey the concepts involved. It was an engineering demo, really. I should have gotten a bad grade on the eighth grade science fair assignment, but the allure of something home-made that spins really fast must have hypnotized my teacher.

---

27. http://guybenary.com/work/silent-barrage/
28. https://steveMpotter.tech

Reflecting on this, I resolved that my students' projects had to educate, not just demonstrate.

I really enjoyed my shop classes. Most of my peers were afraid to set foot in a shop class because of the stigma associated with them — they were considered "remedial" classes that only poor students and delinquents took. I went out of my way to take them instead of the AP courses my teachers and counselors were pushing on me.[29] I took woodworking in eighth grade, and spent a long time making a curvy bookcase out of solid mahogany. I still use it, to remind me of some of the people who inspire me (Fig. 5).

In high school, I took woodworking again, and made a few things of my own choosing and design. One was a rack for my growing collection of New Wave cassette mix tapes (this was 1980, when synthesizers really hit the music scene). I was motivated by getting to make something I actually needed. I made the tape rack out of laminated layers of mahogany and alder (Fig. 6). My instructor could not understand why I wanted to make them diagonally laminated, but he trusted me and let me do it. I was not sure myself, I just knew it would come out looking better than if the layers were horizontal. The diagonal laminations added complexity to the building process, but I learned many new woodworking techniques along the way. For my own teaching, I try to follow my wood shop teacher's approach: I learned that it is a good idea to trust my students' creative ideas, even if I don't quite understand them.

I took a crafts class in high school, one of the few males who did. I learned to tool leather and to weave. I made a belt that held up my pants for many years. Our crafts teacher let us decide what type of projects we wanted to do, and gave us the tools, materials and basic instructions to get started. But mostly he left us to work on them at our own pace, developing self-discipline and planning meta-skills in the process. I loved it!

I took metals class in high school and again in grad school. I learned TIG (tungsten inert gas) welding in order to build a part I needed for my customized mountain bike. By making something I needed, I was much more motivated to learn TIG welding than if I were just instructed to do a few practice welds on scrap metal, and then move on to the next topic, as my other classmates did.

---

29. After burning up all my free time in tenth grade taking AP World History and preparing for a European History AP test, I quit taking AP tests. I decided it was a bad bargain: Study really, really hard for 4 years in high school to maybe get one year of college credit.

4. Lessons I Learned

Figure 5. Mahogany bookcase I made in 8th grade wood shop class, displaying some of my inspiring heroes.

MOTIVATING STUDENTS   I. My Unconventional Background

Figure 6. Cassette rack from wood shop class. I still enjoy listening to the mix tapes I keep in this rack that I made in the 10th grade.

I learned more by doing self-motivated projects outside of school. For example, I learned more welding when I visited my brother Scott's workshop. He is an expert self-taught welder who was making beautiful welded sculptures and artsy industrial lamps at that time. I had a specific project that needed doing: to build a hang glider rack for my new car. As a postdoc, I had finally bought a car that was not a jalopy, my beloved Toyota Rav4, for climbing up the mountains I flew off of.

We immediately voided the Rav4's warranty by cutting up the bumper and welding a custom rack to the car's frame (Fig. 8, p. 50). I learned from Scott all sorts of tricks we had not covered in metals class, such as how metal expands and contracts during welding and how to clamp it properly so it does not get distorted as it cools. Scott taught me the importance of practicing by welding something and then hammering it until it breaks, to understand which welds will be strong and which won't. This kind of "learning by destroying" is a technique I have used often in my maker projects at home and at work, as I mention about soldering in the **Student-designed Experiments** section of Chapter 11.

By breaking or wearing out many of Scott's drill bits, I learned how much tougher it is to work with stainless steel than regular steel, not to mention how much more expensive the stainless steel was! He warned me about these things when I told him I wanted the hang glider rack to be made of stainless steel. By actually doing the project, the differences in hardness and cost between stainless and regular steel were permanently etched into my memory.

The project was an intensive team effort over a long weekend in Scott's shop. I got help and ideas for both the mechanics and aesthetics, not only from my brother Scott, but also from my good friend and fellow hang glider pilot, Scott Eliason, and my Dad. I learned some things about leading a team and taking their ideas on board.

All my experience with art taught me that "art" projects can range from wacky to useful. But all of them helped train creativity, appreciation of aesthetics, refinement by iteration, domain-specific skills and meta-skills that have also been useful outside the art world.

My Introduction to Real-World Assignments

I had a teacher in 9th grade, Mr. Barnes, whom I thank for being perhaps my most influential K-12 teacher in my approach to teaching. He taught *Urban Studies*, which in anyone else's hands might have been a throw-away social science class. But for him, this class was about how to be a good and effective citizen in the world. He was the only teacher in my 4 years of high school who assigned real-world problems to his students.

One of these assignments was to visit a house that was for sale during its Open House, and with the realtor's blessing, draw its floor plan, and ask questions about it as if we were going to buy it. The realtors seemed to welcome this amusing diversion from the usual open-house visit, a chance for them to relax and reveal something about their trade to a curious teenager.

Another assignment was to interview an old person in our family. I learned all sorts of things about my grandmother Mamie's life and how things were in the early 1900s. But in those pre-web days, my recording and report were not shared with anyone but Mr. Barnes. My sister, Sandra Brown-Potter ("Ms. B-P"), had her 3rd-grade students interview older relatives about their immigrant experiences and post the interviews on the web. I love the fact that anyone can benefit from her students' work by visiting the Storycorps Archive.[30]

Mr. Barnes also had us interview a stranger about her or his job. It could not be a relative or friend. We had to choose someone whose role we respected. I decided to interview the head of the Pasadena Public Library. I recall writing a script on a piece of paper before making the call to ask for an interview. I was so nervous, I practiced it over and over. It turns out, Mr. Conover was totally cool and said he was happy to be interviewed. The interview happened in Mr. Conover's office and I learned all about how to run a library.

Mr. Barnes really pushed us out of our comfort zone with this assignment, but the experience gave me confidence. This came in handy in future years, with interviews and cold calls I would have to do. As you will read in Chapter 10, I tried to pass these communication meta-skills on to my students with a similar assignment.

Another very useful real-world assignment he gave us was to do comparison shopping for groceries at stores of three sizes. I chose a mom-and-pop store, a small grocery store, and a big supermarket. I went around the stores with my clipboard, writing down the prices and sizes of a set of common groceries. We learned about Unit Price Marketing tags that tell you how many cents per ounce each item is, and why buying big packages is usually cheaper in the long run. We learned how to fend off worried store managers who came around as soon as they saw a clipboard. We learned that prices are inversely proportional to store size and the underlying reasons having to do with economies of scale. We learned about sales, coupons, and other incentives. For two years (age 17-18), I worked as a grocery clerk in a

---

30. https://archive.storycorps.org/user/the-evergreen-school-3rd-grade-immigration-project/

big supermarket (see p. 36), and having done that assignment helped me in many ways.

My most important learning experiences with Mr. Barnes were not in his Urban Studies class, but thanks to his role as the Faculty Advisor of the John Muir High School Ski Club. My parents did not have money for any luxuries like skiing, so I got a job painting houses at age 15 (see below) and saved my summer earnings for ski trips in the winter. Mr. Barnes' relatives had a cabin in Big Bear in the San Bernardino Mountains outfitted with an array of bunk beds. About 30 students would go up there for two or three exciting weekends of skiing each year. I observed how deftly Mr. Barnes kept a mob of unruly teenagers under control by keeping us on a long leash. He was very clear and strict about certain rules ("No experimentation with drugs or sex") and otherwise let us do what we wanted.

The Southern California ski area by the cabin often did not have much snow. Afraid of damaging rented skis by skiing across bare patches, and eager to explore new terrain, I organized two ski trips to other areas that were colder and have more snowfall. The first was to Mammoth Mountain, a beautiful day's drive up the Owens Valley in California. The second was a week-long trip to four ski areas in Utah, by bus. Mr. Barnes trusted me to organize these ski trips with my club-mates, using his Big Bear ones as examples, and they went off fantastically, with no broken bones, unplanned pregnancies or drug overdoses.

I learned a lot about advertising, logistics, group dynamics, economies of scale, safety concerns, and how to orchestrate transportation and chaperones. I suspect most of these would make very dry topics in a classroom setting. But when they were learned in the context of making an exciting outing in the Real World possible, the learning was extremely effective.

Mr. Barnes taught me many meta-skills I still use today. I gained first-hand experience learning how motivating it can be to do useful things in the Real World. I tried to give my own students a variety of opportunities to experience that themselves.

Juvenile Delinquents are People Too

Why has work experience for adolescents become increasingly rare? My painting job at age 15 was educational in a way that is hard to pull off in a classroom setting. Since the law at the time said that most places could not hire anyone until they were 16, I failed to get my desired summer job after tenth grade, which would have been to work in a record store. I learned that there was a loophole for 15-year-olds. I could apply for a job working for the City of Pasadena: a program to fix up houses of elderly and disabled people with free yard work and new exterior paint. I did not realize until after the interview that this was a program to keep juvenile delinquents off the streets. I thought something was odd during the interview when the man who would soon be my boss asked if I could read. Although I had not had any run-ins with the law, and had no experience painting houses, for some reason I got the job.

When I met my crew later that week, I found I would be working with four guys whom you normally would not want to meet in a dark alley. Turns out, we all became great friends and I learned that even juvenile delinquents are real people with many good qualities.

I learned to paint by just diving in and doing it. My crew chief, Edwin, gave me some instructions, but mostly I watched what the others were doing and asked many dumb questions. At the end of each day, Edwin would patiently point out all the places I had missed or painted poorly, teaching me the importance of attention to detail.

Although my crew-mate Raymond was a dangerous looking boxer, he was actually a sweet and friendly guy. He was illiterate. I realized this one day when I found a book discarded in the weeds, *Everything You Ever Wanted to Know About Sex But Were Afraid to Ask.* Raymond often told us stories about his sexual exploits, so as a joke, I said, "Here is the book for you!" and handed it to him. He said, "What does it say?" He could not read a word. In that awkward moment, I learned why, when we finished fixing up one house, he was always driven by the boss to the next job site, while the others on our crew were given an address on a slip of paper and expected to find our own way there. "Adult literacy" was not in my vocabulary. Until then, I had never considered the ways an illiterate young man would be disadvantaged by that.

By making friends with a crew of juvenile delinquents, I gained more appreciation that my poor upbringing was not *that* poor, and my dysfunctional family was not *that* dysfunctional. Mostly, I learned to look for the good in every person. I did not often interact with criminals and thugs in school. I had tried to avoid delinquents, who would whip me with wet towels in the locker room. After that job, I could understand them better and deal with their teasing. I grew up a lot that summer, thanks to Edwin, Dwayne, Raymond, and Manuel.

This job gave me some meta-skills that later helped me get into the mindset of students of mine who were struggling due to their unfortunate life situations. Edwin taught me how to give my students constructive, iterative feedback to help them continually improve.

Learning to be Extroverted

My high school had a "work-study" program for seniors. If we had fulfilled all our required courses, instead of taking electives, we could take a part-time job in the Real World. I think this is a great idea. A real paying job is

4. Lessons I Learned

much more beneficial and rewarding than a short-term internship or throwaway elective classes.

Beginning in the summer after my junior year, I worked as a clerk at a large supermarket, Vons. I stayed on during my senior year as a work-study student, biking home from school around noon. It was a very busy store, so we were never bored. I enjoyed bagging groceries much more than I expected, kind of like an extended game of Tetris.

I was a very introverted child. I spent most of my free time alone, doing my own thing with electronics, chemicals or model airplanes. I really grew in my social skills working in a supermarket. Vons had a policy that all clerks must greet each customer and thank them, so I had to stretch way out of my comfort zone and be very social to hundreds of people a day. I carried out groceries and loaded them into people's cars while trying to make conversation. I collected shopping carts. I cleaned up messes, rushing to the scene of an accident with the mop whenever the call went out, "CLEAN-UP ON AISLE 3!"

I got to know all the regular customers and began to see the value of small talk. I learned how to turn around bad customer experiences into good ones. We had a very challenging customer whom we called The Scarf Lady because she had about 10 scarves tying up her hair (and wore at least three dresses on top of each other). When she arrived in the store carrying her two old suitcases, other clerks made themselves scarce. But when she was checking out, I dutifully stepped up and packed her goods into her suitcases, always trying to see if I could remember and follow her complex set of rules, such as what could touch what, and which direction the cans must face. If I got it wrong, she did not hesitate to yell at me. I think she appreciated my efforts, and I succeeded in not getting balled out a couple of times. Learning to appease odd characters was a skill I have used many times later in life.

Because our store was the busiest Vons around, we served as the training center for new employees. After working there for a year, I was chosen to be a clerk trainer. Training complete newbies was good experience for me as it forced me to verbalize many of the skills and tricks that I had acquired randomly or by watching others. It also helped teach me to put myself in my former shoes and those of my trainee, trying to recall what were the most difficult aspects of the job when I was just beginning. Years later as a teacher, this experience would help me empathize with my students.

In addition to learning the grown-up skills of getting to work on time and generally being responsible, I also learned how to save money. Once I had a real job at Vons, I seemed to be making huge amounts of money, compared to my $1 per week allowance. I saved most of my earnings for the winter ski trips. Saving for something I loved was a great motivator to do well at my job and to keep getting assigned more work hours. I continued to work at Vons for a year after high school. (I delayed going to college for a year.) Some of my earnings got used in the arcade with my friends, and also for buying electronics supplies for the synthesizer I was soldering together.

In the middle of my last year of high school, Dad decided to quit his job at NASA's Jet Propulsion Laboratory (JPL) and become a roving nomad on his own, living out of his Ford Country Squire station wagon in Mexico and along the California coast. He was upset about all the military projects JPL had become involved in. For example, under the guise of exploring the surface of Venus with side-looking radar, they were developing the next generation of cruise missiles, which depend on the same technology. For a few months after Dad quit his JPL job in preparation for his vagabond phase, I was also buying food for him, myself and my brother. Working in the supermarket, I knew which were the cheapest foods to buy. When Dad left and we moved in with Mom, she kept us fed so I was able to save more.

From my supermarket job, I learned many things. Most importantly, I realized that being social is a learnable skill. If one of my students was not born an extrovert, I let them know that I was once very introverted and that by practicing social skills, speaking up can become habitual and even comfortable.

Computer Programming Applied to Projects

My undergrad university is where the programming language *UCSD Pascal* was created by one of my professors, Ken Bowles. My first-year roommate, nicknamed "Zucke," took Pascal Programming (EECS61) a semester before I did. He warned me, "Bowles will expect you to spend 10 hours of lab time per week for this class! It's brutal." It turns out my lab partner, John Caratti, and I loved programming so much we basically *lived* in the EECS computer lab. We became what was known at UCSD as "EECS Geeks." We spent every free moment there, adding to the cacophony of the clicky keyboards of rows and rows of IBM-AT computers. That ended up being WAY more than 10 hours a week embellishing our class projects and writing extra silly code we didn't need to do. We got intoxicated by the power of writing our own software to make computers do our bidding. My Pascal programming experience came in handy later in grad school, where I programmed the Macs in our lab to analyze data and to study model neural networks. (The Macintosh operating system was originally written in Pascal.)

Why was I so motivated, while my roommate absolutely hated the class and programming? I saw computers and programming as incredibly empowering. Zucke told me he saw them as a ball and chain. His father was a computer professional and had put pressure on his son to become a computer professional and work at his firm. It was clear to me (and Zucke) that this was not his calling. Zucke was fantastic at understanding people's motives and was always thinking deeper and more philosophically about things than most people around him. He probably would have made a great therapist or philosopher. He was also quite a singer, songwriter, and guitarist.

But he had a rough time in college. All that pressure on him to succeed in his first computer course and to fulfill his father's dream was too much. When he got to the topic of *recursion* in the course and didn't understand it, he had a nervous breakdown. Recursion nearly killed him. He jumped out of our suite's second-story window. He survived with a broken ankle, but had to quit college and recuperate not only from the broken ankle but from a deep depression. He was eventually diagnosed with manic depression, now called bipolar disease, and responded well to medication.

Thus, some pressure can be motivating, but too much pressure, combined with some self-destructive beliefs that one is destined for failure, can be devastating.[31] Having my curiosity encouraged by my parents and teachers was crucial in providing me with a view on recursion that was 180 degrees from Zucke's: recursion is a fantastic gem in the coding world, a deep concept[32] that excited and motivated me to work on my recursive programs into the wee hours.

In contrast to Zucke's father, my own father never put any pressure on me to do or be anything. He just inspired me by example and never tired of my questions (Fig. 9, p. 52). He was doing computer programming to design and model antennas since the 1950s for the Jet Propulsion Laboratory in Pasadena. When I was really small, Dad often brought home a Teletype, which he used for programming JPL's mainframe computers via its acoustic modem. When he wasn't around, my sister and I amused ourselves making modem-like noises and whistling into its microphone to see what nonsense it would type.

Dad did very high-level antenna engineering and simulations, so I had no clue about what he was programming at the time.[33] But I sensed the awesome power at his disposal as he went through roll after roll of thermal paper, conversing with huge machines across town at JPL.

---

31. The good news is that Zucke eventually got a degree (in Communication) and became a successful and happy insurance agent. The sad news is that he died unexpectedly from an aneurysm in his early 40s, leaving behind his beloved wife, daughter, and many friends.
32. Recursion is when a subroutine calls itself. Sounds simple, but the results can be amazingly complex.
33. My father (Philip D. Potter) designed the antennas on the first US satellite, the *Explorer I*, the *Voyager* spacecraft, and key parts of the *Deep Space Network* antennas NASA still uses to track all interplanetary spacecraft. See: https://en.wikipedia.org/wiki/Horn_antenna. He died at age 87 in 2019.

I got another small glimpse of what computers could do in 1974, when I was 9. He bought the first programmable pocket calculator (the HP-65) for about $500 (nearly $3000 in 2020 dollars). He used it, among other things, to calculate what angle to aim a solar panel he was inventing, an idealistic scheme that never came to fruition because my parents broke up about that time.

Neither Mom nor Dad ever imposed their dreams on us. With my laissez-faire parents, I learned to be self-motivated early on, and came up with my own goals.

I continue to love and practice programming to this day. Lately, it has mostly been for Arduino microprocessors that control my hobby projects.[34] But all the programming languages I have learned since Pascal share a common core principle: Break up complex tasks into subroutines. Prof. Bowles used to say, "If your program does not fit on one screen, it is time to break it down into separate procedures." Bowles' rule also got recursively applied to procedures themselves. This lesson is useful for everyone, especially students faced with a seemingly impossible project. I coach them on how to begin to break a complex task down into manageable pieces until that process becomes natural to them.

Programming in the Real World

I gravitated toward using computers in a real-world context. In high school, my calculus and physics teacher, Dr. Duncan, had a computer room where geeks were welcome to hang out as much as they wished. Although I did not yet know how to code, I enjoyed hanging out there with my friend, John LeMoncheck. He made the computer talk and coded up a perfect emulation of one of our favorite video games, Q-bert, complete with funny Q-bert-speak. Dr. Duncan also let us play with his physics equipment — lasers, gyroscopes, Van de Graaff generators, etc. — before school and at lunch. From Dr. Duncan, I learned the value of giving students knowledge, tools and gadgets and then stepping back to see what they will create.

John got an Apple II computer that he programmed in BASIC. I was soldering together my own analog synthesizer at that time. I recall one day when he showed me how to make a tone of any frequency with a certain command, I asked if one could use the computer keyboard to play music. "Sure! Let's do it!" he replied. I watched John quickly turn his computer into a digital synthesizer. Not only was he a genius programmer, he was also quite a

---

34. For example, see this device I made to monitor our heating oil level: https://bit.ly/2ZIglzW

musician, and was playing the latest Tears for Fears song on his Apple II in just a few minutes.

During my second year in college, I used a friend's Mac to design my résumé using every possible font. In 1985, when the first Macintosh had recently come out, using different typefaces was not common and really surprised people who saw my résumé. I wanted a laboratory summer job at Caltech, but got a programming job instead, somehow. I had taken one class of programming (Pascal, as described above) but had also learned BASIC on my own with my tiny TRS-80 computer, a gift from my Dad. I had programmed the TRS-80 not just to play music, but to compose original tunes, making good use of the RND() function. They weren't great.

I worked for Prof. John D. Roberts in the Chemistry Department at Caltech that summer. He was a friendly and low-key boss whom I only met weekly to show him what I was up to and get my next tasks. I worked by myself in his small computer room. I learned Fortran to debug a huge program his son had created to calculate the molecular orbitals of organic molecules. I learned serial communications in order to get his computers all talking to each other via their serial ports, and to hook up a digitizing tablet to an HP-9000 workstation. Hardware like that drawing tablet did not come with drivers back then, just a paper manual with a list of ASCII commands you could use in your own custom home-made software, to control it and to collect data from it.

On the beloved HP-9000, I wrote a software package to draw molecules in 3D and plot them on a pen plotter. I learned 3D graphics and user interface design, all by just doing it, with little or no supervision or advice from anyone. I just consulted software manuals and books when I needed help. There was no Google I could search for help in 1985. I learned responsibility and self-sufficiency and the power of intrinsic motivation. I would often bring home manuals to read until bedtime and zip off to work on my bike as soon as I woke up, excited about another day of solving real-world problems by coding.

I was strongly motivated because I was not doing some toy problem in a programming class, I was writing code that my professor actually needed for his research, and that he would use long after I had gone back to UCSD to continue my undergraduate "education." Prof. Roberts really let me manage myself in his lab, just suggesting various assignments I might work on, and pointing me in the right direction when I needed help. One of these assignments was to write an article for a trade magazine about Kermit, a serial communications program I had used often as I got all his computers connected to each other.[35] That was my first official publication.

---

35. There was no Wifi or even ethernet back then — it was all done through the RS232 serial port with AT commands.

From my summer working at Caltech, I learned how motivating it can be to work toward a difficult goal that will benefit the Real World. I reinforced my appreciation of Bowles' Rule, as I kept breaking my tasks down into easily doable chunks.

Becoming a Scientist

The following summer, after my third year in college as a biochemistry major, I tried harder to find a job doing laboratory work. I was determined to be a scientist! I got a job working for Kelco R&D, a division of Merck, Sharp & Dohme. They make all the gums and thickeners you see in ingredient labels: Xanthan gum, Gellan gum, carrageenan, etc. I worked as a physical chemist, measuring the viscosities and physical properties of mixtures of gooey and gelatinous compounds. Years later, I noticed that one of the novel gum blends I characterized and wrote a report on for Kelco was used in jalapeño flavored Tabasco sauce, so my research was not for nothing!

I made the boring physical chemistry research interesting by adding computers. At that job I learned about spreadsheets (Lotus 1-2-3), to tabulate all my viscosity data. I realized that a spreadsheet could be used as a programming language — not merely a place to type in columns of numbers, but to transform them with formulas. When I created a spreadsheet that calculated the linear least-squares fit to my data, and drew a plot of it, my coworkers acted as if I had used magic. Their approach was to hand-draw a graph and use a ruler to eyeball a line that seemed to fit the data.

The company was all about polysaccharides; their thickeners are long molecules related to sugar and carbs. I realized that the program I had written for Prof. Roberts the previous summer at Caltech could also be used to plot 3D models of their polysaccharides. I ported my code to one of Kelco's computers and taught them how to use it so they could visualize the chemicals they were trying to improve. I used it to draw 3D renderings of several of their top-selling polysaccharides on the pen plotter. This got the attention of my boss, and the next time the CEO was in town, he brought him by for a demo.

Getting a visit from the CEO of this huge company to look at my program in action was highly motivating, as you can imagine. I was delighted to create 3D molecular models of Kelco's gums, especially because it meant I would not be spending as much time doing the extremely boring work of watching a viscometer spin in a beaker of gum and taking down measurements for hours. My computer-generated polysaccharide drawings ended up on the cover of Kelco's Annual Report that year. Talk about real-world impact! Contrast that with all the effort I put into my cookbook programming projects in EECS61, which got used for nothing other than to get me a grade.

This was my first and only lab job in Industry. I decided working in industry was not for me. I learned that even in the Research and Development arm of a big company, it is not the norm to ask questions and be curious. When I asked questions, the usual reply was, "I don't know. It doesn't matter. We do this because that's what makes us money."

I did learn many useful lessons and lab skills at Kelco, however. I learned careful note-taking in a lab notebook with signed pages. I learned how useful and important it is to be very quantitative and meticulous about everything in the lab. I learned how statistics actually works to allow you to believe your results. More importantly, I saw how following one's interests (in my case, programming and 3D photography) and merging them into what you are doing for "work" can sometimes lead to useful accomplishments that are highly motivating. Thus, as a teacher, I continually sought opportunities where I could let my students include their interests into a course project.

Although my jobs as a painter, a grocery clerk, and a physical chemist were not what I would have most liked to do at those times, I enjoyed them all and I managed to get some useful lessons that would eventually help me teach the value of doing difficult projects in the Real World.

A Class With a Motivating Real-world Project

In grad school at UC Irvine, after 17 years of grade school and college, I was finally doing a class project that seemed meaningful, in an *Electronics for Biologists* elective class. Profs. Ian Parker and Bob Josephson taught us the basics of electronics and then set us loose building something electronic of our own design that was supposed to be useful for doing our own PhD thesis research. This free-form assignment really helped inspire my NeuroEng. Fun. lab course years later.

I chose to design a circuit that would help me do chromatography and prevent loss and radioactive spills. I was doing mostly chromatography in my advisor's lab for my PhD thesis work. The job of chromatography is to separate complex mixtures of chemicals into their components. This was HPLC (high-performance liquid chromatography), in which I had to collect drops dripping out of a tiny plastic tube into little test tubes. I used a fraction collector, our trusty Gilson FC80, which holds a rack of 80 test tubes and moves the dropper tube from one test tube to the next according to a timer. I might collect ten seconds of drops per test tube, for example. I was expecting that the valuable purified peptides I was studying would be eluted into one or two tubes of the rack. As I watched the robotic fraction collector moving from one test tube to the next, I noticed that often a drop would fall between the tubes and onto the rack. When this happened at the crucial moment that my valuable peptides were coming off the chromatography column, it could mean that a substantial amount would be wasted, perhaps thousands of dollars worth, if measured in the labor and supplies that went into purifying them. Worse, if they were radio-labeled, it could mean that radioactivity had spilled onto the rack and might contaminate the lab.

I was working with tritium radioactive labels, which are notoriously hard to deal with because you can't detect them with a Geiger counter. You have to do "swipe tests" in which you swab every suspected area of contamination with a small piece of wet tissue and put it into a scintillation counter. This process is like the TSA officer who swabs your luggage for traces of explosives, except you have to wait until the next day to see the results from the scintillation counter, during which time contamination can get spread around the lab if one is careless. Everyone in the lab was taught to be meticulous with tritiated chemicals because they could cause cancer or radiation poisoning if ingested or inhaled.

My idea for preventing waste and radioactive contamination was simple: when it is time to move to the next test tube, tell the fraction collector to wait until a drop falls into a tube and *then* move to the next tube, instead of moving strictly according to its clock. My task was made more complicated by my advisor forbidding me from opening up the fraction collector and messing with its internal circuitry. He was (perhaps justifiably) worried I would ruin this valuable piece of lab equipment we all depended on. I had to build a box with my own timer and replicate much of the circuitry already inside the Gilson FC80 fraction collector, without ever looking inside (Fig. 7). For over two weeks my lab desk was covered with wires and electronic components. After several prototyping cycles, the fraction collector had a new brain.

While designing the Drop Saver, I was thinking about digital circuits when I went to sleep at night. I rushed into the lab each morning to resume working on it as my advisor probably wondered when the hell I would get back to doing my research. The Drop Saver was already working and being used for my research before our class Demo Day.

4. Lessons I Learned

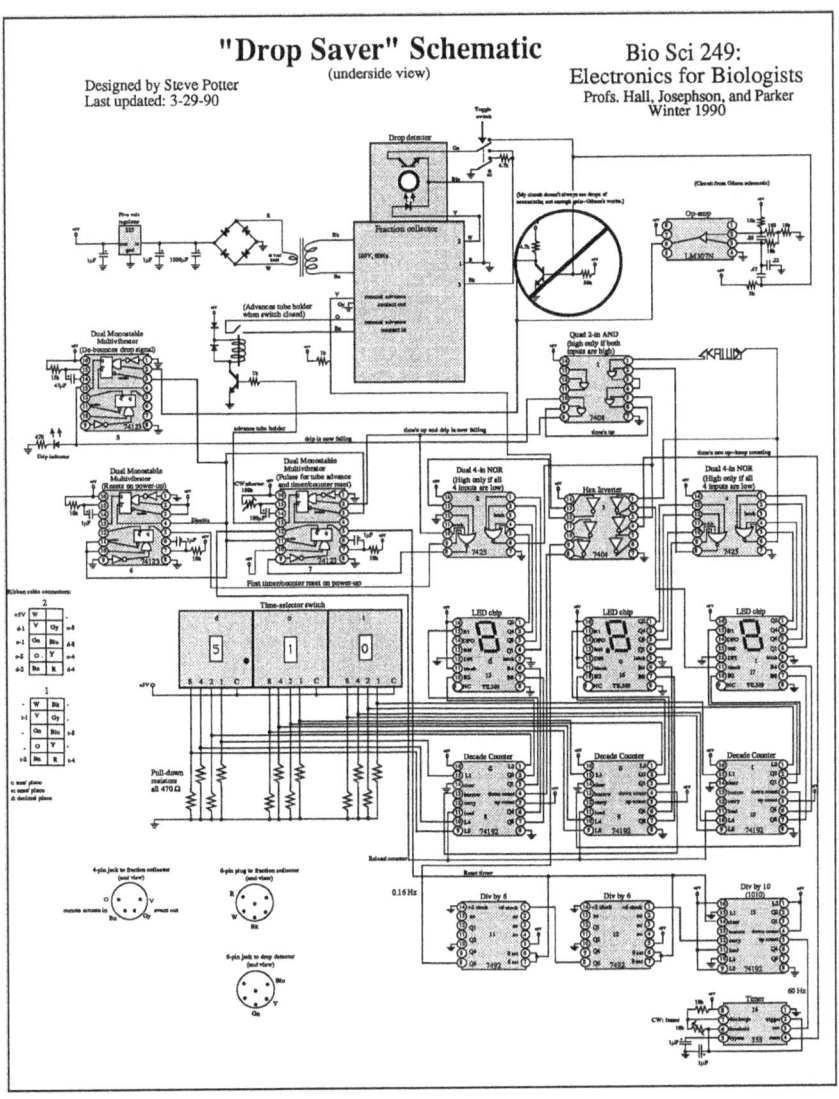

Figure 7. Circuit diagram for the Drop Saver, an external brain for controlling the Gilson fraction collector. After I tested it with actual use on the HPLC, I found that my transistor amp was not a sensitive enough amplifier to detect drops of certain solvents. I needed to use an op-amp instead. In the interest of reminding my future self what not to do, I kept in the part of my design that did not work (the crossed-out circle), *a good example of learning from failure*.

How was I so motivated? One reason is that this was the first time I had ever used digital electronics. I had done analog electronics before, building a modular synthesizer when I was 17. But learning digital electronics was like a religious awakening for me; I had not experienced electronics that were so orderly and well-behaved. I finally realized why computers are digital!

It helped that I had a long history of tinkering with electronics, so it was not so scary. But the main reason I was so enthusiastic about my project may have been that I was building something that I actually really needed for getting my research done. It was a *real-world project*. If I were not to get enough purified peptides because some drops were wasted, it might mean I would have to make another horrible trip up to the worst part of L. A., to the slaughterhouse to get some cow brains, and spend another two weeks in the 4°C (39°F) refrigerated room purifying proteins. (Yes, grad school was hell — not quite as bad as digging up dead bodies in the graveyard…)

It was not only me who needed the Drop Saver. A couple of years after I got my PhD, a younger grad student friend who was still working in my old lab told me, "I still use your Drop Saver all the time."

Real-world projects are motivating. Stretching yourself a bit is motivating. Learning about a whole new field is motivating. Having the proper background and tools is motivating. Having good mentors is motivating. Having the pressure of a demo day in front of your mentors and peers can be motivating (or terrifying, if you are not ready).

What Did I Learn in Grad School?

I did not get much out of my other grad school classes. They were just piles of old papers to read. Most of my professors would rather be doing research than teaching, and they did not bother to update their reading lists or come up with creative assignments. Some class papers I wrote were useful learning experiences. But what I learned most from in grad school was how to learn from trial and error as I conducted research in the lab. I was lucky to have excellent, patient mentoring from a postdoc in the lab, Dr. Brett Johnson. Brett was exceedingly organized and his lab notebook was a work of art.

I was always building things and fixing things, which I love to do. I recall my advisor telling others about the time I impressed him early on when our electrophoresis gel rocker broke down. Instead of asking him to buy a new one, I just took it apart and fixed it the night it broke. Hey, I had gels to rock![36] I couldn't wait three weeks for a new rocker. Taking the initiative in his lab was not always appreciated, I later learned. I resolved that when I had my own

---

36. Each clear acrylamide gel required a long process of staining and de-staining in the rocker to make the proteins show up as blue spots or bands on the gel.

lab, I would let my students make as many decisions as they felt comfortable with, and learn from the consequences if things didn't go as planned.

Aside from learning the obscure art of how to analyze isoaspartyl peptides in grad school, I did learn a few transferrable skills. I learned many things about the brain by attending conference talks and departmental seminars. I learned how to read scientific papers. I learned how to be a careful scientist from my advisor. He helped me improve my writing skills greatly. He would take ages to return the drafts of my research papers to me because he went through them with a fine-toothed comb. Because my first drafts were so poorly written, they were completely covered with his edits in red ink. After several back-and-forths with him and the reviewers, they were eventually published, and my PhD dissertation was successfully defended.

One of the best learning experiences for me in grad school was teaching. I taught the biochemistry class for the incoming psychobiology grads as my advisor's **TA** (teaching assistant), which basically meant that I was in charge of the lab part of the course, purifying proteins, while he did the "lectures" (discussions of old papers). This experience taught me many organizing skills. I had to order supplies and equipment, and get everything ready for each lab. Then during the lab, I had to do hands-on instruction of how to purify proteins, how to use all the equipment (including rocking the electrophoresis gels), how to run the assays, etc.

I spent time before class imagining in my head and on paper how the lab would go and what we would do next. I visualized what we would need, and what might go wrong, based on my own experience doing similar things for my PhD research. If I did a good job teaching that lab, a bonus for me was that my students would have a good yield of the protein they were purifying, calmodulin, and I got to use that for my research after the class was over. Therefore, I was highly motivated to help them succeed in learning protein purification.

I note that this was a traditional cookbook lab, with no effort to give some control to the new grad students taking it. I suspect they would have learned more if they were allowed to choose which protein they had to purify, and if they developed their own strategies for doing so. Such scripted labs may have a place when the instructor wants to be sure to cover specific material, or to increase the likelihood that every student will get the same final product, making grading easier. But I feel the benefits of student-driven learning far outweigh its drawbacks.

Car Mechanics for Learning the Scientific Method

I have often said that I learned more fixing cars than I did in 6 years of grad school. I had a series of jalopies as my first few cars, a 1966 Datsun 411 wagon in college, then a 1969 Toyota Corona and a 1967 VW Beetle Baja Bug in grad school. They were constantly breaking down. I was too poor to take them to a mechanic, so I did all the repairs myself. Sometimes at the side of the highway; I drove with a big box of tools in the back.

Diagnosing their many problems required me to use the scientific method. Like the time a rubber window gasket caused the Toyota's engine to stall. Yes, really. I inherited this car from my beloved grandmother, Mamie, who drove it only rarely in the years before she died. After days of scientific detective work, I finally realized that the gas tank was half filled with water. It had leaked around the rear window (which had an old cracked window seal), dripped into the trunk, through a carpet, around the spare tire and filled the well that the spare tire was sitting in, which is the top of the gas tank. This eventually rusted through over the years and began to drip the rusty rainwater into the fuel. This being sunny California, I did not suspect anything related to rain and lingering puddles could be the problem! But when I pumped gasoline from the tank into a glass jar, I could see that over half of it was water. Diagnosing this problem was a lesson in how complicated a causal chain can be.

One time, my Baja Bug mysteriously began to drive itself up hills. I was using it to go up steep dirt roads with my hang glider rolled up and tied to a ladder on the roof, to unfurl it and fly off the tall mountains of Southern California. A Baja Bug is a VW Beetle that has been converted to a poor-man's SUV by jacking up the suspension and putting huge off-road tires on it (Fig. 8). My Baja Bug had become possessed! On the steepest roads, the engine would rev even when I was not pushing the gas pedal. I had to push in the clutch and turn off the engine quickly to avoid driving off a cliff. My VW repair manual did not mention any such strange behavior.

A careful analysis of the throttle and carburetor revealed nothing wrong, and I could not replicate the problem in my driveway. But by scientifically following the causal chain of events that lead to an engine revving, and considering all the parts that might affect engine speed, I finally realized that I had a broken motor mount. Once again, an old piece of rubber was to blame for engine problems.

Going up a steep hill, there is high torque on the engine, so it tries to rotate against its motor mounts. Newton's Third Law in action: The more force on the wheels (e.g., going up a steep hill), the more reactive force on the motor mounts. For every force, there is an equal and opposite force. If one of the motor mounts is broken, the engine can rotate several degrees, and this caused it to pull on its own accelerator cable. It was self-revving!

Where did I get the skills and confidence to fix my own cars? The summer after my first year in college, my younger brother, Scott, with his new driver's license in hand, bought a jalopy of his own, a Fiat 850 Spider roadster.

He found a second Fiat Spider rusting in a vacant lot, which he used for spare parts. He and I spent the whole summer of 1984 rebuilding the engine of the rusty junker and getting the car working. We had a good Haynes repair manual, and just went through it carefully, page by page, piece by piece. Sadly, Dad was off somewhere in his vagabond phase, so we could not ask him for help.

To completely disassemble, clean, fix, and rebuild an engine is a great way to learn how engines work, much better than reading it in a "How Things Work" book or having a mechanical engineering teacher lecture about it. Of course, as Scott and I were doing this all for the first time and with zero supervision, certain things did not work perfectly. We had to diagnose the problems, and do more repairs, such as replacing the head gasket when we saw green coolant squirting out of the exhaust pipe. By the end of the summer, after much hard work, many do-overs and with grease embedded in our hands, Scott was able to zip around in his "new" Fiat roadster and we were both pretty good mechanics. I learned an important lesson I still use often: Use a variety of color-coded wire for any electrical project. We had used only white wire on the Fiat and this made diagnosing its electrical faults much harder.

All that car repair experience taught me to be fearless in taking things apart to help understand them better. It turns out, this is what biomedical scientists and engineers do for a living. The reductionistic, mechanical approach can be applied to the study of all sorts of biological systems.

Figure 8. VW Baja bug and Rav4, set up for carrying hang gliders. ***Top, Middle***: Me with my 1967 VW Baja Bug, on a hang gliding outing, and just after cleaning and polishing it to sell. ***Bottom***: The Bug's replacement, a new 1996 Rav4, with the home made stainless steel bumper and hang glider rack, ready for adventure!

When I finally got the Rav4 and sold my Baja Bug, there was a hilarious snafu. Although many parts on that old VW were worn and needed me to replace them over the years, the ignition was always good and I kept the engine tuned up — the Baja Bug always started right up. I sold the car to a nice middle-aged man who wanted a cheap off-road car to take fishing. I took his money, kissed my beloved low-budget SUV goodbye, and he drove off happy. I was shocked a few minutes later to hear him call me from a gas station two miles away, complaining that the Bug had died and now would not start! He was stranded. "You sold me a lemon and I am not a happy camper!" he sternly scolded me.

I told him to calm down and I would be right there to figure out the problem. When I got there, I confirmed what he said. The engine was turning over but not starting. What!? It had never behaved this way in the 5 or 6 years I had it.

I put on my scientist hat and said, "There is a reason for this, let's do some investigating." I pulled an ignition wire and saw a very weak spark coming from it when I brought it near the engine block as he cranked the engine. "Engine turns over well = strong battery. Why the weak spark?" I thought. Then I took the rubber protective cover off the distributor and we both saw water pour out. Aha! It turns out the problem was that I had thoroughly washed and polished the car to get it ready to sell. A Baja Bug's engine sticks out the back with no hood over it (Fig. 8). Apparently, I had squirted water into the ignition system with my over-zealous cleaning. I had never washed the car before, because it was a jalopy and I did not care about its looks. After I blew out the water that had pooled inside the distributor cover, the car started up instantly as before, and my customer drove off into the sunset, happy again.

I left out many details in the above stories of all the little experiments I had to do to figure out what was wrong with my jalopies. The meta-skills I was learning were to read manuals carefully, to be patient and keep testing hypotheses, and to observe carefully what happens. This is what scientists do for a living.

I learned to be an auto mechanic by watching, asking, and doing! I watched my Dad fix his old cars when I was a kid and asked many questions (Fig. 9). He was happy to explain every little thing.

Dad sometimes used his lessons to teach me something unrelated, such as when he showed me a very clogged fuel pipe he had just removed, and explained that this is what happens to your arteries if you eat too much fatty food. He was quite a health nut. Hands-on analogies are a great way to learn and remember things. He would sometimes solicit my help to reach a bolt with my small hands, or to clean parts. The best thing was when he would give me worn out car parts as toys. I can still recall the sound of piston rings jingling as I hooked them together in a chain.

Figure 9. Young Steven asking lots of questions. Here I am as 6-year-old getting a lesson from Dad in how an SLR camera works. Photo by Gordon Potter.

Learning by Making Microscopes

Although getting a PhD marks the official end of schooling for academics, my time as a post-doctoral researcher at Caltech was the most educational 8 years of my life. I knew I wanted to learn two techniques to pull off what I hoped to pursue for my career: to study learning in a system where one could watch the brain circuits learn under a microscope. I had read papers by Prof. Jerry Pine at Caltech and knew he was the only one in the world doing both of these techniques: microscopic imaging of neural activity with voltage-sensitive dyes, and micro-electrode array recording. I called him during my final year of grad school to ask for a job, and he gruffly told me to go away, that he did not have funds to hire any postdocs.

Persistence pays! I asked if I could come up and meet him and get his advice about whom else I might work with, and he agreed. I spent a day with him at his lab at Caltech, and by the end of the day we were fast friends. He expressed regret that he could not hire me, so I left with a promise to go find a fellowship to pay my way. A week later, he called me to say he had been talking with his colleague in Biology, Prof. Scott Fraser, who thought that he might pay for half of my postdoc position. I headed back up to Caltech to meet Scott, and, like Jerry, he realized that all three of us loved to build things. So I was hired by both of them! This was wonderful, as Scott was the head of the Biological Imaging Center, with many microscopes and extensive experience imaging living specimens. Both were fantastic hands-on mentors who trained me in their labs when I needed help and otherwise left me to do as I wanted (Fig. 10).

Figure 10. Prof. Scott E. Fraser and Prof. Jerome Pine were my two postdoc mentors from 1994 to 2002 at Caltech.

For my first task in Scott's lab, he asked if I wanted to build a new type of microscope, a 2-photon laser-scanning microscope (TPLSM, now called **MPLSM**) which had been recently invented by Denk, Strickler, and Webb at Cornell.[37] Scott had the lasers and parts ready and waiting for someone who likes to build things, so I showed up at the right time. Seeing my enthusiasm,

---

37. Here is a short paper about this technology for the curious: Steve M. Potter, *"Vital imaging: Two photons are better than one,"* (1996) Current Biology, 6:1595—1598

Scott trusted me, even though I had virtually no experience with lasers or optics. Scott populated his lab with an amazing variety of people with different backgrounds, including art, mathematics, chemistry, physics, and neural development. Scott taught me a policy I emulated later when hiring people to work in my own lab, that **experience is less important than enthusiasm**.

I didn't know where to begin on this huge new microscope project. I was working on building a high-speed neural imaging camera in Jerry's lab, and I used that as an excuse to drag my feet on getting started on the new microscope in Scott's lab. I was waiting for Scott to give me specific instructions. But he was very busy running a large research lab.

One day, he did a brilliant thing to motivate me. I was supposed to convert an old confocal microscope that was seldom used into a multiphoton microscope. He invited a technician from the manufacturer of that confocal microscope to the lab to give us all instructions on how to operate the scope's complex software. During the demo, the scope tech asked "Who is in charge of this equipment?" Scott said, "Steve is. He is going to convert it to a 2-photon microscope!" I realized I was the one in control of this project, not Scott nor any of the other more senior postdocs in the lab. From that day, I took ownership of the project. After getting the software figured out, I soon set about converting the hardware. There were cycles of trial and error involved, but I kept at it for over a year. Scott helped me to break the job down into smaller steps and let me work out the details myself.

The 2-photon microscope (Fig. 11) eventually worked better than all expectations for 3D imaging of living specimens, like brain cells in fruit flies and mouse embryos.[38] This microscopy technique went on to become hugely popular in biomedical research.

Scott always encouraged me to present my work at conferences and to reach out to others interested in MPLSM. I became known as "The 2-photon guy" because I not only took ownership of the project at Caltech, but also created a popular online forum for hundreds of other researchers across the globe who were building and using multiphoton microscopes, called the MPLSM Users.

I really thrived in Scott's lab because he made sure we had all the resources we needed, and he gave us a huge amount of autonomy in terms of

---

38. See, for example: S. M. Potter, C. M. Wang, P. A. Garrity, and S. E. Fraser, *"Intravital imaging of green fluorescent protein using 2-photon laser-scanning microscopy,"* (1996) Gene 173: 25-31; and S. M. Potter, C. Zheng, D. S. Koos, P. Feinstein, S. E. Fraser and P. Mombaerts, *"Structure and emergence of specific olfactory glomeruli in the mouse,"* (2001) Journal of Neuroscience 21: 9713-9723.

what we chose to study and how exactly to study it. I applied these lessons both in my research lab and in the Neuroeng. Fun. lab course.

Figure 11. Fraser Lab 2-photon microscope, circa 1997. I enclosed the microscope in a heated mylar compartment to keep brain slices alive for hours during imaging, with the help of Dr. Adam Mamelak's heart-lung machine on the cart behind me. Hidden behind the microscope are two giant lasers, which I spent many hours aligning in complete darkness, looking through night-vision goggles to find the infrared laser beam.

When I became a professor at Georgia Tech, I went through the process of building another multiphoton laser-scanning microscope. There were quite a few researchers in Scott's lab who were still using the one I had built at Caltech to image development in a wide variety of living specimens. I was lucky to be part of the *Center for Behavioral Neuroscience* in Atlanta, which funded this expensive project to build our own MPLSM in Atlanta.

I gave a grad student and a postdoc in my lab the job of building it under my direction. Unlike my first 2-photon microscope in Scott Fraser's lab, this one was built from scratch, not a conversion of an existing microscope. They got it to a minimal level of usability after over a year of hard work. Around that time, a new building for my department opened, and we all moved our labs into it. As the recently operational MPLSM and all of its lasers were built upon a huge and massive anti-vibration air table, it all had to be completely disassembled to move it (Fig. 12). Unfortunately, before we could get the microscope rebuilt and fully usable, both the grad student and the postdoc left my lab. Its parts were scavenged for other purposes for a couple of years while I tried to find grant money to hire another postdoc to rebuild it. Eventually, I realized that the quickest way to get it functional, and to improve it, would be for me to get in the lab and do it myself. Therefore, I spent two summers doing almost nothing else but working on the MPLSM, solo. I reassembled it, improved it across many iterations, completely reprogrammed it, and built a life-support system for it.

Figure 12. Custom multiphoton microscope at Georgia Tech in its first iteration, just before being enclosed in insulation.

Here is what intrinsic motivation looks like: One morning when I was immersed in the microscope-building project, as I walked to my building from the parking lot, I was surprised to hear my alarm watch going off to wake me up! I had gotten up before the sun because I could not wait to write the code I had thought up as I dozed off the night before. I had a phone installed in the room where the MPLSM was because my wife sometimes had to remind me to come home in the evenings (our lab was electrically shielded and had very poor mobile phone reception).

For two summers, I was in heaven, doing what I love most: learning by making. I spent many long hours in the lab calibrating, testing and debugging the hardware and software with an oscilloscope and other sensors. I learned much more about optics, LabView programming to control hardware precisely, image processing, and many other technical skills. It was exciting to see the tangible results of my efforts: Cool images and time-lapse movies of live neurons in the process of growing and learning.[39]

Enhanced opportunities for social interactions are a side benefit (and motivator) of many projects. Folks in my research group were not used to seeing me actually working in the lab until those summers, a sad fact. My lab members and I benefited from the extra, random conversations we would have thanks to sharing the same workspace. Regrettably, once summer was over, it was back to my office, back to the rat race that kept the lab in business, and kept the university in the black.

The microscope building and re-building experience taught me a few important things. It taught me the importance of regularly checking in on folks in my lab, since some students and postdocs may not take the initiative to let me know if they are stuck. It taught me that complete immersion in a project may be the only way to make substantial progress. I applied these ideas in designing and running my Neuroeng. Fun. lab course in such a way that students could really get into their projects, with regular oral and written progress reports to me and their peers.

***

Of all the important lessons I learned while growing up, shockingly few of them happened in a traditional classroom. All those years of sitting in rows, doing a boring pre-planned lesson in lock step with my classmates seem to me in retrospect to be mostly a big waste of time.

---

39. Here are the first neuron movies from the 2-photon microscope I made at Caltech: https://sites.gatech.edu/potterlab/time-lapse-movies/

The knowledge and skills I still use on a daily basis to be a successful adult and teacher, I learned by actively doing things I cared about, in the Real World. These include communication skills, empathy, persistence, teamwork, initiative, how to break big tasks into manageable pieces, how to organize my time, how to set long-range goals, and many others. These meta-skills can be taught in the classroom, and are being taught, by progressive teachers. Sadly, that describes very few of my own teachers.

By setting students to work on projects they help design, and giving them the right **scaffolding** and feedback, teaching these important lessons becomes a natural part of schooling. Project-Based Learning is not an extra assignment to do at home, but the way students should learn *in school*. Projects should not be thought of as fun diversions from the main classroom activity of learning. They ARE the learning.

Ponder your own stories about how you learned the important lessons of your life, the knowledge and skills you use on a daily basis to do your job or just to get on in life. Whether they happened in school or out in the Real World, see if there are ways you can create a similar learning experience for your students. Going through this recollection process was the main inspiration I used to guide me in designing my curriculum.

Part II

The Neurobiology of Learning

Given that this book is about learning and motivation, and that I dedicated my career to studying the brain, brain/mind stuff will come up a lot. My approach to motivation is pretty pragmatic and based on my experiences, rather than theoretical. That said, some neurobiology and psychology concepts are useful in understanding the teaching approaches that I found to be successful. I was not usually thinking of these concepts explicitly when I implemented my teaching practices, but as I tried to understand what worked over the years, and in writing this book, I did some research that was helpful in putting what I did in a psychological context. I wish I could go back and tell my earlier self about these things. By telling you about certain aspects of the nervous system worth keeping in mind as you teach, I hope to save you some of the trial and error I went through in motivating my students.

CHAPTER 5

Humans are Learning Machines

Let me admit at the outset that I am primarily a neuroengineer and neurobiologist, and only an armchair psychologist. I have taken some psychology courses in college, but my PhD is in neurobiology. Sadly, there is still such a big chasm between our understanding of brain structure and function (neurobiology) and why people do what they do and feel how they feel (psychology) that these are still considered different fields of science. Many experts in psychology are still dualists in the sense that Descartes laid out: He believed that there is the physical stuff (res extensa) and the mind stuff (res cogitans).

> Strangely, the only place these met, he hypothesized, is in the pineal gland, a pea-sized brain nucleus at the center of the back of the brainstem. Most brain parts come in left-right pairs. Descartes' logic was that wherever the soul was located, it must be in part of the brain there is only one of, like the pineal gland. It turns out that the pineal gland secretes melatonin and helps regulate our sleep-wake cycle.

I am a materialist: I firmly believe that all human behavior has its basis in the biological mechanisms of the nervous system. But this is more my faith than science, because we really know surprisingly little about how the brain works.

I once had a blind date with a cognitive psychologist. I liked her, but I made a big mistake. In our discussion about what we each do for a living, I told her that I believe cognitive science is a subset of neuroscience. She vehemently disagreed and that was our last date. I have faith that eventually my assertion will be true, but she was right, it is not yet.

My grad school, the University of California, Irvine, was built around a big circular park. It is telling and sad that the School of Biology is completely on the opposite side of Aldrich Park from the Cognitive Sciences department. I was one of the few grad students in my department (then called Psychobiology) to venture clear across the park to hear many excellent Cognitive Science talks. I was hoping to see the connections between cognition and what I was learning in my very reductionistic Psychobiology department.[40] Researchers in my department used animal models, while those in Cognitive Sciences studied mostly undergrad "volunteers"[41] as the subjects of their research.

Humans are special. For us, learning is more crucial than it is for other animals. It is debatable whether we are the smartest animals on Earth, and we certainly don't have the largest brains. A dolphin's brain weighs about 1.6 kg and an elephant's brain weighs 5 kg, compared to the typical adult human brain, weighing in at 1.3 kg. But no one can deny that humans have more technology and culture than any other animals on the planet — stuff we made, and which we had to *learn* to make. An orb spider can spin a beautiful web, but how it does that is hard-wired in its neural circuits. It did not have to be taught how to spin webs. A mountain goat can walk and avoid cliffs within hours of being born.

We humans, by contrast, know little at birth (we have comparatively few innate skills[42]), and spend years wiring up our brains with the help of our parents or other carers, peers, the environment, and when we hit school age, our teachers. I am struck watching toddlers at how they are constantly doing little experiments to explore the world around them and their own capabilities and senses — they are little scientists. Chimpanzees and other Great Apes have twice as many opposable thumbs as we have and use tools, so it's not manual

---

40. Now called Neurobiology and Behavior, in the School of Biological Sciences. The Cognitive Sciences department is in the School of Social Sciences.
41. Many psychology and cognitive science professors bribe their students with better grades if they volunteer for research studies.
42. I will refer later to some innate skills or instincts that humans do have.

dexterity that makes humans special. It's our voracious appetite for learning new knowledge and skills.

We have more learning circuitry than any other animal. We have a large general-purpose **cortex** to store memories of our learning experiences. One thing that sets humans apart is how much of the brain comprises **the prefrontal cortex**, the part of the brain that evaluates the long-range consequences of our actions, and prevents us from taking the easy but foolish way out of a situation. Neuroscientists say the frontal lobes are responsible for **executive function**, or the choosing and monitoring of one's behaviors and goals. The frontal cortex tends to inhibit the impulsive parts of our brain. I bet you can imagine just how many aspects of what goes on in the classroom are closely linked to brain activity in the frontal lobes. Crucially, the frontal lobes support many of the meta-skills described throughout this book. Executive function is something children learn gradually from experience and instruction.

Other Learning Systems of Mammalian Brains

Learning circuitry is not found only in the cortex. All mammals have several brain circuits dedicated to helping remember things that went well or poorly for them, enhancing their chances for surviving and/or reproducing. Some of these circuits are called reward mechanisms, and they involve activity in the **dopamine**-releasing neurons of the ventral tegmental area (VTA), which is deep in the brainstem. The dopamine neurons of the VTA branch out with **axons** (the wires of the brain, collectively called white matter) which send signals all over the cortex, especially to the frontal cortex, and to a few other important reward-related nuclei such as the nucleus accumbens. (For a nice diagram and more nuanced explanation, see https://www.sainsburywellcome.org/web/qa/diversity-dopamine-neurons.)

The **neurotransmitter** dopamine is being released at some background level all the time, like a drip irrigation system. A brief increase in this release rate signals the expectation of something good. If it happens, the related memories are reinforced, and the behaviors that led up to that reward are more likely to be expressed in the future. A sudden reduction in the ongoing release of dopamine happens when something surprisingly bad occurs or an expected reward fails to materialize. This triggers learning to avoid that situation in the future.

This signaling of expectation and surprise is crucial for learning. If you were to measure dopamine release from the VTA of students while they were engaged in building something, you would see a big spurt each time they got another part working, and this would help them remember the things they did right, and add to their toolbox of useful skills. You might also see dips in ongoing dopamine release when a part failed or when they were criticized by someone for doing something the "wrong" way. This would help them learn to avoid going down that path next time.

Another circuit that evolved to help us and other mammals learn is the **noradrenergic system**. Norepinephrine (called noradrenalin outside the US) is another neurotransmitter released by neurons deep in the brainstem under extreme situations that tend to activate one's **sympathetic nervous system**. If you become angry or scared, your sympathetic nervous system causes adrenalin (epinephrine) and noradrenalin to be released into your bloodstream by your adrenal glands located on your kidneys. This activates your whole body to either fight an attacker or run away as quickly as possible. But noradrenalin is also released in the brain by the locus coeruleus, and, assuming you survived the incident, this causes you to keep replaying memories of what led up to the perilous situation. Noradrenergic circuits are responsible for reinforcing these traumatic memories, sometimes causing post-traumatic stress disorder (**PTSD**) in those who experienced very traumatic events. We know this because blocking norepinephrine receptors with beta-blocker drugs soon after a traumatic experience, or inhibiting the sympathetic responses to a frightening stimulus, greatly reduce one's memory of such experiences.[43]

Yet another reward circuit in the brain is the **opiate system**, where endorphins are released when you accomplish good things. Endorphins are the neuromodulators responsible for the "runners' high" that kicks in while running a marathon. They knock out pain and give one a great feeling of accomplishment

---

43. See Steven M. Southwick et al., *"Relationship of Enhanced Norepi-nephrine Activity During Memory Consolidation to Enhanced Long-Term Memory in Humans,"* (2002) Am. J. Psychiatry 159:1420; and Larry Cahill et al., *"Beta-Adrenergic activation and memory for emotional events,"* (1994) Nature 371:702

and contentment. Thanks to learning strengthened by endorphins, many runners keep repeatedly putting themselves through grueling experiences. Opiate-related drugs of abuse and pain medications also work by acting on the brain's opiate receptors, making them highly addictive.

There are other reward neurotransmitters or neurohormones, such as vasopressin and oxytocin, involved specifically with sexual experiences, childbirth, pair bonding, territoriality, maternal care, toxic food aversion, etc. These trigger their own specific learning circuits under the right circumstances. Although important to the survival of our species, these learning circuits are less likely to be important in the classroom and I will not discuss them further.

Put simplistically, you have **dopamine** circuits to help remember and repeat good things (or avoid mildly bad things), and norepinephrine circuits to help remember and avoid really bad, dangerous things. The main point here is that the brain, especially the human brain, has many, many chemicals and circuits that evolved to help us *learn to be successful* at survival, reproduction, and being a valued member of one's tribe. There are probably as many different kinds of learning as there are skills and facts to be learned. The brain's learning systems are used in varying combinations across the learning process. Instead of being preloaded with many useful instincts at birth, like those of most other animals, humans' brains are *plastic* or moldable. This allows us to adapt to diverse environments and situations.

Although we share the same learning circuits with all mammals, we have much more real estate in the human brain in which to store complex memories, skills, and things to seek out and to avoid. And we have powerful symbol systems (such as spoken and written language and numbers) that allow us to organize and record this mass of information as it is learned. Harnessing the power of the brain's learning systems — **plasticity** mechanisms — is tricky but worth striving for, when designing your approach to teaching.

CHAPTER 6

What Motivates Students?

Where does motivation come from? I will go over what I believe are the six most powerful forces that motivate students and make learning happen. These are based on my observations of what worked and what didn't with my classes. I will attempt, if possible, to include some of the mechanisms behind these forces, in terms of neurobiology. I will try to answer the question, "How can teachers make the best use of the nervous system that evolved in humans?" I divided this material up into six categories that make sense to me, with an emphasis on motivation. These topics have many interactions and overlap — a good metaphor for how the brain is wired up.

How does a student decide if a topic to be learned is interesting and worth learning?

1) Motivation from Excitement!

The topic excites them.

2) Motivation from *ATTENTION*

The topic is challenging and holds their attention.

3) Motivation from Accomplishment

The topic gives them a sense of accomplishment and purpose.

4) Motivation from Interaction

The topic promotes good interactions with others.

5) Motivation from CONTROL

Students feel in control of their learning of the topic.

6) Motivation from Play

There is something fun about the topic or the learning approach.

I will now delve into each of these sources of motivation. As you read, try to come up with ways to apply them in your own teaching environment.

1) Motivation from Excitement!

Imagine yourself on a lazy weekend afternoon. You are tired or bored, and can't seem to get around to doing anything on your to-do list. Then a good old friend rings you, one you have not heard from in ages. He happens to be in town and he wants to visit you. Suddenly you are full of GO! You now have no trouble finding the energy and motivation to change out of your pajamas and tidy up the house. What happened there? One minute you can't think of anything worth doing; the next minute, you have no trouble knowing what to do and doing it. Hearing your old friend's voice gave you a shot of adrenalin that made you excited. That was your **sympathetic nervous system** in action. You expect that you both will have a great time catching up on each others' news and reliving the past. That's dopamine setting up your reward circuits with the expectation of good things. Your brain makes its own drugs (neurotransmitters and neuromodulators) that can have powerful effects on your mood and behavior. They can snap you from lethargic and bored to excited, enthused and moving in a second. The anticipation of rewards is inherently exciting.

Imagine how your students' attitude suddenly changes when you tell them to put away their books because it is a beautiful day and you decided that the class is going to the park to collect some interesting bugs or plants. If you frame it as a fun learning experience and provide the right scaffolding, such as a guide of specimens to look for, your enthusiasm will spread to your students. When they get back to class, to study a weird bug they found is much more exciting than studying a dead specimen mounted on a microscope slide decades ago. Such an outing could be focused on what bugs do for our environment, such as decomposing fallen trees and enriching the soil. If we make it easy for our students to see the potential rewards of new understanding, they will become excited and motivated to learn.

The sympathetic nervous system kicks into action for both good and bad excitement. It is often called the "fight or flight" part of the autonomic nervous system, but it plays important roles in preparing you for quick action, whether in a scary context or an exciting but pleasurable one.

Excited!

In an interesting experiment done in the 1960s,[44] subjects were given injections of epinephrine (adrenalin) while a "stooge" or confederate pretending to be another waiting subject did things that influenced the subjects' emotional interpretation of how they felt. Subjects were told they were getting a drug that might improve their vision, and would soon have a vision test. It turns out, the real experiment was being carried out in the waiting room, with experimenters taking notes behind the mirrored window into the room.

The confederates had a fun acting job to fool the subjects and rope in their emotions: In one group, the confederate expressed anger about a form they had to fill out that asked personal questions. In another group, the confederate goofed around with paper airplanes and hula hoops. The subjects, who were beginning to experience diffuse physiological excitement from the adrenalin injection, including sweaty palms and their heart beating fast, took their cues from the confederates and either became angry or happily excited about what was to come next. Because the drug didn't come from their own adrenal glands, the subjects did not know whether it was a good or bad sort of excitement they were feeling. The subjects were primed by the adrenalin to notice any cues that might reveal the answer to why they suddenly felt excited. The confederates provided those cues at just the right moment in the waiting room. What is interesting is that the subjects' interpretation of their situation almost always matched the one portrayed by the confederates (either playful or angry), and their mood went up or down accordingly.

---

44. Stanley Schachter, *"The Interaction of Cognitive and Physiological Determinants of Emotional State,"* (1964) Adv. Exp. Soc. Psychology 1:49-80.

It turns out that excitement from good things and excitement from bad things both feel pretty much identical. The lesson for teachers is that we can switch our students from feeling anxious or annoyed about a new learning activity to feeling positively excited about it, by providing the right cues. If we are genuinely excited about a new activity, our students will pick up on that. Conversely, if we are not careful, we or other students can provide cues that will rapidly turn on anxiety circuitry that demotivates some students. For example, a seemingly empathetic comment like, "The first time I did this I was terrified, too" might make them terrified when they were only a bit excited. They become demotivated. In the bug collecting example above, if the teacher or other students emphasize how disgusting or dangerous bugs are instead of how interesting they are, it could quickly demotivate the students.

Excitement in the classroom is a good thing — in moderation. With too much excitement, things may devolve into pandemonium. The **Yerkes-Dodson Curve** (Fig. 13) is a useful image to keep in mind while running your classes. Yerkes (rhymes with "turkeys") and Dodson realized that performance for any task is highest at a certain middle level of excitement. Their inverted-U-shaped curve of performance as a function of excitement level has a peak representing the optimal level of excitement for that task. To the left side of the curve's peak is poor performance due to boredom, sleepiness, or actually being asleep. To the right side of the peak is reduced performance due to inability to focus one's attention and inability to sit still. At the extreme right are hyperactivity, ROFL, anxiety, mania and hysteria.

6. What Motivates Students?

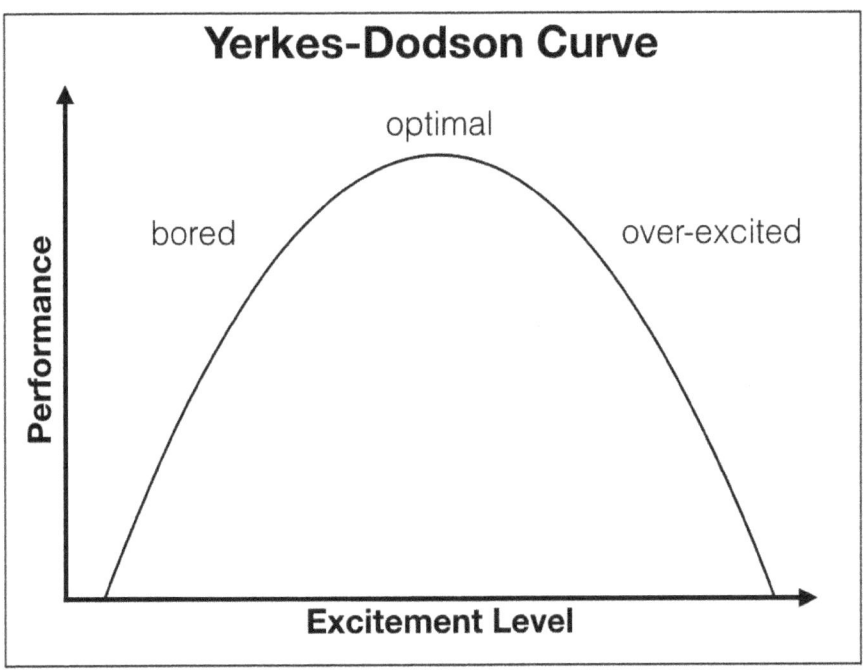

Figure 13. Yerkes-Dodson Curve, showing how performance is optimal at some middle level of excitement. This is not a bell curve (statistical distribution), but an "inverted U" function with no long tails. It hits zero on the left when the subject falls asleep, and on the right when they become too manic to function at all.

Note that the curve is not about how nice it feels to be in these moods. It is just (in our context) about how well a student can perform a given task that is part of a learning experience. It may be enjoyable to be rolling on the floor laughing or relaxedly daydreaming, but learning is not optimal. Our job as teachers is to try to keep students at the peak of the Yerkes-Dodson Curve as much as possible. If they are too bored, they need more excitement. If they are too excited, they need to be calmed down.

Moderate anxiety or stress can be used to motivate, such as when students are facing a deadline. The key is to move students rightward from the low side to the peak of the Yerkes-Dodson Curve, not past the peak. A good example of stress effectively motivating learners can be seen at a hackathon. These are usually one- or two-day high-intensity events, for example, the all-girls coding hackathon described at aihacks.org. Teams face a hard deadline to come up with an idea, build a prototype, and often give a sleep-deprived pitch to potential funders at the end. The sheer amount of creative output that hackathon teams produce is astonishing. The short deadline and high intensity of these events force participants to learn many details about their chosen project, as well as about team and planning skills.

In addition to the Yerkes-Dodson Curve, a key concept that is useful in understanding motivation is the idea of a **threshold**. I will define **motivation** as *whatever it is in one's brain that compels one to act*. And *to act* almost always means movement of some sort. A threshold is a barrier that takes some effort (energy, movement) to cross. Thresholds are applicable at many scales, all the way from a single voltage-sensitive ion channel in a neuron up to a student deciding to do their reading: in crossing a threshold, movement happens. A switch is flipped on. Something gets done. Ion channels let ions through the cell membrane, neurons fire action potentials, the brain circuits controlling hands and eyes become active, the student begins reading.

Any complex task worth doing involves crossing many thresholds, carrying out many movements. There are many, many factors that have an influence on our behavior and raise students up and over the threshold that divides doing nothing from doing something. As teachers, it is helpful for us to become experts at knowing what those factors are and how best to manipulate them in the brains of our students. Neuroscientists also talk about raising and lowering the threshold itself, making it either more difficult or easier to cross. In simple terms, things get done with more excitement *or* reduced difficulty.

We want to push students across the threshold of **active learning**, usually moving them to the right on the Yerkes-Dodson Curve. If they are already to the right of the peak (too excited), they may be crossing all sorts of irrelevant thresholds, such as getting up for no reason, hitting or shouting. With too much excitement, extraneous stimuli cause distractions. Internal urges or comments by classmates trigger irrelevant or even disruptive behaviors. By keeping students at the peak of the Yerkes-Dodson Curve, they can more easily cross the learning thresholds we set for them, while avoiding crossing irrelevant or counter-productive ones.

It is worth repeating that learning is always active. There is always some movement involved. Even if it is just turning their heads or only their eyes, students need to move to pay attention and to learn. Even listening, which seems like it might be passive learning, students must sit up and not go slack and fall asleep. There are many more aspects to active learning than just movement. For the purposes of this section, the important point is to do what it takes to raise students' excitement.

Don't confuse the Yerkes-Dodson Curve with a **learning curve** (Fig. 14), which shows performance on some task as a function of time (or learning trials). The X axis of the Yerkes-Dodson Curve is *excitement level*, while the X axis for a learning curve is *time*.

6. What Motivates Students?

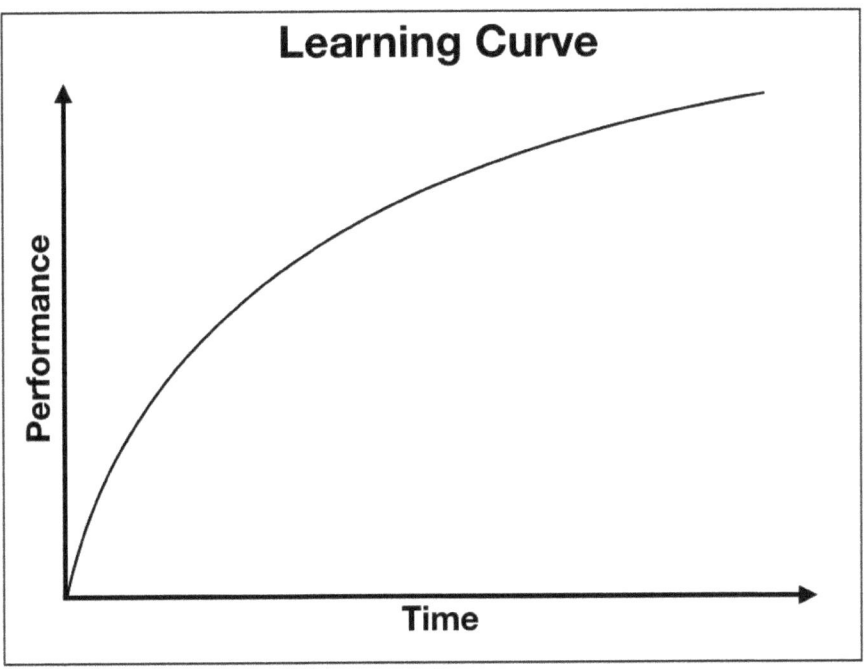

Figure 14. A learning curve is a plot of a learner's performance as a function of time or the number of learning trials.

To build excitement in your students is a great way to get them motivated to accomplish a seemingly difficult learning task. I say "seemingly" because I have observed, both in my students and for myself, that how difficult a task feels can change dramatically with motivation. If your students are complaining about an assignment, you *could* make it easier (lowering the threshold). Instead, I recommend that you ramp up their excitement. They will lunge forward with the job, and they will feel a greater sense of accomplishment once they complete it. The easiest way to do that is to convey through your words, tone and body language your own excitement about the task.

You can also show your students how excited and glad others became when they did an assignment. Videos or comments from previous classes are helpful for that. With motivating next year's students in mind, record interviews of your students when they are proud and excited. You might ask a former student to come visit your class and describe how things went for them. Some of my most enthusiastic students asked to be my teaching assistants (TAs) in following semesters. They were then able to validate, from a student's perspective, the reasons for doing an assignment and the rewards they felt when they were taking the course. As TAs who had been there and done that recently, they were very helpful in improving the course, in case some things did not go as well as they could have. They were also helpful in answering anxious students' questions, moving them leftward on the Yerkes-Dodson Curve.

Motivation is contagious. Being in a class full of excited students scurrying around doing fun things, it is hard not to get pulled into the excitement emotionally. However, it does not always spread to every student. There may be students who feel they don't fit in, or are having a bad time due to family circumstances or health problems, and may tend to sulk or zone out when others are having fun. It is our job as teachers to notice them and find ways to get them involved. I have found that the best thing to do is to give them a very specific and doable task that is something others need done. Once they do it, and see how it made others glad, they may break through their malaise. Or the others may be more inclined to bring them into a project.

Variety is inherently exciting. Keep things changing, but also have some recurring familiar Good Things to look forward to. Both surprise and anticipation can be exciting and motivating. However, fear of the unknown can lead students to dread a learning task. Most of us are familiar with the experience of procrastinating with a tough assignment in school, only to realize that once we finally got into it, it was not nearly as tough as we thought it would be. If you (perhaps with help from your TAs) can better explain the task, or break it down into more manageable sub-tasks, you can change that worry into excited anticipation.

Students who are too excited need to be calmed down and moved left on the Yerkes-Dodson Curve. If students know what is expected of them and what the next task is, they will realize they need to calm down to get it done. They can learn to regulate their own excitement and calm themselves down to focus on what is next. As instructors, we can help them with that, for example, with mindfulness meditation exercises or other relaxation and focusing rituals. Their peers can also help, if a culture of mutual respect is established, by politely urging disruptors to calm down and pay attention.

Human physiology comes equipped with its own pharmacy of neuromodulators for adjusting excitement levels. There are many triggers for dispensing those natural drugs and optimizing learning. Each student may need their own unique "prescription." It greatly simplifies our job as instructors to know this: **much of the complexity of motivation can be distilled down to the one axis of *excitement level*, and that the optimum for learning is in the middle.**

Excitement and hyperactivity

Hyperactivity has a surprisingly complex relationship with excitement. When a person is excited and motivated, they will learn (including elderly or learning-disabled students). Only a serious disability like being locked in (completely paralyzed) or narcoleptic (unable to stay awake) might prevent learning. ADHD (attention deficit hyperactivity disorder), in my opinion, should not be considered a disability but more like a recurring mood that can lead to behavior that makes learning in a quiet classroom difficult. Consider the harm done labeling a student or one of your children as *being* ADHD. That is how I have heard it from parents and teachers: not, "They have ADHD," but "They *are* ADHD." It becomes their defining identity.

The causes of ADHD are still not clear, but most of the symptoms point to not enough activity in the prefrontal cortex. As described earlier, this part of the brain controls **executive functions** and normally inhibits other more impulsive brain circuits in order to make one's behavior socially appropriate. When the prefrontal cortex is doing its job, social norms are considered, dangerous or inappropriate impulses are not followed through, distractions are ignored, and long-range plans are carried out. The inhibition from the prefrontal cortex allows attention to be focused. With reduced inhibition, as in ADHD, hyperactivity, distraction and misbehaving happens.

We came to understand the executive functions of the frontal lobes by observing those with damage to this area of the brain caused by accident, disease or stroke. These unfortunate people suffer from an inability to plan their lives, and exhibit impulsive and socially inappropriate behavior.

Brain Damage Reveals Brain Function

An early and often-cited example of how neuroscience is advanced by studying those with head trauma is the curious case of Phineas Gage. He suffered brain damage in 1848 when a pointed metal tamping rod accidentally shot up through his face and out the top of his head. He survived, but this formerly responsible and respected railroad foreman was transformed into an irresponsible "child" no longer able to keep a job:

"He is fitful, irreverent, indulging at times in the grossest profanity (which was not previously his custom), manifesting but little deference for his fellows, impatient of restraint or advice when it conflicts with his desires, at

> times pertinaciously obstinate, yet capricious and vacillating, devising many plans of future operations, which are no sooner arranged than they are abandoned in turn for others appearing more feasible. A child in his intellectual capacity and manifestations, he has the animal passions of a strong man." [45]
>
> Gage's skull was found in a museum and scanned, and computer models were used to determine that the tamping rod had damaged his left frontal cortex and the white matter tracts connecting it to many other brain regions.[46]

---

45. John Martyn Harlow, *"Recovery from the Passage of an Iron Bar through the Head,"* (1869) Publications of the Massachusetts Medical Society, 2 (3): 327–47, David Clapp & Son.
46. Van Horn JD, Irimia A, Torgerson CM, Chambers MC, Kikinis R, et al. *"Mapping Connectivity Damage in the Case of Phineas Gage,"* (2012) PLOS ONE 7(5): e37454.

What is important for teachers to realize is that activity in the prefrontal cortex (as with other brain circuits) can be dialed up and down by the brain's own neuromodulation circuits. The most familiar and obvious example of this is sleep: a good fraction of your prefrontal cortex is switched off during REM (rapid eye movement) sleep, when we are likely to be dreaming about doing things we would never do in our awake life, even when we don't realize it is a dream.

Knowing that ADHD is a *tendency* toward lower-than-normal frontal activity — the prefrontal cortex is not operating at full steam[47] — helps explain how ADHD symptoms can be reduced or eliminated by anything that modulates frontal activity back up to normal levels. Relevant to this book, that includes exciting and engaging activities. It also includes ADHD drugs (which cause widespread increases of dopamine and norepinephrine) and self-stimulation (which may explain some of the hyperkinetic behavior). Although a doctor or parent may have labeled a student as "being ADHD," I suggest that teachers should be open-minded to the possibility that this diagnosis signifies the *potential* to be in a certain mood or state. It is not a

---

47. Frances Kuo & Andrea Taylor, *"A Potential Natural Treatment for Attention-Deficit/Hyperactivity Disorder: Evidence From a National Study,"* (2004) Am. J. Public Health 94:1580.

fixed disability, like brain damage that would prevent a student from learning or taking part in classroom activities.

All children (and many young adults) are still developing their executive functions, wiring up their prefrontal cortex. This is something that can be improved with the right practice and good role models, enhanced by adequate motivation that encourages the student to pay attention.

When students are paying attention, all types of learning are much more effective (see next section). This includes learning better executive functioning. Executive functions can be enhanced across the *minutes* time scale by varying amounts of the brain's own neuromodulators, and across the *days and weeks* time scale by brain plasticity — strengthening frontal circuits that control the ability to focus, to inhibit impulses, to plan, and to imagine goals. Any student can improve by exercising these brain functions, just as an athlete would exercise certain muscle groups.

2) Motivation from *ATTENTION*

Paying attention is almost always a prerequisite to learning. Unfortunately, humans have only one conscious processing circuit with which to pay attention.[48] It is impossible to pay attention to two things at once. Therefore, to be distracted means to stop paying attention to the task we are working on. If that is a learning task, learning is halted until attention is brought back to the task. Research on multitasking in humans[49] shows that unlike computers, we are pretty bad at it. It often takes over 10 minutes to get back to a tricky task after a distraction. This is why it is crucial that we as teachers do our best to reduce distractions and make it easier for our students to stay focused on learning.

We also need to teach students **how to stay focused**, how to master their attention mechanisms. Admonitions to "Pay attention!" are not enough. After getting the level of excitement right, the next step is to teach students how to reduce distractions. I had my students turn off their phones, tablets and computers, and keep conversations on task and quiet. You could ask your students for their own suggestions regarding what they find distracting and how they eliminate distractions.

The conscious circuits of the brain evolved to enhance learning of complex tasks, bodies of information, or skills, by allowing the brain to focus

---

[48]. As discussed in detail by Daniel C. Dennett in *Consciousness Explained*, (1991) Little, Brown & Co.
[49]. Summarized well by John Medina in *Brain Rules: 12 Principles for Surviving and Thriving at Work, Home, and School*, (2008) Pear Press p.84.

on only the relevant sensory input. All the inputs hitting our senses need to be filtered down to what is relevant to the task at hand. The conscious mind does that, under the direction of the prefrontal cortex, keeping goals and plans in mind and inhibiting extraneous impulses.

It helps teachers to appreciate just how much is going on "under the hood" in students' brains. They are always taking in a lot more information through their senses than they need, and most of that is either being ignored completely, or it is being monitored by various unconscious circuits. These background circuits evolved to be fast and vigilant, not smart, always on the lookout for attention-grabbing stimuli. They command our attention and quickly activate the appropriate reflexive orienting and protective responses, for example, cringing when a loud noise happens, turning when someone says our name, ducking when something is moving quickly towards us, scratching when we feel a bug crawling on our skin, or sniffing and looking around when we smell something burning unexpectedly. Teachers should avoid activating these vigilant unconscious circuits unless desired.

Consciousness kicks in *after* reflexive responses, to help learn from the situation. In the classroom, students' single-track conscious processor is gathering relevant input, such as instructions spoken or words read, and it is making connections between that input and what is already in their brains: relevant memories, skills, and ideas. This type of conscious learning involves activity across the entire cortex. It is what humans excel at.

Sensory-Motor Learning

In the case of learning physical skills, an important input is **interoception**, the internal feelings our own body is sending to the brain, such as position and movement of body parts (proprioception), and movement of the self through space (kinesthesia and vestibular senses of balance and acceleration). Even though much of interoception is unconscious, learning a skill is faster and more enduring when we apply our conscious attention to these internal feelings along with external sensory input related to performance. A master, coach, or teacher can help their protégé learn by calling their attention to subtle internal and external cues during practicing.

Skill learning requires not only cortical activity (e.g., processing instructions, associating memories) but also subcortical activity in the cerebellum and basal ganglia. As skills are mastered, less and less cortical activity is required, freeing up the one-track conscious cortical processor to do other things

> while the basal ganglia and other subcortical circuits execute well-learned routines. We say something has "become habitual" when it is burned into our basal ganglia and other non-conscious circuits.
>
> You are probably already familiar with this transfer of skill-related knowledge from the cortex to subcortical brain structures. Most experienced drivers are able to have a conversation while driving, yet when we were learning to drive, every bit of our attention was required to monitor our speed, road signs, the dashboard, lane markings, and how well we were steering. The instructor would have us pull over and get our full attention before giving us a complex instruction. New, faster and more efficient subcortical neural connections are created (in part) by conscious cortical mechanisms.

Thus, conscious attention aids all types of learning, whether they be the learning of motor skills, facts, calculations, events, or pretty much anything.

How can we optimize our students' attention? In the "sweet spot" or optimal peak on the Yerkes-Dodson Curve is a state called **flow**. In the flow state, students stay focused on the task at hand, filter out distractions, and are enjoying making progress. Flow is usually associated with being self-motivated by the intrinsic rewards of an activity. Flow involves continuous feedback on progress toward difficult but attainable goals.

Goldilocks Tasks and *Flow*

The most motivating tasks are those which a person feels able to accomplish, with focused effort. It helps if the person is genuinely excited about the task. Note that I much prefer the term "effort" to the term "work." "Work" has too many negative connotations. We often draw a hard line between work and play, time on the clock and time off. It is much better to tell your students, "Put in more effort!" than, "Work harder!" "Effort" can mean all sorts of things, including work *and* play. For example, ask any athlete how they became so good at their sport and they will certainly mention hours and hours of practice, much of which was fun.

Effort by students can and should be fun. It *will* be if students see accomplishments building up, or see improvement in their skills — these are intrinsically motivating. If a task can be accomplished with little or no effort, students may become bored or may not see the point of doing the task. If they do the easy task, they get little intrinsic reward. They will probably feel like they just wasted their time doing something trivial or something they already knew how to do well.

On the other end of the effort scale, if the task seems impossible, they are likely to become frustrated and will want to give up on it. Frustration demotivates. If the task is in the *Goldilocks Zone* of just-right levels of doability and effort and they accomplish it, they are rewarded by a great sense of internal satisfaction. This intrinsic reward is usually in proportion to how much effort it was to accomplish.

When in a flow state, students know what to do next from moment to moment, and trust that they can handle any difficulties. We should strive to keep our students in the Goldilocks Zone of doability as much as possible. Therefore, one of the most important things teachers can do is to monitor constantly how students are doing and adjust either the task difficulty or the students' perception of it. If students feel it is impossible, maybe it is! Maybe we need to change what we expect our students to accomplish. Or maybe the students just need a pep talk to improve their self-confidence.

Different students will progress through a complex task or project at different speeds. For this reason, it is best to allow students to set their own pace, which they will naturally do to avoid becoming bored by moving too slowly, or overwhelmed by advancing too quickly. This may be more tricky for the instructor, compared to the tradition of having everyone do each task at the exact same time for a predetermined amount of time. But in my experience, the benefits in terms of student motivation are well worth it.

"Self-paced" does not mean that the students work in isolation. Self-paced learning requires input from the instructor. There should be a number of checkpoints to see how the students are doing and to give them useful individualized feedback (Chapter 11) so they feel they are continually progressing, building new skills and learning new and useful things. Some of the burden of monitoring progress can be carried by the students' own classmates. If students are working in groups, they will gladly monitor their group-mates' progress.

Because attention is a limited and valuable commodity, there are many things competing to get some of it. One of the hallmarks of being *in the flow* is that intense concentration or immersion in a task seems to happen effortlessly. In fact, it was named "flow" by psychologist Mihály Csíkszentmihályi because people described it to him as like being carried away by a stream. Things that are normally distracting can be easily ignored during flow states. Even bodily signals like hunger or a full bladder can be completely overlooked during prolonged flow episodes. Time seems to zip by unnoticed.

Here is an extreme example: When I was in high school, I was addicted to playing an arcade game, *Robotron: 2084* (Fig. 15). I once played with a single quarter for over 8 hours, pausing only once to run to the toilet after I assigned an onlooker to play for me. He was not quite ready for the task; by the time I returned, he had nearly killed off all my extra men. But I persisted and accomplished my goal of "rolling over" the top score back to zero, which erased the leader board. This is an extreme example of flow: it felt like the 8 hours whooshed by. It highlights that too much flow is not necessarily a good thing if it causes you to neglect other important things!

Flow defeats insecurity. When in the flow, because attention is concentrated on the task at hand, there is little or no attention left to focus on one's own self image. This means that students experiencing flow tend to be less self-conscious, which is great for those who might be inhibited or worried by thoughts of how they look to the teacher or their peers. Being in the flow can be a group activity, such as with a music ensemble or sports team who know each other well and perform at the top of their game when with their group.

Figure 15. Robotron: 2084 video game. My former grad student, Dr. John Rolston, found a working *Robotron* game at the boardwalk arcade in Santa Cruz, California. The next time I was in Santa Cruz, I was compelled to go there and play it to get the top score...for old time's sake, right? Photo courtesy of John Rolston.

More often, flow happens during an engaging solitary activity. Many athletes describe their peak performance during flow states. I have experienced flow many times while hang gliding.

How I learned to fly is a good example of keeping tasks challenging but doable. I learned to hang glide gradually across an entire summer by flying a few feet above a sand dune, and at higher altitudes, hanging next to an instructor in a tandem glider. My excellent instructor, Dan Skadal, was careful to keep each task within or just beyond my abilities at that moment, and therefore, not too scary. When I was finally flying solo at high altitudes, the challenges of finding thermals and landing safely stretched my abilities but were within the Goldilocks Zone where I was confident I could do them (Fig. 16).

With the Yerkes-Dodson Curve in mind, contrast my hang gliding with my few attempts at rock climbing. I was given a harness and set loose climbing up a cliff, with little instruction. I was not very good at it and was terrified of falling, even though I was theoretically protected by a rope. My excitement level was way to the right side of the Yerkes-Dodson Curve, making my progress halting and clumsy as my heart raced. The key to helping students get in the flow is to make sure the task is well suited to their beliefs about what they can accomplish. You may suspect their beliefs are way below what they can actually accomplish. In that case, break the scary task into smaller and less imposing steps, the way my hang gliding instructor did.

How to monitor your students? It is usually not hard to tell when students are working at the correct level of difficulty. They believe what they are trying to do is possible with effort, so you see them expending a fair amount of effort, often stretching themselves in new ways. You see their excitement. You see them delving more deeply into something with little or no prodding. You see them spending long periods in the *flow* state. Students in flow are highly motivated to surmount the hurdles facing them at this moment. By watching carefully where their eyes are looking and what their hands are doing, you can tell whether they are deeply engaged in a task or not.

Be careful, though: flow can resemble stubbornness, which can lead to frustration. I have had many experiences with amazingly persistent students who kept trying to solve a problem that was not yielding to their efforts. They were "spinning their wheels," as if trying to move a car that is bogged down in mud by just hitting the accelerator. Therefore, when students seem very focused, it helps to check in on them occasionally. Ask them face-to-face how things are going and what, specifically, they are working on right now. Do they feel they are moving forward? The instructor-feedback cycle will get them unstuck or prevent them from giving up. This happens much more quickly if done orally than with a written assessment or assignment.

6. What Motivates Students?

Figure 16. Hang gliding in California. ***Top***: I'm visualizing my flight plan before launch at Crestline, California, with my friend and fellow hang glider pilot Scott Eliason's help. ***Middle***: I'm searching for thermals (rising air), just after flying off the cliff at Crestline and into the San Bernardino smog. On the ground, my 18-foot glider was awkward and heavy. As soon as I was flying, it always felt as though it magically shrunk to a nimble 6 feet and became a part of me. I was figuratively *and* literally in a flow state. ***Bottom***: I'm happy to have made a safe landing after launching from Kagel Mountain near Sylmar, California, ready to process and reinforce what I learned during the flight by writing in my Flight Log. Photos by Robin Eliason and Scott Eliason.

Everyone agrees that being in the flow is a good way to learn things, but it is not the only way. The Yerkes-Dodson Curve is the key to understanding why. Getting your students in the flow state is not as important as keeping them at the peak of that curve. Plenty of good learning happens when not in flow. The important thing is **ATTENTION**, which engages the cortical learning circuitry: The more one's attention is focused on the learning, the better. The enemies of attention are distraction and boredom, the two parts of the Yerkes-Dodson Curve on either side of the optimum.

3) Motivation from Accomplishment

What's the Purpose? Why spend so many years in school?

It is absolutely crucial for students to understand *why* they are being asked, or often compelled, to learn the things school aspires to teach them. It is nearly impossible to be motivated entirely by trusting an authority figure who just says, "Because I said so." Parents and high school counselors sometimes make a complicated argument to motivate learning, such as,

Student: "School sucks. It's BO-ring. Why bother?"
Authority Figure: "If you do well in class and put in the hard work, you will get good grades."
"What use is a good grade?"
"They might prepare you to ace the SAT."
"Why should I care about the SAT?"
"A high SAT score and a good GPA are crucial to get into a good college."
"Who says I am going to college?"
"You bet you are! Getting a degree from a good college is essential for getting a well-paying job when you grow up."

Are a good grade point average or high test scores really accomplishments? The default assumption in the US these days is that everyone in high school should be heading for college. The parents and school counselors suggest that with a well-paying career, happiness is guaranteed. Observant children often need to look no further than their own parents' lack of happiness to notice some flaws in this story. Even if it *were* a true story that money equals happiness, the further off in the future a goal is, the harder it is for a young person (whose frontal cortex is not fully developed) to visualize and be motivated by it.

In my case, I did not get the "prize" of a well-paying tenure track professor job until after 10 years of college and 8 years of postdoctoral work. If I were *not* intrinsically motivated to learn at every step along the way, I would never have made it that far. In fact, I was happier making much less money as a postdoc than I was as a professor, because I was busy inventing and building things every day during my postdoc years at Caltech. I got happiness and motivation when learning from my mentors, Jerry Pine and Scott Fraser, from learning self-taught skills, and from making high-tech gadgets. Almost daily, I could see tangible accomplishments being made. Money ≠ happiness!

Perhaps some day, students will not spend so many years in school in the hope of *some day* being happy. Right now, however, teachers can structure school so that it becomes more intrinsically rewarding and beneficial, both for the student and for those whom their projects may help.

Accomplishing Real Things is Rewarding

How do you feel when someone says "Good job!" to you? Every time you accomplish a good thing, your reward circuitry sends a spurt of dopamine and other neuromodulators throughout your brain. Even when no one compliments you, as long as you see value in what you did, you probably feel a jolt of energy, enthusiasm and self-confidence. That might seem to be not very useful, if the motivating feelings only come *after* you do something of value. But that dopamine release triggers learning, strengthening the brain circuits that were active and crucial in getting a good thing accomplished. The result is that in the future, it will be easier for you to do similar things, when you find yourself in a similar situation.

Thanks to humans' large prefrontal cortex, we are good at generalizing, imagining the future and anticipating such intrinsic rewards while engaged in a difficult multi-step task. We can instruct our students to imagine or visualize success to help them experience how it will feel to finish a tricky project or assignment. Coaches do this all the time, "Keep your eyes on the prize!"

I have found that students can easily see the value of doing projects that have some real-world aspects to them. When people outside the classroom benefit from students' efforts, the motivating reward students feel upon accomplishing the project is amplified tremendously. For example let's compare a traditional term paper with a real-world research report. For all the term papers I wrote, I had to wait until I got them back from the teacher and saw my grade to get any sense of reward. That is, assuming I got a good grade!

And even if I did, I now had a term paper that would be seen by no one else, and probably would soon be tossed out.

Imagine instead that you have your students do research for a busy professional out in the Real World (the "client"). You could help the students find clients and determine what their research needs are. The students then carry out the research and write it up for the client. This could be in pretty much any field, for any subject that has applications out there in the Real World. It could be library research, online research, research in a laboratory, interviews, environmental measurements, or many other information-gathering activities.

It helps if instructors and clients can set up the projects so that there are multiple sub-goals to accomplish. That way, each one provides the accelerating motivation to take the project further. In the case of the real-world research report, the client could look at material gathered throughout the project and give the student periodic feedback on how useful it is, and what else needs to be researched. During the compilation and writing stage, outlines and drafts could be graded, not just the final report.

Incremental assessment is key to getting an excellent result for any project. I have found that when I used this approach with my students (serving either as the instructor or as the client, when Senior Design (p. 198) students built things for my lab), I was almost always able to get an incredibly useful document in the end. Many of their reports lived on as reference material for my research lab for years. I made this fact clear to my students at the outset, so they believed that this was not just an exercise or toy project to "prepare them for the Real World." It was them actually compiling information others would use and depend on.

Even young children can be involved in such projects, as presented in a video about the research of Halvorsen and Duke on Edutopia.org. A class of second-graders studied their local park and made recommendations to a City Councilman about how it could be improved. Their process involved repeated refinement of their initial information-gathering.[50] Their ideas eventually resulted in improvements to their park. I imagine that those kids will always remember what they learned during that assignment, especially when they visit the park again.

---

50. Halvorsen and Duke 2017, Michigan State University https://www.edutopia.org/video/project-based-learning-raising-student-achievement-all-learners

Mastery?

Mastery is a popular buzzword in education lately. For example Berger et al. consider *Mastery of Knowledge and Skills* to be one of *The Three Dimensions of Student Achievement*.[51] To master something is intrinsically motivating. One of the problems with the term "mastery" in the context of education in grade schools or universities, is that it takes much more time than we have available as teachers to enable a person to become a true master at something. This is what apprentices take years to do. It has often been said that it takes at least 5-10 years or 10,000 hours to master something. Therefore, the idea of mastery is an aspirational goal we can shoot for, but it is important for our students to know that this is an *ideal*, so they do not become discouraged if they do not perform perfectly.

As I mentioned earlier, a **learning curve** is a graph of how an ability is improved by practice over time, or with learning trials.

---

51. Ron Berger, Libby Woodfin & Anne Vilen, *Learning That Lasts*, (2016) Wiley, p. 4.

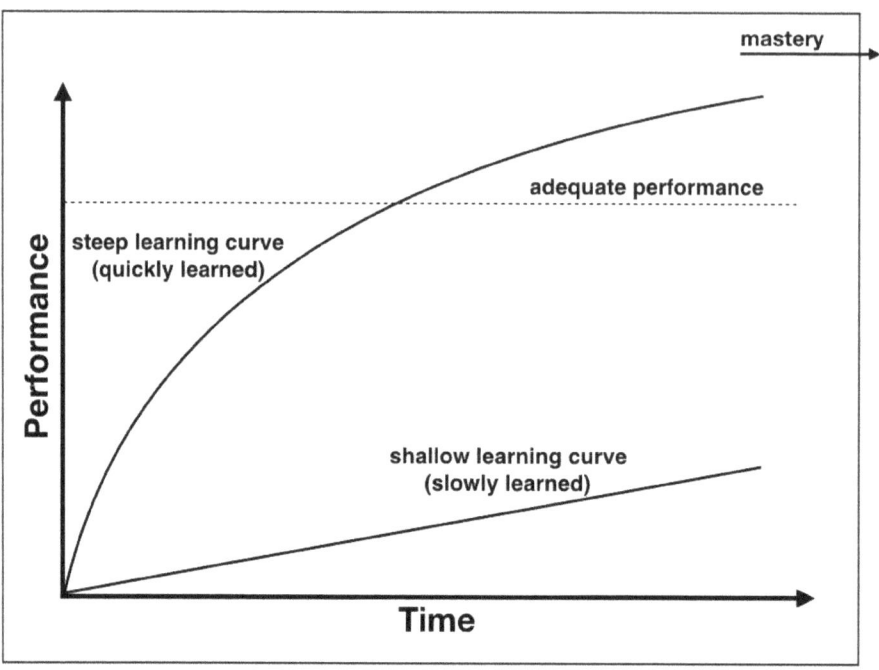

Figure 17. Shallow and steep learning curves. This cartoon representation shows two learning curves of a student's performance as a function of time or learning trials. The upper curve is for an easy task or a fast learner, and the lower curve is for a difficult task or a slow learner. Note that true mastery only happens with years of experience, way off the right side of the learning curve. Most educators who are talking about "mastery" these days actually have in mind some level of adequate performance after which the student may move on to the next task.

As a scientist whose research involved many learning curves, I can say that the top of the learning curve (complete mastery) is usually only reached asymptotically, that is, never quite (Fig. 17). A "steep learning curve" would be one where some capability is learned rapidly, contrary to how it is often used in the media and by lay people.[52] Usually, after a skill is pretty well learned, the curve begins to flatten out. This is the hard part of learning: a long, shallow (not steep) learning curve that takes the learner from good to outstanding across a long time and with much practice.

---

52. The misuse of scientific terms and phrases by the media and then by lay people is one of my pet peeves. Please say, *"A long learning curve"* if you must use a learning curves metaphor to emphasize how difficult a thing is to learn. Do not say the incorrect phrase, *"It has a steep learning curve,"* because that means it is easy — learned quickly.

Students need to know that each step toward mastery is worth taking, and that *the first steps are usually the easiest*. That is, the most gains can be achieved with the least effort early on in the learning process. Unless we are talking about apprenticeships or other long-term endeavors, we should avoid the demotivating and unattainable term "mastery." Instead, we should focus on very specific accomplishments that demonstrate that a student has learned *enough*, or as much as we can expect or hope for, given the time constraints we have to deal with.

Salman Khan, the creator of the Khan Academy, emphasizes "mastery learning" in his book, *The One World School House.* He proposes what I believe is an excellent way to reform education: instead of giving lessons across a fixed time interval, let students take them online in their own time, for however long they need to "master" a specific concept. He acknowledges that students can only approach mastery asymptotically. He says, *"Mastery learning simply suggests that students should adequately comprehend a given concept before being expected to understand a more advanced one."* This seems like a great idea to me. A key word here is "adequately." How much "mastery" is "adequate"?

He uses the analogy of constructing a multi-story building. You lay the foundations, and you have the inspectors come to inspect them. They say, "You are compliant with 85% of all the structural safety regulations." You probably should not then go on to build a big tall building on top of foundations that failed to meet 15% of the safety regulations. But this is what we often do with our students, letting them proceed to the next topic when they did not fully understand the previous one. We often accept way less than 85% as a passing mark. At some point, Khan suggests, the building will collapse, or from the student's perspective, they "hit a wall" of frustration, where they feel so far behind they give up trying to learn more.

While I think that this model of online learning where the student can independently repeat and practice what they need to work on is a good idea, there is still much merit in a scheduled lesson plan led by a living teacher in the room or on a live 2-way video feed. We can incorporate self-directed learning tools like the Khan Academy as one component of our in-person teaching practice.

Certainly we should think carefully about what we expect from our students, and communicate that to them early. It is also important to be flexible and adapt these goals and expectations to the circumstances. For example, an ice storm closed down the entire city of Atlanta for a week one winter. People were ice skating down a deserted Peachtree Avenue, Atlanta's main street. Universities were closed along with everything else, so we missed some lectures and had to readjust our expectations. Certain missed topics were important — I gave my students some autonomy in deciding which topics they felt were worth covering, and I took their opinions on board when adjusting the schedule.

As opposed to mastery, I emphasized other goals that were actually attainable by my students in the time we had. For example, to be *conversant* about the course topic is one good goal for an introductory course. Can the students go to a conference and have an intellectual conversation with a scientist or engineer there about the subjects they learned in class? If they are conversant, they will have the confidence to have many such conversations in the future, and continue the learning process.

Another attainable goal is to be able to think deeply and critically enough about a topic to begin to solve problems that are not yet solved. In my Problem-Based Learning classes, students used the foundations they learned in lecture classes and in reading the literature to solve real-world problems. I didn't expect them to have solutions already in their heads, but instead to have confidence and bravery that they knew enough to begin to tackle a tough problem. As they uncovered deficiencies in their knowledge, they should know where to go to get the answers. As a Facilitator, it was my job to teach them the problem-solving process.

Not knowing something is not a depressing failure, but a motivating call to action. Learning how to solve problems (in groups or individually) and learning how to obtain new knowledge in a self-driven way are two important and realistically attainable goals. Mastery is not required.

For a Khan Academy-style self-paced learning approach, there is likely to be a recurring motivator, that is, getting promoted to move on to the next topic, project step, or unit of study once the last one has been "mastered." Each advance gives the students a spurt of dopamine, reinforcing the good habits that got them this far.

Watch out for the negative motivation or discouragement that may happen for students who take more time to make progress on a topic, or who perceive themselves as struggling. This could be partially balanced by the extra attention they may get from their instructors or peers who are willing to help them out. Remind them that **it is the process that is important** and their rate of advancement does not define them.

It is a fine line to know how much fanfare to make of "leveling up" or getting promoted, so as not to make it a competition. I prefer to let the students find their own motivation for their accomplishments rather than passing out medals or gold stars to everyone as they advance. I certainly complimented students who deserved commendation, but I made it specific about *what they did*, not about *them*, and tried to encourage them to tell others how to do as well as they did.

Addiction and False Accomplishments

We evolved neuromodulators like dopamine, and reward circuits in our brain, to motivate us and help us learn to accomplish useful things. Unfortunately, some chemicals such as opiates, cocaine and amphetamines can spoof the system, misleading the brain into thinking something good was accomplished when all that happened was that a drug was taken. Learning circuits, under the misleading and powerful influence of illicit drugs, reinforce the drug-taking behaviors and addiction happens. The reward circuitry is *hijacked* by addictive drugs.

Thanks to our own endogenous drugs (neuromodulators), one can become "addicted" to anything — not just drugs — that activates the reward pathways in the brain. Gambling is a good example. No drug is consumed, but the unpredictable rewards of winning at the slot machine or blackjack table can be highly addictive. To win money by gambling may be an accomplishment involving skills worth reinforcing, up to the point where it begins to deplete one's bank account and ruin one's life. Addictions, by definition, cause a person to persist with the addictive behavior even when it is understood by that person to be detrimental. That is, only when the reinforced behaviors are *destructive* do we consider it an addiction. In high school, I kept playing *Robotron* even when I was developing painful tendonitis in my elbows. That's addiction.

When someone really gets excited about learning, it can look a lot like addiction. The key difference is that the behavior is productive, not harmful. When activation of reward circuits reinforces *productive* behavior, we call it a successful learning experience by a highly motivated person. Therefore, it is important for instructors to take humans' reward circuitry into account and to leverage it to optimize learning. To do this, we should provide many opportunities for students to receive a spurt of their own endogenous "drugs" (dopamine, endorphins, serotonin, norepinephrine) when they reach goals and accomplish tasks along the way. Complimenting them for any learning and mental growth from their efforts, even after failures, is important.

As I mentioned above, I did not dole out many compliments to individual students, unless they did something outstanding. I didn't want to be seen as having favorite students. I gave out compliments more to the group: "Wow, I really enjoyed reading your write-ups!" Watch out for compliments that lead to a fixed mindset by labeling the student. Say, "Good question!" rather than, "You are very clever to ask that!"

Setting things up so students also receive compliments from their peers, clients, parents, and others in the Real World can really encourage the release of reinforcing neuromodulators in students' brains.

We must also give students the time and resources to *reflect on what has brought them to an accomplishment*, while they are still under the influence of those neuromodulators. This will help them strengthen habits of how to be productive, and reinforce the meta-skills of how to learn, how to deal with failure, how to come up with new approaches, etc. Students must understand that successfully completing an assignment is only one important accomplishment. Learning the meta-skills that can be applied to future projects is just as important, if not more so. Therefore, I encouraged my students to make it a habit to reflect, note, discuss, and celebrate their accomplishments.

Creating Enduring Digital Artifacts

There are more and more opportunities for students to create things online, which gives them a great sense of accomplishment. It was Tim Berners-Lee's original intention when he invented the World Wide Web that all web pages would be editable, living documents created by consensus. This dream of his has come true in many ways, with Wikipedia, GitHub, YouTube, blogging, and of course the social media websites. It is likely that somewhere on the web is the perfect digital venue for your students to make their mark.

I provide evidence of the motivating potential of online projects in Chapter 10, where I describe assignments in which my students wrote articles for Wikipedia and book reviews on Amazon. I have found that when students create lasting artifacts that they know will be of value to others out there in the Real World, they are highly motivated to do an outstanding job. They invariably learn a lot about the specific subject matter they worked on, but they also learn many meta-skills, ones that will continue to serve them well as they become adult citizens who regularly contribute to society through their work and avocations. Such meta-skills include writing and communication skills, how to work in groups, how to collaborate with strangers who may be far away, and web page design.

4) Motivation from Interaction: Social humans

It is seldom truly appreciated how intensely social our species is. We evolved in small groups of close-knit relatives. Our ancestors maximized their reproduction and survival by evolving (across generations) and learning (across each lifetime) mental strategies that benefitted the tribe. Many of these are social strategies. Those tribes had dominance/respect hierarchies. They had altruism. They employed cooperation to accomplish large tasks, such as big game hunting, building a house, and farming. They cared for each other. They shared food and resources to survive. Crucial learning was passed from older to younger members of the tribe.

There are always going to be rules, laws, norms, traditions, and etiquette to encourage a group to function well. Our ancestors who were quick to pick up on social subtleties survived and reproduced well, and now much of this social intelligence is instinctive. It is hard-wired into our neural circuitry or more easily learned than if we did not have such a social evolutionary history.

In structuring our classrooms and courses, we might as well take advantage of students' social brains. I have noticed that some of the most powerful things that motivated my students to perform well (learn, behave, advance) tie in to their social nature. The long list that follows emphasizes just how extremely important social forces are in regard to student motivation. I tried to mix in useful and specific advice related to each one.

These powerful social motivators ...

*... **lead to new friendships.*** Instructors can assign group or pair work. Use name tags and getting-to-know-you activities at the beginning. Be sure to incorporate free or less structured time into the students' day, where conversations can happen. Make a contact list so classmates can exchange information and bond outside of class.

*... **are influenced by mating instincts.*** Be sensitive to who may be attracted to whom. On the first day of each year as a student in school, I was very excited to find out which girls I might be seated next to, even if I didn't know why. Sometimes, those feelings present more of a distraction than a helpful motivator, well known by those in favor of all-boy and all-girl schools.

*... **spread excitement.*** Allow students to make suggestions or to come up with new directions. Take hand-raise polls often to sense the group mood. Allow exclamations, cheering, high-fives, hugging, selfies, etc.

*... **boost status.*** Praise students' efforts and encourage students to compliment each other when appropriate. Post an accomplishments board, on the wall or online. Have students share their good work with the class. Consider awards, ribbons, trophies, certificates, or badges, but be sure to tie these to tangible accomplishments and *effort*, rather than use them to

label students. Promote students to the next level of difficulty if they earned it and are ready.

These powerful social motivators also …

… prevent embarrassment, humiliation or shame. Don't let students put shoddy work out there in a presentation or on the Internet. Give students a chance to fix up a disappointing effort after discussing what went wrong. Try to reduce the chances that you or the students' parents express disappointment. Let those doing group work know at the outset how not to let teammates down.

… improve peers' opinions of each other. Give students chances to impress their peers, especially when working in groups. Google Docs is great for collaborative writing. Encourage students to pose thoughtful questions in class, and to be prepared to answer the teacher's questions. Allow students with creative ideas to express them freely.

… build respect. Give students opportunities to excel or to be unusually creative. Give them chances to help or teach others. Allow students to take on as much responsibility and leadership as they wish.

… enhance feelings of belonging. Mention how fortunate your students are to be here, doing what they are doing. Praise exceptional efforts by groups. Remind them of things to be proud of about their situation. Let the students come up with Team Names for their group projects. Allow freedom of expression that may bond a group, such as custom T-shirts or nicknames on the backs of their chairs. Encourage group outings, such as meals together.

… result in kudos from others. This could include parents, clients, authorities, or online acquaintances. Showcase presentations or material on the Internet. Nominate outstanding students or groups for awards or special recognition or press in the media. Hold an open house for the general public to learn from and admire students' work.

… give warm fuzzy feelings from helping others. Include opportunities for students to help those in need, including classmates as well as strangers.

... enhance fairness. Respond quickly and forcibly to cheating. Don't have Teachers' Pets. Be constantly aware of favoring any student or even giving the appearance of playing favorites. This is why compliments must be based on effort and tangible accomplishments.

... reduce FOMO (fear of missing out). Be sure to communicate all opportunities and options that students may pursue, in multiple ways and times, so that no student will miss an important or potentially rewarding experience. Investigate reasons why a student failed to get permission from their parents for a field trip or special activity, because they may feel devastated by being left out.

These all have human interaction in common. Think about it: if we were a solitary species, none of these would matter.

Many of the projects and problems I had my students work on were done in teams. There are a number of advantages to team work compared to solitary work. It helps students learn social skills such as the importance of being responsible or how to be critical in a constructive way. Most importantly, it really increases their level of excitement and engagement, thanks to all that social circuitry in their brains.

Google did a quantitative study across dozens of its teams, of what makes teams perform well.[53] It found that the number one parameter that predicted success was **how safe team members felt:** *"In a team with high psychological safety, teammates feel safe to take risks around their team members. They feel confident that no one on the team will embarrass or punish anyone else for admitting a mistake, asking a question, or offering a new idea."*

Teachers and facilitators can help establish a culture of openness and acceptance that make student teams feel safe with each other. I usually had some "getting to know you" exercise right after teams are formed, such as having each person tell the group about some hobby of theirs, or favorite music, TV shows, etc. One good way to do that is to have pairs interview each other and present the results of their interview to the group. At all stages of a project, I was quick to correct a student who said a mean or disrespectful thing

---

53. https://bit.ly/2ZDxDMF

to another team member, reminding them to always keep criticism constructive.

Number two on Google's list of key parameters of successful teams was **dependability:** *"On dependable teams, members reliably complete quality work on time (vs. the opposite — shirking responsibilities)."* There is a lot more to being responsible than just being on time. Good communication between team members is crucial for making sure everyone knows what they are doing, and letting others know if they need help. I made sure that on the first day, everyone on a team had everyone else's contact information, and encouraged them to communicate as much as they needed to outside of class. That ties in with Google's third most important parameter, **structure and clarity:** *"An individual's understanding of job expectations, the process for fulfilling these expectations, and the consequences of one's performance are important for team effectiveness."* These "job expectations" come from their peers as well as the teacher.

What is most interesting about Google's study is that it did not help if the team was filled with geniuses. Teams of mediocre achievers did better than teams of over-achievers. Instead, the top three most important features of productive teams were about how well they interact socially. These social skills can be taught and learned. I have observed many students metamorphosing like a caterpillar into a butterfly, from being poor team members to super-motivated ones, once they figured out the social rules.

The social aspects of education can have a negative side. Some of the strong motivators above are related to the fear of letting others down, or of letting oneself down. But we could also talk about *demotivators* related to interpersonal interactions. Humans have an innate sense of fairness and consider even a small amount of unfair treatment as worse than many more tangible or serious problems.

Even monkeys are keenly aware of being treated unfairly, as Frans de Waal describes in his TED talk.[54] He and Sarah Brosnan gave one capuchin monkey a boring slice of cucumber, while its neighbor in the cage next door got a sweet grape. The first monkey, seeing that he missed out on getting a grape, shook his cage and tossed the cucumber back at the experimenter, even though if both had gotten cucumber slices, they would have eaten them happily.

If students notice any unfair treatment in school, they may become outraged like the capuchin monkey. They may just keep it bottled up, becoming demotivated and losing respect for the teacher. I have found that by creating an environment where students can say how they feel about how things are going, either privately or in class, they will quickly bring any

---

54. https://www.youtube.com/watch?v=meiU6TxysCg

perceived unfairness to my attention. I always responded quickly, explaining my logic if I felt I was being fair. If, after a discussion, another student or I were found to be unfair I instituted the needed changes.

Students in BME at Georgia Tech were often the top students in their high schools, used to getting only As. A student sometimes felt that I had singled them out for unfair treatment if I did not give them an A, while others in their group got As. I was careful to share with them my grading **rubric** and got good at justifying how I came up with the grades I gave (e.g., our Problem-Based Learning grading rubric, Fig. 22, p. 197). To do that, it helped to take careful notes about each student's shortcomings, and to scan all exams before returning them, in case they might be tempted to cheat by altering what they had written during the exam.

Comparing

Status is one of the most powerful motivators of most people. Humans' obsession with status probably dates way back to protohumans fighting to be the tribal chief or alpha. Or even further back — many animals use their status to improve their mating opportunities and survival.[55] What I find interesting about status is how prone it is to adjustment by observing one's peers. It is not about the absolute amount of wealth, the cost of a house, car or pair of fancy shoes. It is not enough to think, "Isn't my house comfortable and good at keeping out the rain?" We need to compare it to all the others on the block before we can decide how proud or ashamed we are. We look at our friends, neighbors and coworkers and continually ask, "How am I doing *compared to them*?" When I was a child, I was called out by one of my teachers for wearing tattered pants with holes in the knees, and was terribly embarrassed. Nowadays, when it is stylish for expensive designer jeans have holes in the knees, a girl may look at her peers and make it top priority to get ripped jeans too. It is all relative.

For students, this can be about all sorts of things. Grades are an obvious one. Most students want to know not just how did they score, but how did they do relative to the rest of the class. "What was the mean score?" was always asked immediately as I handed back graded exams. It was nearly impossible for me to fight their instinct to keep comparing themselves to each other. I had to keep reminding them that I graded on a straight scale based on what they

---

55. See Robert Sapolsky's excellent book, which includes many of his observations of dominance hierarchies in groups of wild baboons that he studied: *Behave: The Biology of Humans at our Best and Worst* (2017) Bodley Head.

learned and did, not on a bell curve based on their classmates' scores (I discuss grading in Ch. 9).

But grades are just one aspect of where students derive their status. Students may also be comparing themselves to each other to elevate their relative status. This could be in terms of who gets the most toys from Santa, whose family goes to the most exotic places for vacations, who is the strongest athlete, who looks the cutest, or who has the coolest and most expensive smartphone or shoes. They may also hope to raise their status by hanging out with or being "followed" by the cool crowd or getting "likes" from the most popular or good-looking student. Much of the dominance or respect hierarchy is established these days online in social media, where it is easy to track who follows whom.

The key point here is that students — and most humans, in general — are preoccupied with status, and the status instinct can be leveraged to help motivate them to love learning. But it is not easy to develop a curriculum that somehow boosts the status of everyone. I accomplished that by giving all of my students an opportunity to create something they are proud of, something that changed the world for the better. They can then use that to impress others outside of class if they wish. Or they may just use it to bolster their self-confidence, to feel more empowered to make positive, enduring changes.

I am conflicted on the merit of competition in school. Clearly, competition can be used to get people motivated and excited, such as at a sporting event. I have seen it work well to get teams of engineering students to learn the basics of robotics. For the ME72 class taught to undergrads at Caltech,[56] groups are each given the same box of robot raw materials, and challenged to design and build a robot to accomplish a specific task. The students put a huge amount of creativity and work into building their robots, culminated by a well-attended public robot competition. The winning team members each get a trophy.

I think the things that make Caltech's ME72 robot-building competition a success are a culture of friendly cooperation the instructors foster among all students, and that it is a low-stakes competition. I have seen students become mean, and even sabotage other groups, during competitions, so I avoided competitions in my courses. Higher stakes can bring out the worst in students, such as if the prize is a $20,000 angel investor grant to start a company, or if their grades depend on winning top place. Losers, especially those who got second or third place, may be bitter or feel like they wasted all their effort.

Given how important it is for students to compare themselves to each other, if you can leverage that drive into good-natured low-stakes competition, it may be worth a try (as I did for my *Peer Ranking* assignment, p. 167). Just

---

56. http://www.mce.caltech.edu/events/me72

make sure that everyone knows that it is the process and the learning that are truly important, not who wins.

Social Fear

Fear can demotivate and many fears are social. Students may not always behave respectfully to others and this can damage the self-worth of their target. An extreme example is bullying. But even wisecracks or put-downs that seem like joking can be harmful and really sap a student's motivation. We can help prevent this by establishing a culture of respect in the classroom and by not tolerating disrespectful behavior.

Performance anxiety may not only be demotivating, but for some students, it may be paralyzing or terrifying. Speaking in front of a group can evoke the fear of embarrassment or humiliation. I used to be very shy. I learned gradually that I can stand in front of class and give a presentation without any disasters happening. In fact, sometimes when I survived a small disaster, (such as misspeaking or answering a belligerent question) I got more confidence: I *can* deal with things not going perfectly! I still get some nerves before giving a talk or at the beginning of class, but I am so used to it that I think of nervousness as a necessary part of giving a good "performance." The extra adrenalin keeps me on my toes and sharpens my mind. It moves me closer to the peak of my Yerkes-Dodson Curve. Inevitably, once I begin speaking, I don't even notice being nervous anymore.

We can remind our students that fear and excitement are almost the same thing (p. 69), and that excitement is useful. We can help them reduce pre-performance worries by making sure they are well prepared and by creating a supportive atmosphere where shyness is accepted, mistakes are forgiven, and students are expected to have to *learn* to be good presenters. Very few are born knowing this skill.

To reduce students' anxiety about shaking, stuttering, blushing, sweating or other signs of nervousness, let the whole class know that these are normal physiological signs that the presenter cares a lot about what they are presenting and how it is received by their audience. These sympathetic nervous system responses are nearly impossible to control consciously but can usually be reduced or eliminated with experience and the confidence that comes from being well prepared.

Relaxation techniques can also help reduce sympathetic responses. For example, deep, slow breaths activate the **parasympathetic nervous system's** relaxation response, which opposes the sympathetic "fight or flight" response.

Another interesting approach that may help is power posing,[57] recently given the more scientific name, *postural feedback*. The idea is to adopt poses associated with powerful people (think of Wonder Woman standing arms akimbo) before and during presentations. It has been shown that this can provide real boosts in confidence and even alter the levels of circulating testosterone and cortisol, two hormones associated with status, confidence and drive.

The Importance of Communication of All Types

Of the adaptations that promoted survival and reproduction in our prehistoric tribal past, those serving communication purposes are likely to be the ones that required our cortex to become as large as it is. Those who did not develop a large cortex to help them communicate well failed to thrive, survive and reproduce.

Communication includes much more than spoken and written language. For example, how many other animals move their eyes as much as humans do, and have "whites" visible on their eyeballs, making it easy to see the direction of their gaze? Knowing where someone is looking is an important means of communication. Even infants watch their carers' gaze direction to learn what they should be paying attention to. When hunting as a group, it was probably important for our ancestors to be able to coordinate silently with the others using eye gaze and a minimum of gestures. If you want to know what your students are paying attention to, just look at where their eyes are pointing.

Humans also have elaborate languages of gesture, body language, and facial expressions. Can you think of any animals that express as many things by moving their facial muscles as we do? Even the briefest of facial twitches, called micro-expressions, can betray a lie, according to psychologist Paul Ekman. Some of these nonverbal communication methods are innate, but many are learned and are culturally dependent.

Students use all these nonverbal cues to send and receive a wide range of important social information. Communication helps them bond to their friends and to the teacher. It determines their status or rank in social groups.

It helps to keep asking yourself, "What is my body language communicating? My tone? My eye movements?" Eye-to-eye contact can be highly motivating, so it is a good habit to try to make that bond with each and every student regularly.

In the modern age where online communication is becoming increasingly common, keep in mind the huge benefits of rich 2-way

---

57. Amy Cuddy, *Presence: Bringing Your Boldest Self to Your Biggest Challenges,* (2015) Little, Brown & Co.

communication. The asynchronous low-bandwidth media, such as text messages, Twitter and Instagram posts, and Facebook comments are terrible for promoting understanding. Slightly better is email, where one can be verbose, but written expressions and smileys are poor substitutes for seeing and hearing all the non-verbal cues present in face-to-face communication. Phone conversations are a big improvement, adding the benefit of emotions conveyed by intonation, and the simultaneity that allows misunderstandings to be cleared up quickly. One-way communication by recorded audio and video is higher bandwidth, but still prone to misunderstanding and confusion. Videoconferences are better, adding the benefits of immediate feedback via body language and facial expressions,[58] and the asking of questions. Therefore, when communicating with your students outside of a classroom context, whenever possible, choose simultaneous (2-way) high-bandwidth modes of interaction, i.e., live audio and video.

Learning With Words

Another thing that sets humans apart from other animals is our extremely versatile ability to communicate with spoken and written language. Humans are uniquely good at symbol processing in general, making analogies, pretending, and understanding that something stands for (represents) something else. Large portions of the brain, poetically called "eloquent areas" by brain surgeons, are crucial for us to speak, read, write, and understand speech. If you get a stroke that damages any of these circuits, you have serious problems with language, called aphasia. Many brain parts other than just the eloquent areas are involved in the process, of course, such as the visual cortex for reading, the auditory cortex for hearing, and motor cortex for writing.

Written language has allowed humans, in a very real sense, to be taught by generations of dead ancestors. The only way other animals get that (wisdom from their ancestors) is via the MUCH slower process of evolution. Neural circuits evolve across many generations to develop hard-wired skills (instincts). Individuals that, by chance, could do a bit of the skill survived and reproduced better than those who had none of it.

Cultural transmission is much faster. Knowledge can be transferred more veridically, more quickly and more broadly from generation to generation via written texts, than orally or by demonstration. The sum total of that accumulated wisdom is what we call culture and technology. Written knowledge can easily skip generations. I can read a copy of Newton's *Principia* from the early 1700s and get a lesson straight from one of the

---

58. However, eye contact is often problematic, because the webcam lens is not where one is usually looking during a videoconference.

greatest scientific minds of all time.[59] My parents probably would not be able to teach me that stuff, but in this modern world where the classics have all been scanned thanks to Google and many volunteers, it is easily accessible to anyone.

A good fraction of modern instruction is verbal, whether oral or written, and verbal skills vary widely. Therefore, it behooves instructors to make sure students are understanding the material. The "Aha!" moment students get when they suddenly understand a tricky concept, whether through their ears or eyes, is a great motivator. Conversely, getting stuck due to poor or ineffective communication can really sap students' motivation. While giving lectures, I continually asked if anyone had questions, and gauged students' understanding from their questions. Daily quizzes that I used for taking roll also tested their understanding of any written material they were assigned to read. Students who have communication difficulties such as dyslexia or impaired hearing or vision must be accommodated to make sure they are able to absorb the course material in the most effective way they can. I made good use of Georgia Tech's Office of Disability Services, which helps students with special needs. They supplied signers, aides, note-takers, or special test proctoring as needed.

When you add them all up, in my experience, social factors are the strongest motivators, inside the classroom and out. It is imperative for instructors to understand them well enough to take advantage of them, rather than fight them.

5) Motivation from Control: Give Students Agency

A feeling of being in control of one's life is motivating for anyone. Conversely, being under someone's thumb is demotivating, demoralizing or even devastating. Being an active agent in one's education should be the norm for all students, but usually it is not. We expect students to conform to our list of required courses, to the schedules of our curriculum, and even sometimes to where they must sit in the classroom. By doing that, we are training conformity. This is boring at best and demotivating or humiliating at worst. It is saying to students, "We don't trust you to make decisions about your education."

When students feel a sense of **agency**, that they are in control of at least some aspects of their education, they become much more motivated. They may even take ownership of the process, a huge advance in maturity for any student, and usually a requirement for successful completion of difficult

---

59. Newton's book: https://bit.ly/2qRhTZf

projects in the Real World. This helps develop the executive functions of their frontal lobes.

Doing Project-Based Learning does not necessarily mean students have more agency. There are many types of projects. The standard, traditional approach is what I experienced in all of the science lab classes I took: follow the instructions written by the teacher, and everyone is expected to get the exact same result. I am not a fan of teacher-designed projects. Students are much more motivated when they have a hand in deciding what to do and how to do it.

Here is an example of a bad project: Coming up to Christmas vacation, my third grade teacher dictated the way every student in the class would make a Santa Claus candy jar. She meant well when she laid out the materials (baby food jars, felt cutouts, cotton puffs, glue). We dutifully glued on the felt beards and hats she had cut out, and at the end of the day, everyone's Santa jar was identical. There was no room for any creative input by us students. Even as a third grader, I could tell what a lame project this was. If I had decided to glue the beard on the lid where Santa's cap goes, she would have scolded me and not let me fill it with candy until I fixed it.

In all my courses, I tried to give my students as much autonomy as possible. Autonomy is a powerful motivator, while outside control (a lack of autonomy or outright oppression) can be a powerful demotivator. Although my grad school advisor was a good mentor and a very careful scientist, he was a micromanager. He preferred to give everyone in his lab complete and detailed instructions about what to do next. He did not appreciate us making our own decisions, no matter how trivial. This management style clashed often with my unusually independent personality. He vetoed most of my attempts to set the course of my PhD research, and that lack of autonomy wore me down and sapped my motivation.

By contrast, beginning my postdoc at Caltech, I suddenly had two mentors who trusted me to make most of my own decisions. I nearly felt like I had been released from prison.

Based on my own experience as described earlier in Chapter 4, however, too much autonomy can lead to a feeling of being lost if an insufficient amount of scaffolding is provided. I was often too hands-off with my own research group. One of my grad students told me a few years after getting his PhD in my lab, "I wish you had cracked the whip more." Some students thrive with more direction and flounder without it.

Figuring out the right balance of autonomy versus guidance for each student is a tricky thing. For the courses I taught, I found quite a few ways that I could let my students choose aspects of the assignments or projects that they did. However, a project can be a disaster if students have too much "**voice and**

choice" and not enough direction. Often they do not have the necessary background to make good decisions.

My students sometimes got frustrated after coming up with impossible projects. I realized the solution was to develop the projects *with* the students, collaboratively, and with several iterations or cycles of refinement.

Usually, I would have the students begin with a brainstorming process in which they create **mind maps**[60] (Fig. 18) of every single idea they can come up with related to the project. I would sit back and enjoy their brainstorming until they started to gain a sense of direction in where they wanted to go, or how exactly to proceed. Only then would I intervene if needed, to serve as a reality checker, and let them know what was feasible with the time, equipment, or supplies we had available for the project.

Here is where scaffolding becomes important, at the beginning stages of defining a project. I tried as much as I could to let my students direct the scaffolding I provided, by asking me (or other experts) for advice and help, rather than foisting it upon them and risking limiting their creativity. When they realized that the project was largely their creation, they took ownership of it and derived great pride and motivation from this fact. If you give students as much agency as you can, but stay involved enough to keep them from floundering, they will accomplish great things with enthusiasm.

---

60. https://en.wikipedia.org/wiki/Mind_map

6. What Motivates Students?

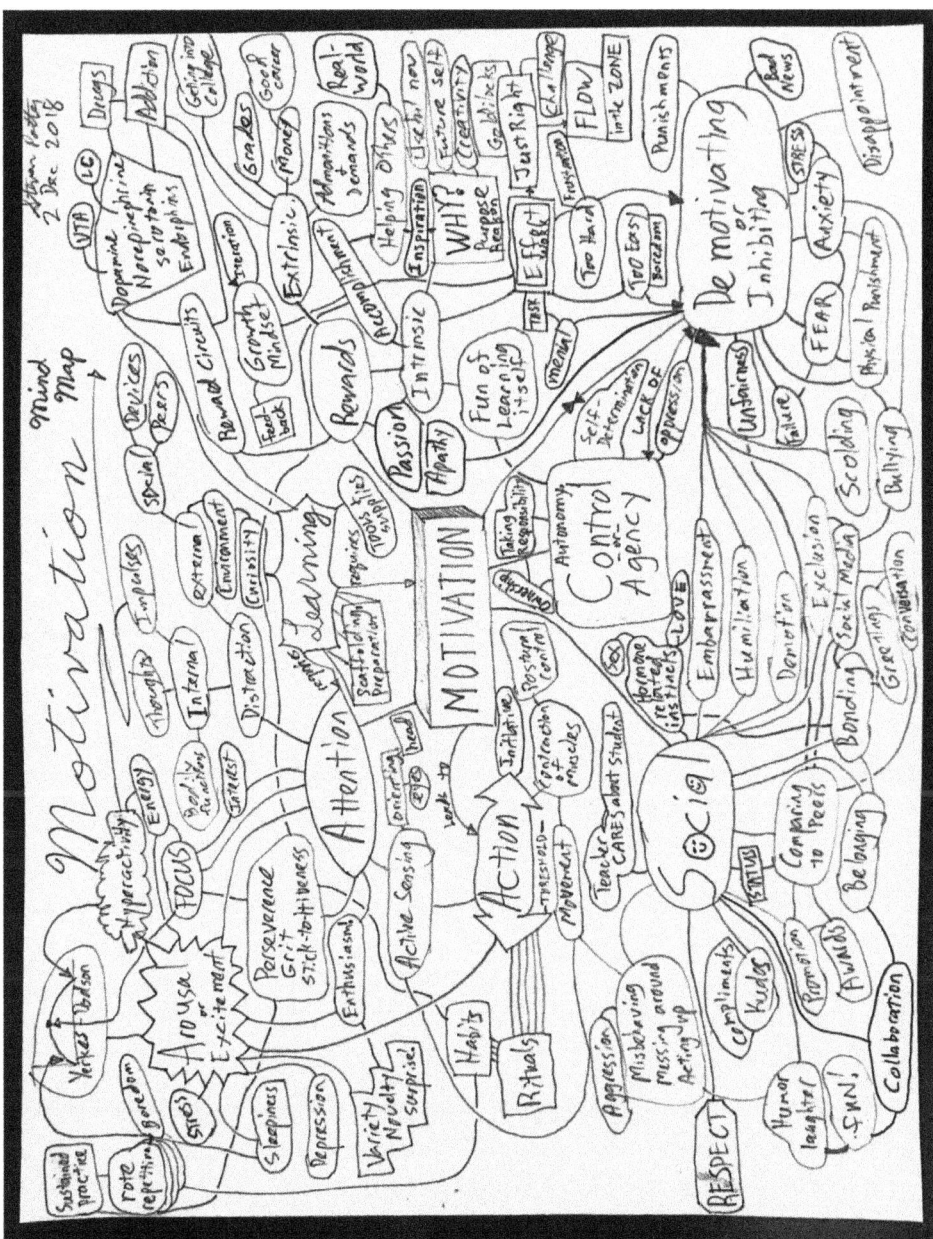

Figure 18. Example of a mind map, one that I created while writing this book.

6) Motivation from Play

Children love to play. Play is characterized by excited movement, laughter, screams of delight, and self-directed and free-form activity. It is often in a social context, though not always. It may involve pretending or imagining — make-believe. This is a kind of learning that children do not need to be coerced into doing. They are intrinsically motivated to play. They are curious, energetic, and love to explore and try new things, always seeking novelty and surprise.

Watch children play. Through play, they learn and practice the types of things they will be doing as adults. Seeing how strong the play instinct is in humans and other mammals, we can guess that most learning early in life is from play. Play is how children and other young animals learn all about their world, its potentials and limitations. Play leads to all sorts of learning, often without rules, a teacher, or even any particular goals. With humans, play includes frequent complex verbalization (even when done alone) and imagination that depends on human verbal processing circuits. Play is how children build models of the Real World in their heads as they experiment and pretend with their toys and playmates. It is how they learn the rules of social interactions.

How can we take advantage of humans' love of play in an educational context? Contrast the playground with a typical school classroom. Class resembles a Time Out punishment. "Sit still and be quiet!" Perhaps if schooling resembled what our brains evolved to learn from, it would be more effective. Some types of home schooling, such as **unschooling**, promote self-directed play as the main way to learn things. Montessori schools do an excellent job of giving kids the scope to learn while playing in a more structured environment. This was the original idea behind kindergarten.

As we get older and less energetic, we mostly move on to other ways to learn. Play may become tinkering, or participation in sports, playing music, doing hobbies or club activities. All are intrinsically motivating learning experiences. I have often felt that my building and fixing things in the lab and in my workshop are much more like play than work. They are the most enjoyable and, in many ways, the most educational part of my work.

There are many aspects of Project-Based Learning that resemble play, especially if projects are tackled by groups of students. As instructors, we can use play to raise the level of students' excitement to the peak of the Yerkes-Dodson Curve. Of course, we must be wary of it going past the peak into chaos. Students may be having more fun, but are not making progress or learning much if they are acting on every impulse and distraction.

Inquiry-based Teaching and Learning

How can we merge play with teaching, to enhance student motivation? Inquiry-based teaching does that. My postdoc mentor, Jerry Pine had a big influence on my teaching style. He founded, with Prof. Jim Bower, the Caltech Pre-college Science Initiative (CAPSI), which developed ways to teach elementary school teachers how to lead inquiry-based lessons. They built teaching kits, led workshops, and transformed the 22 elementary (K-6) schools of the Pasadena Unified School District, including the very schools I had attended as a child. Before CAPSI, there were roving science teachers that visited classes only once a week for short science lessons. After CAPSI training, *all* teachers were expected to be able to lead inquiry-based science modules.

The idea of inquiry-based teaching and learning is to set the students loose on a poorly defined problem or topic in which there will be many mysteries and unknowns that the students might ask about. Unlike typical K-6 lessons, the teacher is not meant to be the expert in the topic, but merely a facilitator in the learning process. That process is supposed to be driven by the students, using their own intrinsic curiosity, in a playful way.

If the teacher doesn't know the answer to a question, they are trained to help the students come up with their own tests and experiments to try to answer it themselves. For example, as part of a module called *There's No Away*, Grade 6 students each made and watered their own mini-landfill full of trash and soil in a bucket. They later dissected it to see which waste decomposed and which did not. A *Daytime Astronomy* module had fifth-graders tracking the Sun by measuring how shadows change over hours and weeks, and building physical models of the Solar System to understand what they were seeing.

Although I was focused on my research rather than teaching during my postdoc years at Caltech, I could not help learning a lot from Jerry about his inquiry-based teaching and learning efforts because we worked closely — literally. I often worked *in his office* because it was also a mini-laboratory. While working there, I saw and heard him interacting with his CAPSI colleagues. He told me about his various K-6 teaching modules, and also about the project-based teaching he did with the physics undergrads at Caltech. I wished I had had a teacher like Jerry in my K-12 years.

Jerry was a great hands-on mentor with a playful attitude. Like me, he loved to build things, and almost all of the equipment in his lab was made in-house by him and others in his lab. We worked together for several years building a high-speed camera for imaging activity in brain cells. As I observed how he led me through design-build-test cycles, I learned a lot about how to deal productively with failure and how to diagnose a wide variety of electrical, optical, and programming problems. Being a physicist, he had all the math we needed to design the camera well on paper. From all my tinkering with cars, computers, and electronics, I had (or soon learned) the hands-on skills to build, test and improve it. We made a great team and eventually got a patent for the camera (US patent 6,633,331).[61]

Jerry had no patience for anyone who did not put the work into understanding what they were doing in his lab. His gruff Long Island style of exposing an experiment's weaknesses with loud profanities sometimes had his grad students in tears. But I loved it and thrived in his lab.[62] Making that camera took two or three years of tinkering in the lab. I found this process highly motivating and seemed like play to me.[63]

***

As I will describe in the following chapters, I had great success exploiting the power of social interactions to help motivate my students. Think about how you can restructure your classroom and curricula to take advantage of the excitement that comes from interacting with fellow students and others, but also from accomplishing meaningful things, being in control, expressing curiosity in a playful context, and immersing one's full attention in a project. By having students work on real-world projects that they helped to choose and design, letting them interact freely, keeping them on a very long leash, and letting them have fun, you can tap into the prehistoric brain circuits that evolved to allow effective learning.

---

61. https://patents.google.com/patent/US6633331B1/en
62. Jerry kept doing his innovative teaching at Caltech right up until he died at age 89 in 2017.
63. One day, after I had solved a particularly tricky problem with the camera's circuits, I found on my desk an honorary diploma. Jerry conferred upon me the degree, *"Master of Experimental Electrical Engineering,"* from the *"Jerome Pine School of Hard Knocks."* I proudly display this diploma on my electronics workshop wall, as a reminder of how valuable hands-on real-world teaching and learning has been to me.

Part III

The Learning of Neurobiology

My Introduction to Neuroscience ("IntroNeuro") course was expected to be a traditional lecture course: Professor at the lectern talking for 50 minutes about neurobiology while about 100 seniors in BME and Biology take notes in a big lecture hall. In this Part, I will describe the ways I strayed from the beaten path with IntroNeuro, by making the lectures more discussion-based, and by focusing on real-world projects to help motivate my students and teach them skills that will be useful to them long after they have forgotten the factoids. I had my students write articles for Wikipedia, create YouTube videos, interview experts, write book reviews for Amazon, and go to talks by neuroscientists about their latest research. My students' comments and accomplishments have convinced me that Project-Based Learning and lecture-based classes can work well together to motivate students.

CHAPTER 7

Engaging Lectures

Lectures can be an effective tool for teaching and motivating students, if done well. As a professor, I have given many "lectures" for my courses. I put "lectures" in quotation marks because they usually were not traditional lectures, which tend to be one-way communication, teacher to students. Judging from my students' course evaluations, and from the large amount of effort they voluntarily put into my elective courses, I developed a number of effective strategies for conveying information that got them excited to come to class and to be active participants in my "lectures." They were especially motivated by interesting stories, discussions, and the enthusiasm shown by my guest lecturers and me.

Anonymous responses from IntroNeuro students in answer to the question, **"What was the greatest strength of the course?":**

> *"Everything, but if I had to choose one it would be the desire to have the class involved in the lectures."*
>
> *"Made the class interesting!! Had great stories and discussions to keep you engaged in the material."*
>
> *"Professor Potter's enthusiasm was a great motivator. His discussion driven class was one of the more entertaining classes."*

And from anonymous Neuroeng. Fun. students,

> "Dr. Potter's enthusiasm for the class and what we were learning made the class so much better."

> "His passion and knowledge of everything and anything Neuro related. It really made the class enjoyable."

I will try to describe my strategies below in this traditional one-way medium of a book, but if you have any questions, you can email me![64]

I feel the main shortcoming of the lecture format is the likelihood of poor *engagement*. Engagement means, "To occupy the attention or effort of." Not paying attention and not exerting any effort leads to very poor retention of the material. We pay attention to things we wish to learn. A bad or even so-so lecturer may fail to capture students' attention or to generate any enthusiasm in them. Or maybe the student is good at paying attention by taking extensive notes, but doesn't see the point of what the teacher is lecturing about.

I had a World History teacher in tenth grade who said he was doing us a service by "Preparing us for how class will be in college." When we walked into his class, he had already completely covered the chalkboard with notes on whatever epoch of history today's lesson was about. We spent ten minutes quickly transcribing the board to our notebooks while he paced around watching the clock. At ten minutes and one second into the class, he launched into a monolog that did not pause for the next 45 minutes, while we quickly annotated our notes with more details. Sadly, my World History teacher was correct. Many of my college courses were like that: facts force-fed to us with little or no explanation of why, and no discussion.

Now more than ever, I feel this style of teaching is inappropriate because students can always just look up who won the Crimean War, or who Chandragupta Maurya was, on Wikipedia if they ever need to know that. (Those are two poorly recalled World History sound bites floating in my head, completely unconnected to any other things I know.)

It is useful to ask ourselves as instructors what we hope our students get out of lectures in the modern era of free and easy information access. I hope they get some context for the material that bolsters their enthusiasm and raises their curiosity. If your students are enthusiastic and curious, you will have their

---

64. Emails related to this book should be sent to me using this address: motivate2lovelearning at gmail.com.

attention, and what you say will stick in their heads and change their thinking by making new connections.

> "Dr. Potter has consistently proven that he is a more involved educator than most. His own passion for the subject matter makes learning that much more exciting. The fact that he consistently espouses the virtues of graduate school and science at large provide stimulating relief in a major that all too often becomes about burying yourself in details."
> - anonymous IntroNeuro student

The most important thing for me was to make class more of a discussion than a lecture. Having two-way communication really motivates students. Knowing the teacher cares about what they think motivates them. Getting their questions answered and their frustrations or misunderstandings respectfully addressed engages them well. Discussions also helped me set the direction and level of my lecture. I heard right away (not after the midterm) what the students were understanding and what they were confused about.

Guest Lecturers

In Elementary school, I recall loving to hear about what my classmates' parents did for a living when we occasionally had one visit our class. Sadly, most guest lecturers in college are merely substitute teachers filling in when the prof couldn't be there for some reason. In IntroNeuro, I always had about a dozen guest lecturers visit my class (during a semester of about 45 sessions). Many of my students felt this was the most educational aspect of my courses. One anonymous student wrote in the end-of-course survey,

> "I also enjoyed the guest speakers. They were always relevant, interesting, and well integrated into the course material. You could tell the guest lecturers were selected with the overall course in mind instead of being poor substitutes for a busy professor."

Another anonymous student wrote,

> "The interaction of the lecture made it much more interesting than any lecture I've ever had, and the guest lectures really opened my mind to different areas in the field."

My guest lecturers were usually researchers or clinicians from the Atlanta area. I was always present to introduce them,[65] to take notes, and to lead discussions if they did not take the lead themselves. I chose guests whose research complemented material I planned to give lectures on. I instructed them to talk about their lab's research and their latest experiments, not give a general introduction to their field. It was exciting for my students and me to hear about cutting-edge neuroscience research, including work in progress that was not even published yet. Because my students had been told by me that no question is too dumb to ask (p. 121), we always had to leave time for questions during and after the guest lectures. Thus, another job for me was to keep track of time and warn the speaker when it was time to wrap up their lecture.

Before the semester began, I had to plan out the lecture schedule and invite the guest lecturers. I eventually got better at doing this far enough ahead of time to avoid any shuffling of lectures after the semester began. To my recurring surprise, I was never turned down when I invited a potential speaker. Perhaps that is because I made it clear that there might be benefits to them, such as recruiting future grad students or getting fresh perspectives from my students about the research the guests presented. If one of my students got fired up by a guest lecture, they might approach the speaker afterwards to inquire about working part time in their lab.

The majority of undergraduates in the BME department got some experience working in a lab during their time at Georgia Tech. My own research lab usually had between two and five undergrads working alongside the grad students and postdocs. Some of them met me when I had given a guest lecture for one of my colleagues. I sometimes invited guests to IntroNeuro whom I had not met before, based on reading their papers or studying their website. I became good friends with a number of these guests as a result. A guest lecture was not used as a "day off" for me. Having guest lecturers was a win for all involved.

One of my most popular "guest lecturer" days was a graduate student panel discussion. Many of my students were in the process of applying to grad schools and/or med schools, and often had no clue what they are really like. I could tell them about my own experiences in grad school, but that was ages

---

65. Except once: I had told my guest from Emory Med School to meet me at my office before class so that I could escort him to the lecture hall. As class time drew nearer, I paced the floor waiting and waiting for him. Eventually, I messaged my students via the learning management system the sad news that there would be no class today because our speaker was a no-show. Then I got a reply from a student saying, "He is here and giving a great lecture!" Somehow, he had found his own way to my classroom without me. I was careful to exchange mobile phone numbers with my guest speakers after that.

ago, and was pretty painful so I would rather not dredge it up. I invited about five grad students to class and led a panel discussion and Q&A session. I had each panelist tell the class the basics of where they are, what they are researching, and anything they might like to say about how they got into their program. Then I opened the floor up to questions about anything my students wanted to ask. They might ask about the mechanics of courses vs. basic research in a PhD program. Or they might wonder about how easy it is to get a paper published, or to be in charge of one's own research project. They might ask about the merits or problems of getting married or starting to have children in grad school.

I had an ulterior motive in inviting a panel of senior grad students whom I knew were thriving in grad school. A good fraction of my students think they are bound for med school and a career as a medical doctor. Many of them (so they have told me) have been admonished, "You will be a doctor!" by their parents since an early age. I was hoping to convert a few potential MDs into scientists and engineers, by letting them know there is an alternative to going the med school route. Here is evidence that my course helped to set some of my students on a neuroscience research career path. In 2006, IntroNeuro student Michael Dorman said of my co-teacher Prof. Nael McCarty's and my class,

> "I can't tell you how much I've enjoyed your class this semester; it has inspired me to look twice at the idea of becoming simply a clinician as I pursue medicine, and towards incorporating neuroscience research as part of my career goal. Of course the subject matter itself is unbelievably vast and exciting, but it was through this class that I was turned on to the magnitude of it and where the edges of our knowledge are. Anyway, I don't know if you guys care, but at least someone left your class this semester inspired!"

In an email apologizing that she could not take my follow-on lab class (she was too busy doing real research in a lab), my IntroNeuro student Jenny Kim wrote:

> "I really enjoyed your class and definitely learned a lot. I strongly believe that your class was one of the main deciding factors in helping me realize that I wanted to get a PhD in neuroscience and possibly work with patients with Parkinson's Disease."

Ethics Discussions

For all of my courses, I tried to make the material relevant for my students. I incorporated discussions of how the science and technology we were learning about change society. Some topics were chosen precisely because they were controversial, such as the time that we gave a Problem-Based Learning problem to assess the implications of publishing a paper that described how to manufacture a highly contagious flu virus. A top scientific journal was debating this issue at the time, so the students had the journal's recently published editorial as a starting point.

Other topics might not have seemed controversial, such as cochlear implants that allow the profoundly deaf to hear. I brought up related issues such as how this might impact the deaf community and perhaps cause the death of sign language. I was lucky that with neuroscience and neuroengineering, there are many, many topics that are controversial and can be used to spark a lively discussion.

The rapid advances neuroengineering is developing portend large disruptions in issues as important as, "What is unique about humans, and will Artificial Intelligence ever change that?" or, "Should we keep trying to extend lifespan?" or, "Would it be a good thing to upload your consciousness to a digital repository?" or, "Will the whole idea of *blame* be eliminated when we understand why criminals do what they do?"

Often, I would pose an ethics-laden question and then invite the class to break up into small groups of two to five students to discuss how they felt about it for five to ten minutes, sometimes after thinking quietly to themselves for a few minutes. Then we would go around the room polling each group to summarize the main points they felt were at issue. I learned this approach called "Think-pair-share" while teaching Live Cell Imaging summer workshops from the course organizer, Prof. Jim Pawley. It always got my students excited and engaged with the material, and can be used with learners of all ages.

I had to be on the lookout for quiet students who may sit on the sidelines, hesitant to speak up. They could serve as a note taker for their group. If someone tended to dominate a group, I would try to get them to use their excess energy to solicit input from the quieter ones.

I would often invite an expert who specializes in neuroethics to visit my class.[66] They would start by introducing some of their favorite ethics topics

---

66. For example, Prof. Karen Rommelfanger, the Neuroethics Program Director at Emory University.

and then lead the discussions. The guests always valued hearing what a classroom of 100 college seniors had to say about their favorite topics. The students loved learning from the experts that what we were discussing in class was at the absolute cutting-edge of current thinking in neuroethics. One anonymous student wrote,

> "I think the Neuro Ethics talk was one of the most interesting lectures I've had in four years at Tech. Your willingness to bring in the experts to lecture on what they know best was invaluable."

A lesson for all teachers, even at the elementary school level, is: Don't be afraid to discuss controversial topics in class! They are highly engaging, and to hear others' perspectives on such topics provides a mind-opening opportunity for students.

Make Sure Students Know You Care

Because I did not get proper training in how to teach, I learned by trial and error some key things that every Elementary School Teacher knows, such as the importance of making a personal connection with your students. It certainly is not the norm with college professors, especially for big lecture classes. My students got a surprise on the 2nd meeting of the semester. I spent the first 5 minutes of that class calling each student by name from memory, row by row, even for classes of 100 students. How did I do that? They may have assumed I was a whiz with names and faces or a savant of some sort. Not true at all; I actually have a really hard time remembering names and faces. I have been known to introduce myself to apparent "strangers" at a conference, only to have them remind me how I once toured them around my lab.

Here is my "secret": concentrated effort to learn associations. On the first day of the semester, after handing out the syllabus and giving them a few minutes to read it quietly, I handed out index cards and had each student write their name, major, why they took my class, and a hobby or special interest. I had them line up at my video camera and read these cards and hand them in to me as I greeted each one and tried to repeat their name correctly. Students were allowed to chat and get to know each other while waiting for their turn at my camera. That was on a Monday and the next class was on a Wednesday. That gave me all of Tuesday to watch the video over and over, while reading the index cards and quizzing myself on each name until I could say it as soon as I saw their face.

This was a LOT of work. I spent hours of replaying the video and testing myself with the flash cards. I had to reinforce my name memory before each class by speaking their names and writing them on a printout of their faces, which I had captured from the video. I was building associations: their voice, their face, their name's spelling and pronunciation, their hobby.

This effort paid off. I always addressed my students by name when anyone raised their hand or came to talk to me. As the semester went on, I had more and more associations for each student to help me remember them. This showed them that I cared about each individual student and built respect in both directions. And it made them more responsible. They knew that if they somehow violated the class norms, I would know exactly who was causing the trouble. I had to teach after lunch one year, during the time folks in other countries would be taking a siesta. If my students fell asleep in class, I could wake them up by calling their name and politely inviting them back into the discussion.

The video was also very helpful for getting the pronunciation of their names right. Georgia Tech has many international students whose names would be very tricky for me to pronounce from just reading the roll sheet.

I had my students put down on the card why they decided to take this course. Then I could incorporate their goals with my own goals for the course. I could also set my and their expectations if they had written a goal that was not reasonable or relevant. For example, if they were pre-med and wanted to learn neuroanatomy well, I might let them know that I don't emphasize that topic much in my course. It might also help me make a personal connection when talking one-on-one with them. My individualized care had a big effect on student motivation.

> ```
> "The instructor did a fantastic job in my opinion. I
> was very impressed by the fact that he put forth the
> effort to learn and remember the names of every
> person in an extremely large class."  - anonymous
> IntroNeuro student
> ```

After she graduated, alumna Christa Caesar recalled about my course,

> ```
> "The most memorable thing from your course was on
> day 2, when you recollected each of our names in
> class. (I remember how awe-struck I was that a
> professor actually cared to remember my name, the
> 2nd day of school.) You made the course a very
> personal experience since that day."
> ```

I was not surprised that the names I had learned usually did not stick in my head more than a semester, once I stopped reinforcing them. Some of my former students would say "Hi Professor Potter!" to me in the hallway the next year and I had completely forgotten their name. I just had to smile and say,

"Hi! How's it going?" The problem with names is that they are arbitrary. To recall names well, you need to go out of your way to build more connections from your memories of the person to the spelling and pronunciation of their name. Salespeople know this and become experts at creating name mnemonics, and reinforcing the memories by using the client's name often. Because names are arbitrary and usually not well connected in memory is why name recall is one of the first things to go when we get older and our memories are fading.

If your students know you care about them, you will get much more respect, attention, and involvement in the class. Learning their names is only a start. I tried always to treat each of them with respect. If they came to me with a concern, I listened 100% and tried to address it to their satisfaction. Many students have special circumstances that get in the way of their full participation in class, such as the death of a loved one, or an away game they must participate in if they are athletes. Treating all special needs with care and appropriate attention goes a long way to earning students' respect. It even helped when other students saw how I dealt with those with special needs; they would be less inhibited to come talk to me later if something troubling came up with themselves.

> *"Dr. Potter, Thanks for being such a great professor. **I don't think I've had another professor who cared about what we are learning or gave real meaningful assignments as much as you do. This is honestly the most worthwhile class I have taken at Tech.** I know many of my classmates feel the same way, and we truly appreciate everything you have done this semester.... I've never written a thank-you note on the back of a final before."*
> *– IntroNeuro student Alysia Rudis*

The flip-side of earning their respect is demanding mature behavior and respect from them and not being taken advantage of. It was rare, but occasionally I got bogus requests for special treatment, and had to make a tough decision based on what would be fair to the rest of the class. I think even those students respected me more when I turned them down after listening to their "my dog ate my homework" story and they saw that I made my boundaries clear. I eventually managed to ward off most of those uncomfortable interactions by making my rules and policies very explicit in the syllabus.

Encourage Sharing of Stories

A good way to show my students I cared about them was to encourage them to bring their personal experiences into the discussions we had during the "lectures." I would solicit such personal stories by frequently asking, "Does anyone have any questions? Or related experiences?" For example, in my lecture on sleep and dreams, I would ask if anyone has had a lucid dream. I would invite them to tell us what they did in dreams when they knew they were dreaming. For some of my informal student surveys, I would write the students' suggestions or input on the whiteboard in a list. Then I would look for trends in these and discuss the implications, e.g., how there are different levels of "lucidity" and how this might relate to the arousal system in the brain that determines what sleep stage we are in. I would always take a photo of the whiteboard at the end of class and those lists would often help me make a better lecture next year, or perhaps form the basis of an interesting test question.

Of course, if no stories were forthcoming, I have plenty of my own to relate to make a point, to engage them, and to see that I am a real person too. I noticed that on the index cards I used to learn names, some students mentioned a personal or family connection with a brain disorder as the reason why they took the course. If I were talking with them alone at some point, I might bring it up and invite them to tell me more about that situation. Some were happy to share and ask me questions about that particular brain disorder. Others chose that disorder as the focus of their Wikipedia article (Chapter 10) and subsequently became an expert themselves.

Let Go of Your Need to "Cover the Material"

Many teachers are worried that if they don't lecture like my World History teacher, then crucial parts of the curriculum will be missed. Time will run out. Students will leave class not having heard about some key points that will be on their standardized tests, or perhaps just points that they feel are important. There are many other means for the students to learn those points, if indeed they are important. If curious students are fired up by your discussion and you hand them a list of points you feel are most important, and leave it to them to research them, they will. I strongly believe that **teachers' job in class is to focus more on the *why* than the *what*.**

I make a point of making my important points at least twice during each lecture. At the beginning I say, "Here are the things about this topic that I feel are worth remembering." At the end, I try to summarize those points, tying them together with things brought up in discussions. This follows the advice I learned in Toastmasters: "Tell them what you are going to say. Then say it. Then tell them what you said." It is not just the repetition, but making more connections that enhances later recall, and makes the ideas you convey useful to the listener. If you have slides or handouts that can be accessed after class, then students can follow up on items in your list that did not get discussed due to lack of time.

I usually avoided handing out printouts of slides or outlines at the beginning of class for a couple of reasons. One is that my presentations would often include some engaging surprise or twist that I did not wish to reveal until just the right moment. The other is that I prefer it when students' attention is directed forward rather than down at their desk. However, a good way to keep students engaged is to use handouts that include blank spaces for them to fill in actively, based on a lecture or their own thought process. Either way, I made it clear that my slides would be available online after class, so my students would not have to write down everything I had already included on my slides. Their notes could focus on the extra material related orally in class discussions or media presentations.

No Question is Too Dumb to Ask

I got many good discussions started in my "lectures" with my policy on questions: "No question is too dumb to ask." [67] I was encouraged by my Dad to ask questions. Or maybe we just shared the same curiosity genes. He never ever turned me away when I asked questions (Fig. 9, p. 52). I can't recall how often I asked questions in grade school, but I am guessing I probably did annoy a few teachers. I don't recall any of them embarrassing me for asking a dumb question. I certainly asked many questions during lectures in college and in grad school — so much so, that a fellow grad student forbade me from asking any questions during our friend's dissertation defense.

I would often be the first one to queue up to the microphone at conferences during the Q&A session after a talk. I learned not to be afraid of asking questions when I did not understand something. And from the time I began informal tutoring of my peers in the dorms at UCSD, I also got used to *answering* questions. Being a TA in Chemistry during my junior and senior years in college, I had to stand in front of 20 students and answer whatever questions they had about the recent material from lectures or homework.

---

67. Some other teachers have a "There are no dumb questions" policy. In contrast, I acknowledge that there are plenty of dumb questions, yet still welcome them. Some students were annoyed by my policy, though. From one anonymous end-of-semester evaluation: *"Dr. Potter has far too much patience for irrelevant questions."*

> *"Dr. Potter ... encouraged class discussions and was open to just about any comments we provided in class (no matter the tangent and how stupid)."* – anonymous NeuroEng. Fun. student

My NQITDTA policy accomplished a number of goals. One, it allowed students to clear up confusion early, so they did not fall behind in a lecture. It loosened them up for interacting with me, when they saw how I answered them by name and treated them with respect no matter what they asked. If the question seemed foolish, probably other students had that question too, but were afraid to ask. That student who did ask is the hero, not a fool. It helped me to gauge how well they were comprehending things. It helped me know that next time I teach this material, I may want to explain it differently. It revealed their personal interest in the topic. It got them "classroom interaction" points for the final grade, about 5% of their grade. Even the quiet ones were required to interact in class because I feel this is a life skill that can be learned and which will serve them well.

I often say, "I got where I am today by asking many dumb questions." I eventually learned how not to be shy by repeatedly venturing out of my comfort zone. The NQITDTA policy, along with my unusual policy of holding my "office hours" right after class, right outside the lecture hall, encouraged my students to approach me with very tricky questions. "That is a GREAT question!" was a recurring refrain from me. Some of these really challenged me and encouraged me to go learn something new in order to get back to them with an answer. I have always enjoyed hearing the fresh perspectives and questions of people at my lectures; they often send me on a fruitful excursion, thinking of the subject matter in entirely new ways.

Humor and Fun

I knew from my own experience that I remembered better those lecturers who incorporated humor into their material. For some people this comes naturally — I have to work at it consciously. Like the Yerkes-Dodson Curve, there is an inverted-U-curve for the effectiveness of a lecture as a function of humor: too serious and people may fall asleep. Too funny and they may be too busy laughing and wiping the tears from their eyes to pay attention to what you say next. There is an optimum level of humor to get lasting learning. Somewhere in the middle between sleepy and hysterical is where you want your students to be. Of course, humor is not the only way to increase their level of excitement, but it always helps.

It also sometimes helps in making you seem more approachable or less intimidating to them. Some self-deprecation works well, like when I revealed my ignorance about sports. Half the class was wearing yellow T-shirts. I asked, "What's with the yellow t-shirts?" and they said, "The game!" I asked which sport and everyone laughed. How could anyone at Georgia Tech not know about the homecoming game? I think it was football, but I am still not sure.

Humor that worked well for me sometimes included a build-up that seemed perilous or very serious, and then it was suddenly revealed to be not what they expected.[68] Like when I was giving a lecture about the brain circuits involved in addiction, I revealed to them the shocking truth that I am a former addict. After a serious pause, I showed a picture of the *Robotron: 2084* video game that I was addicted to in high school. Nowadays, to be addicted to gaming is so common as to be mundane.

Be careful with inappropriate or insensitive humor and absolutely avoid any humor that makes fun of a student. Nowadays, many types of humor that were popular when I was a kid are a big no-no. If we don't stay politically correct, we may alienate some students and lose their respect. If you are teaching minors, you should probably steer clear of humor related to sex and other adult topics. But during the sometimes awkward discussion of our reproductive circuitry in IntroNeuro, I found that a little humor helps loosen up the class.

During one of the few chemistry lectures I recall from my undergrad days, Prof. Clark was getting ready to melt some salt with a blowtorch as a demonstration of the strength of ionic bonds. He mentioned how important it is to wear safety glasses, then put on Groucho Marx glasses with a big nose and fired up the torch. Being goofy or funny or doing activities that allow the students to move, interact and have fun can also aid engagement and enhance recall — as long as it does not get out of control and move from the peak to the right half of the Yerkes-Dodson Curve.

Active Learning

What is active learning? It is easy to understand by contrasting it with most classroom instruction: students sit there nearly motionless for about an hour while the teacher lectures, draws things on the board, and shows Powerpoint slides. Students may be busy taking notes but that is a relatively passive process. It is slightly better than just setting out a recording device on the desk and falling asleep. The extreme was parodied in the movie *Real Genius,* when eventually, as days of boring lectures went on, every student in

---

68. Humor theorists say that laughter evolved as a signal to our tribe-mates that all is OK. This explains why it is emitted during play which is often ritualized fighting, or after a fall that did not result in serious injury, like slipping on a banana peel.

the lecture hall was replaced by their recorders. By the end of the scene, even the professor was replaced with a reel-to-reel tape recorder giving his lecture for him.

There is a whole spectrum of involvement; learning is not an either/or, active/passive kind of thing. The next level up from just taking notes is for the student or teacher to ask a question. In my class, I would often poll the students about something by show of hands, e.g., "Who here thinks we have free will?" If this was an emotion-laden question, it might make the students sit up and pay attention for a while. "Has anyone ever lost a loved one to dementia?"

Another level of being active in my class would be to help determine what will be in the lesson. For example, "Raise your hand if you want me to spend another day discussing sleep and dreams. Now raise your hand if you prefer we move on to consciousness."

Some lectures included demonstrations that required the students to do informal experiments with their own sensory or nervous systems: "Push on your eyeball through your eyelid and see the world jiggle. Why is that any different than when you just move your eyes from one part of the room to the other using your eye muscles? Why don't you perceive the world as moving then?" (The answer is: there is no *efference copy*, a signal from one part of your brain to another when you move intentionally.) By seeing the effect themselves by experimenting with their own nervous system, it really brings it home to them.

The Brain Loves to Make Stuff Up

A good example of how getting up and moving helped my students learn was during a lesson on the eyes' blind spots. Instead of just hearing about them, visualizing their blind spots (where the optic nerve exits the retina) cemented the concept in their memories. I could have given a standard boring lecture and said, "The blind spot is a scotoma we all have two of, located about 12–15° temporally and 1.5° below the horizontal and is roughly 7.5° high and 5.5° wide." No one will remember or care what I just said.

It was surprising enough when they found out how huge their blind spots are, but then I showed them how blind spots can be "filled in" by their imagination with hallucinated text, no drugs

7. Engaging Lectures

necessary.[69] Their jaws dropped and they exclaimed, "NO. WAY." But due to the limitations of the projector screen size, this only worked for people in the middle of the lecture hall. An active learner would get up and move to the correct part of the aisle for it to work and then their jaw dropped. A passive learner would see other students react and just get a vague idea of what is going on. They were less likely to remember the concepts of filling in of visual scotomas when it was test time, or years later in med school.

I did this demo without mentioning the boring numerical details and encouraged everyone to get up and move to a part of the room where it worked. I mentioned the fact that the moon is only half a degree, so the blind spot in each eye can completely hide an object 10 times as big as the full moon! And the visual system fills the spot with whatever it thinks is most likely to be there. NO. WAY!

If you are a curious active learner yourself, you can try this demo by cutting a piece of Post-it about 1-inch square and sticking it to the middle of a text-filled right-hand page of this book. Cover your left eye and fixate with your right eye on the corresponding spot on the middle of the left-hand page as you move the book slowly closer from arm's length. At some distance, you ought to see the Post-it in your peripheral vision vanish (even if it is fluorescent pink!) and get replaced by imagined text. Not a blank black or grey oval the shape of your blind spot, but seemingly real words. The instant you move your eyes to look directly at the filled-in words, the Post-it reappears.

---

69. V. S. Ramachandran and R. Gregory *"Perceptual filling-in of artificially induced scotomas in human vision,"* (1991) Nature 350:699-702.

Think about how you might incorporate more movement into your lessons. My sister Sandra teaches math to her third-graders using spatial metaphors and long tape measures that require them to get up and do things. She has them act out scenarios their ancestors may have lived through as a way to teach history.

To force students to remain motionless and seated for an entire lesson is a good way to sap their motivation and keep them on the left side of the

Yerkes-Dodson Curve. Keep them at the peak by incorporating the right amount of movement.

Science Museums — The Exploratorium

I am a huge fan of science museums. My favorite one is the Exploratorium in San Francisco, which may have been the first one to try out the idea of being highly interactive. Instead of mounting plaques beneath static "Do not touch" exhibits behind velvet ropes, they make every exhibit something "To See and Do." I first visited the Exploratorium when I was in the tenth grade, on a road trip. The only rule posted in this cavernous museum was "No skateboarding." Every exhibit had a stack of cards explaining what was going on, in more and more technical detail as you flip more cards over. I was enjoying learning about so many things, I didn't notice the hours passing. They had to kick me out when it was closing time. They now have a hands-on "Tinkering Studio" where kids of all ages can build all sorts of things in workshops or on a drop-in basis.

I go back to the Exploratorium whenever I am in the Bay Area because I always learn new and amazing things there. Most recently, I sat in a chair there that was thumping different parts of my body, while I adjusted a knob to make the thumps feel simultaneous. With this simple rig, one can accurately measure how fast signals travel along nerves. I had taught a "nerve conduction velocity lab" as a grad student TA long ago in Psychobiology. It required killing frogs to get nerves to study and used high-tech lab equipment. I wish we had had those thumper chairs back then. The exhibit designers at the Exploratorium keep coming up with these simple and engaging ways to teach complex ideas in science, technology, engineering, and math (**STEM**). I like that they also incorporate art in many of their exhibits, making the science even more creative and fun — STEAM! As a bonus, their exhibit-making workshop is itself an exhibit that you can watch!

I urge you to visit an interactive science museum like the Exploratorium and imagine how your lessons can be turned into things students can both See and Do.

Skillful Presenters Learn to Engage Students

There are many ways to grab students' attention and hold their interest. I have sat through many talks presented by scientists who nearly put me to sleep, even though they had great data. Maybe the speakers were jet-lagged or maybe they just had not practiced the art of presenting. They may have had a monotonous voice, or one that trails off at the end of each sentence so I couldn't hear the last few words. Or their accent was very hard to understand. Or they just didn't seem very interested in what they were talking about.

I worked on my presentation skills in the Toastmasters, a public speaking club. Toastmasters International[70] has a local chapter near you, pretty much anywhere in the world. If not, you can always start one. They have a very structured way of building confidence and presentation skills in a supportive low-stakes environment, so that when you find yourself in front of a hostile or indifferent audience, you will be ready to win them over. In Toastmasters you get extensive practice giving short impromptu and prepared talks, and get much helpful feedback from your club-mates.

I also found it very helpful to watch videos of myself giving lectures to improve my delivery. Practicing in front of a mirror is not very helpful because while talking, your mind is on the material, not on how you look and sound. Watching videos of myself was painful at first, when I was an undergrad chemistry TA at UCSD. Around that time, I was also a volunteer DJ at UCSD's student radio station, KSDT. It was shocking when I first heard what I really sound like in a recording of one of my radio shows. But those videos and KSDT air-check tapes were great tools for improvement.

Things I still consciously strive to improve when I speak to a group:

- Speaking loudly and clearly. This is especially important if English is not the first language of some of your students, or if you have an accent yourself.
- Adding pauses at the right times to let things sink in.
- Gesturing.
- Asking for questions or suggestions.
- Noting how well I answered a student's question.
- Taking "Raise-your-hand-if…" surveys.
- Taking "Name-something-that…" surveys and writing answers up on the board.
- Avoiding throwaway utterances like "um," "uh," "basically," "like," "so," and "you know."
- Smiling more and using facial expressions.

---

70. https://www.toastmasters.org/

- Making eye contact with as many people in the class as I can.
- Moving around the room, but not pacing back and forth.
- Modulating the tone of my voice in both pitch and volume (but not too quiet).
- Inhibiting habits or tics that might be distracting.
- Keeping track of time and pacing the presentation.
- Not letting the topic wander too far afield, while being open to interesting diversions brought up by the students. Know when to say, "OK, let's move on…"
- Listening carefully to how the microphone sounds. If it is a lapel mic, is it rubbing on something? If it is on the lectern, do I bang into it while gesturing? Is its battery running down? Is there feedback or hum? If you have a naturally quiet voice, consider using a microphone even in a small classroom.
- Scrutinizing how the slides look. Are they readable from way in the back? Is there not too much text on them? Is there a point to each and every slide? Is anyone's view blocked by me standing in the way or by an obstacle like the lectern or a pillar?
- Most importantly, showing my enthusiasm for the material.

After I give a talk about my research at a conference or seminar, I ask for feedback from my host or some colleagues in the audience about how the presentation went, and take notes. If you are open to constructive criticism, you should solicit it and then act upon it. Few will offer such feedback unless prompted. Make it clear you want to improve, otherwise they may just be vaguely complimentary, afraid to be critical.

A simple question could be added to your next quiz or exam like, "What are the best and worst things about my lectures." If you leave it open-ended like that, you might get all sorts of useful feedback, on content, presentation, or other aspects you were not even thinking of. I am never finished with improving — I try to get better with every lecture. I was inspired by a fellow scientist/engineer, Dr. Dave Piston. I once heard him give an excellent talk about his research at a conference. I went up afterwards to ask him some questions, one being, "How did you become such a good speaker?" His response stuck in my head: "I worked really hard at it."

Good communication is not just conveying ideas with your words, but is a holistic mix of your presentation, the environment, and engagement of the audience. If students become disengaged, they cease to learn. If you captivate them, their energy and motivation rises to the peak of the Yerkes-Dodson Curve and they will remember what you say. Many of my course survey respondents mentioned that my passion or enthusiasm for the material struck them:

> "I remember the passion that you had for neuroscience, and the passion you had for getting us interested in the subject. It really carried through to the content of the course, and it made neuroscience more than something to learn for a grade." – alumna Audrey Southard

Enthusiasm does not materialize out of thin air, unless you are a very good actor. How to become passionate about the material to be taught? Immerse yourself in it. Before each lecture, as I fixed up my slides and thought about what I would say, I reminded myself what is exciting or relevant about the specific things I wanted to tell students about. Often, that required me to do quick literature searches and readings of recent papers and news. If I couldn't make that connection, I deleted that topic, leaving more discussion time for the good stuff.

Don't teach something you are not interested in. How can you expect students to be interested in the material if you are not? Every time a subject is presented again, improve the old slides and the material to be covered. Keep reading the current literature. Look for examples in recent media for what you want to talk about. Students not only get bored by stale lectures, but they also resent the teacher for being lazy or not interested in teaching. I had one high school history teacher who was so bored, he actually nodded off during his own lecture!

For many of my "lectures" I kept changing the pace of the lecture by including relevant videos that make my point well. Sometimes, I would include part of an interview of a famous neuroscientist I respected, or whose wisdom I had been trying to impart to them myself earlier. Sometimes, I would show a clinical video of a patient with a certain interesting neurological disorder. Other times, I would show demonstrations of optical illusions that highlight certain of the brain's visual mechanisms or evolutionary principles, like the blind spot demo.

There is an amazingly huge and increasing supply of interesting and relevant clips on YouTube and TED to draw material from. These help keep lectures current; to disregard them is to run the risk of boring this generation of students used to watching their screens nearly every waking moment. I even opened my first lecture with my favorite science music video (yes, that is now a genre), *An Ode To The Brain!* by Symphony of Science.[71] It was great for getting a room full of excited students to settle down and begin to pay attention to the front of the room. Apparently I even did a little spontaneous dance to it one year, because one student wrote in the end-of-semester survey in response to "How could the course be improved?" `"Dr. Potter could do more dancing."`

The Teaching Environment is Important

The environmental details of the classroom are important for allowing students to concentrate and stay focused on what is being taught. A poor environment can be a big demotivator. It is your responsibility as teacher to reduce noise and other distractions, get adequate lighting, and make sure the audio-visual (A/V) system works well and can be seen and heard well from everywhere in the room.

If you teach in a big room, can everyone hear you? Ask them! Don't accept a vague nod, quiz them to make sure they actually can. If not, use a microphone or learn to project your voice like a stage actor. It helps if you have a guest lecturer or student give a speech while you sit in the back to see and hear what it is like back there.

How is the aural environment? Are the seats comfortable and not squeaky? Oil them or add tennis ball feet to the legs if needed. Are distractions audible or visible outside? If so, close the windows or pull down the blinds. Is sound from other rooms or the hallway leaking in? Make sure the doors close themselves; have door closers installed and adjusted if needed.

Are people talking or using their phones or computers in class? If students seemed to be having a conversation about the class, I would invite them to share it with all of us. That actually led to interesting discussions sometimes.

I had a *No Screens Allowed* policy. If your classroom has computer workstations, turn off the monitors until it is time to use them. The same goes for the projector if you are not using it. Some students are like me, sensory-driven people who are magnetically drawn to a screensaver that is moving around. We are transfixed like a cat who sees a moving ball of yarn or a laser pointer spot. Turn them off!

Is the room the right temperature? Know how to work the heating and air conditioning. If it is too warm, students get sleepy. If it is too cold, they

---

71. https://www.youtube.com/watch?v=JB7jSFeVz1U

may be distracted by being uncomfortable. They should not be hugging themselves or wearing heavy coats in class.

Many good lectures at conferences I have attended were ruined by a bad environment. Some teachers may cop out and say, "Well, this was the classroom I was given." I carefully chose my classroom, or tested out the one I was given and improved the things I could. If the room needed refurbishment, I let the administration know. If it had an A/V problem, I called the computer support crew in there to fix it before the semester began.

Some A/V systems are ridiculously complicated and prone to malfunction. One deluxe lecture hall I was in had a wide range of different types of lights with five lighting pre-sets. The first 4 had been set to Full, all the same, and the last was OFF, completely dark (only suitable when no one was in the room). I had the A/V guys come in and reprogram it so there were 5 different levels of lighting appropriate for writing/reading, watching the screen, focusing on the whiteboard, etc., and I switched between them often. It is a lot like a car, a ridiculously complicated technology most adults use every day without thinking about it. All drivers have spent many hours of training learning how to operate a car properly.

If you are a teacher, A/V is your thing whether you consider yourself technical or not. Practice your technology until you know it well and it fades into the background, like using turn indicators in a car. While driving, you don't give up and say, "Well, I am not that good at working all those knobs. It's very complicated." You can have your geekier students help you learn classroom technology. It is there to enhance your teaching, not cause distractions and problems.

The classroom environment is not all about using technology well and preventing distractions. **Social engineering is important for motivation, too.** One semester, I had a class in a beautiful HUGE new lecture hall. I had about 100 students, half the room's capacity. At first they spaced themselves out all across the room. I felt it was much harder to connect with those in the back, even though I was using a microphone, so I just made the back half of rows off-limits. If anyone sat back there, I politely invited them by name to join the rest of us up front. This made a huge improvement in their level of engagement. It had the unexpected benefit of making the whole group much more friendly and social, because they were sitting close to each other.

A few days after compressing my class into the front half of the lecture hall, I came in before class to hear a loud hubbub. "Wow!" I remarked to myself, "There are dozens of great conversations going on here right now. Look how excited they are to see each other and to be here!" It felt like a shame to interrupt them to begin the lecture. In college, it is usually not appropriate to dictate who sits next to whom, but K-12 teachers have long known that adjusting the seating assignments can transform an unruly class into a productive one.

Many of the concerns about the classroom environment mentioned above also apply during Project-Based Learning. However, there are additional considerations I have noticed are important, based on my experience running a research lab, teaching lab classes and leading makerspace workshops.

Because teams working on projects have to do a lot of talking, and excitement may be higher than during a lecture, it really helps if the project space has carpeting or other measures to reduce echos and reverberation. This might include upholstered furniture, sound-absorbing wall hangings, and soft acoustic ceiling tiles. I (and many students) find it very hard to concentrate or have a meaningful conversation in a tiled-floor room full of excited people. Some equipment, such as 3D printers or power tools, make noise that adds to the cacophony. It is sometimes possible to isolate noisy equipment inside a soundproof box, closet or separate room.

Project and design rooms benefit greatly from having furniture on wheels, so that the social dynamics and working areas can be reconfigured easily at any moment, as needs change. This might happen every day, for example, when the class switches from scaffolding or whole-class discussion mode to working in small teams.

When we were designing the research lab space for the new BME building we moved into in 2003, I proposed that we use lab benches on wheels, instead of the traditional built-in benches. Many of my colleagues went along with the idea, and we all enjoyed the flexibility of reconfiguring our labs every so often, to accommodate new equipment or personnel, or just to provide a fresh working area that the grad students themselves could design.

Projects will go much more smoothly if students find what they need close by, as soon as they realize they need it. Thus, it helps to have tools and supplies well labeled and visible, ideally on pegboards, in clear bins or drawers, or in cabinets on casters. Cupboard doors with clear windows help reduce searching time, and felt or rubber bumpers reduce door banging noise.

There need to be explicit rules, traditions and etiquette for how to share tools, space, and supplies, and how to keep everything well stocked and tidy. I learned this working in Scott Fraser's large lab alongside dozens of other scientists. His fantastic Lab Manager, Mary Flowers (AKA "Lab Mom"), was almost psychic in anticipating our every need, optimizing our research in a thousand ways, by stocking supplies, organizing space, and enforcing rules. And because projects of all sorts require computers, whether in a research lab or classroom, it helps to have a top-notch computer guru on hand to keep computers working and up to date with all the right software and peripherals. Dr. Gary Belford was the crucial computer geek in Scott's lab. No I.T. problem was beyond him. The team of Mary and Gary made the Fraser lab the most efficient working environment I have ever had.

To help scaffold projects, I recommend keeping a well-organized library of relevant books and other reference materials close at hand. Magazines, and some free time to flip through them, can also provide creative ideas for students' projects. I recommend *Make:*, *Hackspace*, *Reinvented*, *Elektor*, *Nuts and Volts*, and *Servo* magazines, each of which is full of fun maker projects to inspire and educate your students. Whiteboards at strategic locations where groups hang out promote brainstorming and impromptu peer-to-peer learning.

Many of the student projects I promote are connected to the Real World in various ways. Computers should have good high-bandwidth internet connections, especially for videoconferencing. It is also helpful to have quiet phone booths or small rooms for students to carry out phone calls or quiet 1-on-1 conversations and interviews. Such a room could also be used to produce podcasts or other media to be disseminated. Think of ways your students can or should connect with people outside of class. How can you help facilitate those connections by setting up a productive environment?

How to Convey Tricky Concepts and Ensure They are Remembered: Analogies

Links to things the students care about or have emotional feelings about will help a new concept be remembered and understood. To help remember things, the rule is, ***the more links, the better***. I often use analogies in my teaching. Some cognitive scientists, notably my favorite author of all time, Prof. Douglas Hofstadter, believe that analogy making is the driving force behind all human thought.[72] This probably has to do with the fact that the trillions of connections, the **synapses** and gap junctions, between billions of brain cells are what set humans apart from other animals. It is all about the links, at all levels.

If you have to explain some arcane subject that students may think they are not interested in, make an analogy to something that the student is quite familiar with. Once they connect the dots with your help, the picture of the new concept becomes clear and it is remembered well. Let's try the tricky concept I had to convey about the role of the hippocampus in memory:

> *It is often said that the hippocampus is a brain structure that is crucial for memory. The hippocampus is not*

---

72. Douglas Hofstadter and Emmanuel Sander, *Surfaces and Essences — Analogy as the Fuel and Fire of Thinking*, (2013) Basic Books.

> *where memories are permanently stored, but it plays a key role in the storage of memories, especially episodic memories, e.g., "While I was walking home yesterday, I was splashed with mud by a passing car, but then I found five dollars!" It is often misspoken that the hippocampus is the place in the brain where memories are stored. It is a mistake or great oversimplification if someone says that the memories are first stored in the hippocampus and then 'moved out' to the cortex. The memories always were in the cortex, where the sensory input was originally processed. But the hippocampus coordinates connecting all the different parts of the cortex together into a coherent episodic memory.*

If you found that confusing, you are in good company. Even many smart neuroscientists and reputable textbooks don't seem to get it, judging from what I have read. The famous patient known as HM had his hippocampus removed on both sides (to treat epilepsy) yet could recall many events of his life before the surgery. This showed that his long-term memories were stored elsewhere. He had a very hard time storing *new* episodic memories after the bilateral hippocampectomy procedure. To tell stories about HM is helpful, but analogies worked better.

Let's try a Google analogy on for size. Google News is analogous to episodic memories, which are the speciality of the hippocampus. Is the information stored at Google News Headquarters? No, there is no News Headquarters. There are servers located all over the world, and news media outlets, each storing a bunch of links to news items in local and national publications related to a given topic. Google News gives every incoming story a time stamp, and it lets us know that this story was from ten hours ago and that one was from three days ago. It keeps track of which news source the story is from. This is like the sensory modality (vision, hearing, touch, etc.) of incoming sensory data. Any episodic memory includes information from a variety of senses. Even if it seems that it all came in via the eyes, say the memory of having read something, there was a sensory context around that. Was music playing? Was I hungry at the time I read it? There are many related memories, including links to previous related experiences, or conversations we may have had about what we read.

Google News draws a box around stories related to the same topic, the way the hippocampus makes sure that all the inputs from any remembered episode get linked to each other, and to older related memories, by strengthening synapses. Google News' "View full coverage" is like one of the things the hippocampus does: it puts a memory into context. The hippocampus does that by activating and linking relevant memories all across the brain. It is very well connected to the entire brain, just as Google is connected to everything on the Internet. Like Google, the hippocampus is very responsive and good at processing sensory information as it pours in. It misses very little. And if the hippocampus were to be cut out (as during HM's surgery to treat epilepsy) or destroyed by a stroke, the memories are still there. If Google ceased to exist, the news stories would still be there. But in the early hours and days of a breaking story, the connections Google News provides really do a lot to help ensure that the news item makes a splash and has an impact on society. Likewise, for several days or weeks after a big event happened, the hippocampus plays an important role connecting circuits across the brain and making the memory into a long-term episodic memory that can be used later to guide behavior.

Here is another analogy for us oldsters: Think of the library, full of books, as being a brain full of episodic memories. You could say that *the hippocampus is like the Dewey Decimal System or the Library of Congress Classification System.* A new book comes into the library. Where does it get placed so that we can find it again when it is wanted? The Dewey Decimal System tells the librarian how this book relates to other books, by way of the subject matter contained in it. The librarian looks up the subject categories and classifies the incoming book with them, giving them a specific set of numbers like LB1044.87. This is like the hippocampus taking incoming sense data and tying it to other incoming sense data, and to existing memories. The Dewey decimal system allows the book to end up in permanent storage on just the right shelf between the most-related books in the library. This makes later recall of the book easy because if you find any one book in that topic, you are likely to go to the right shelf and scan it and find just the book you want, and perhaps some other good ones you did not even know about. The book does not get stored in the librarians' desk or in the card catalog, but in the stacks on the correct shelf. The librarian implementing the Dewey Decimal System is like the hippocampus helping to store episodic memories.

This is an apt analogy, but sadly, with electronic storage of information, browsing shelves of books filed by subject has gone out of style, so few of today's students would resonate with this analogy. Choose your analogies with your audience in mind.

Hopefully, one or both of these analogies resonated with your own personal experiences and memories and now you have a decent understanding of the role of the hippocampus. But will you remember it? The next step in reinforcing the tricky concept to be learned is to add some emotional content to the lesson. For my lesson, this might be a video of someone with bilateral damage to the hippocampus. This causes them to keep repeating the same odd comment every couple of minutes, forgetting that they had just said that.[73] You could ask the students if they know of someone who keeps telling the same stories over and over. Evoking the image of a loved one who became or is becoming demented with Alzheimer's or other neurodegenerative disease reinforces the lesson in ways that just listing the facts can never do. This brings it home and makes it personal.

Should We Shock Our Students?

There is such a thing as too much emotion in a lesson. John Medina suggests in his excellent book, *Brain Rules*, to include "emotionally competent stimuli" every 10 minutes in your lecture to "wake up" the students and keep them engaged. Such stimuli could be funny, or may induce shock, fear or disgust, causing activation of the sympathetic nervous system. This has the effect of moving students to the right side of the Yerkes-Dodson Curve and causing the release of norepinephrine in the brain. This strongly reinforces relevant (and ongoing irrelevant) memories surrounding the stressful stimulus, in part by inducing replay of memories. Replay of memories is reinforcing, especially if it reactivates the sympathetic nervous system on every replay. Those would be things that get your heart beating faster or make your hands sweat when you recall them. Blocking beta adrenergic norepinephrine receptors causes poorer recall of stressful events, while drugs such as yohimbine that cause release of norepinephrine enhance recall of stressful events.[74]

To activate the fight-or-flight response by scaring students is probably a memory mechanism that teachers should use sparingly, if at all. I have noticed that when it was done to me, I had a very hard time focusing back on the lecture because my brain was busy reprocessing whatever had scared me. That said, Medina's approach was used quite effectively by my metal shop teacher in High School. He showed movies and told shocking stories of gory shop accidents in the first week of metals class to emphasize dangerous things not to do in class. We remembered to be safe because our sympathetic nervous system got activated by the films, and then reactivated whenever we were using the equipment portrayed in the gory accidents. To get your students' attention back to the material at hand, I suggest evoking milder and more positive emotions than shock, disgust and fear, such as humor, incredulity, patriotic loyalty, curiosity, and friendship.

---

73. For example, Clive Wearing, https://youtu.be/Vwigmktix2Y
74. Southwick et al., *"Relationship of Enhanced Norepinephrine Activity During Memory Consolidation to Enhanced Long-Term Memory in Humans,"* (2002) Am. J. Psychiatry 159:1420.

Science is Not About Truth

My approach to teaching science differs from that of most other science teachers. Many students and even some science professors think that the purpose of science is to Find the Truth. It makes science professors feel holier than their engineer colleagues who are "just building bridges," while they are on a holy Quest for the Truth. This is a myth and a harmful one. It is harmful to students because it suggests that there actually is something called the Truth that is somehow inviolate and must be learned. If you really follow the scientific method, you realize that we never, ever get there. We can only acquire more and more evidence to support (or refute) our hypotheses about what may be true. If you follow any scientific field for a while, you realize that much of what was commonly considered "Truth" at one point becomes embarrassing naïveté at a later point. A commonly used example in neuroscience is *phrenology*, or the idea that mental abilities can be determined by locating the bumps on one's skull. What was considered Scientific Truth in the 1850s is regarded as quack pseudoscience today.

In my lectures, I took most of the pressure to learn the Truth off my students. I told them that there are no absolute Truths, only provisional ones, that work today. The provisional truths can be used to make useful things, and to solve important problems. That is what matters. It is why we do science.

For example, there are many people with Parkinson's disease who are helped by deep brain stimulation (DBS). This is like a pacemaker for the brain, an electrode implanted in their subthalamic nucleus that relieves their tremors and allows them to become "unstuck" when the disease would otherwise lock them in their seat or in mid-step while shuffling slowly along. Although scientists, neurologists and functional neurosurgeons all agree that DBS is a great thing and high-frequency stimulation often helps Parkinson's patients, they don't all agree why it works. There are several theories, and perhaps it will work even better when we have more evidence. For now, our sketchy and incomplete understanding of movement circuits of the brain was enough to develop a useful therapy.

Even the mechanisms of a drug as common as Prozac are very much in debate. Prozac is an SSRI which stands for *selective serotonin re-uptake inhibitor*. It blocks re-uptake (recycling) of the neurotransmitter serotonin, causing it to build up here and there. Great. But it does that immediately upon taking the first dose, yet it requires a few weeks of taking an SSRI before patients' depression begins to get better. Therefore, other things must be going on in their brains when taking Prozac than extra serotonin, but we are not sure what. Sorry, you scientists merely seeking the Truth! In my opinion, we scientists are here to serve the doctors, engineers, and lay people with what we find out. Science was developed as a method to understand the world well enough to solve problems and make things — usually for humans, but also for the plants, animals and environment we love and depend on.

Carrying this idea of provisional truths even further is my belief that there are plenty of "truths" that we even *know* are wrong when we think about them, yet we still believe them because they are useful. Whuh? My favorite example is the idea of *suction*. Most people have an intuitive idea that a vacuum cleaner pulls dirt out of the carpet into its bag. They believe that they pull liquid up a straw when they drink their soda, like tugging on an invisible string. That is what suction is, right? It is a pulling thing that gasses and liquids do, right? No, that is an illusion caused by the fact that we live under immense atmospheric pressure, amounting to about a kilogram per square centimeter. (Thankfully, our innards push back with an equal amount of force or we would be crushed.)

The Concept of Suction — Debunked.

> The simple idea of suction as pulling works in most circumstances, until you need to suck water out of a well deeper than about 10 meters. All of a sudden, you are hit with the fallacy of this "truth" and may now understand that it takes atmospheric pressure to push the water up the hose. One kilogram per square centimeter can only lift up a water column of 10m before the weight of the water equals the atmospheric pressure. (A square tube that is 1cm X 1cm X 10m holds one kilogram of water.) Almost everywhere in the universe (except on pressurized planets with atmospheres, which make up a vanishingly tiny fraction of the universe) liquid water only pushes. If you open a bottle of liquid water in the vacuum of space, you have an explosive water rocket. Your vacuum cleaner motor creates a slight vacuum in its bag by pumping air out against atmospheric pressure. The immense pressure all around us causes air to rush in through the carpet toward the bag and push the dirt with it — pushing, not pulling the dirt.

All that explaining is closer to the truth than the idea of suction as a pulling force. But because the concept of "suction as pulling" works under most circumstances we are familiar with, we go with it. It usually gets the job done. A more common example of a falsehood we like to believe: The sun rises and sets, right? Nope! The horizon gets in its way as the Earth rotates.

I taught my students to go with what is useful, with what works to get the job done. This turns out to be crucial in neuroscience, since we can't wait until we understand everything about the brain before we try to come up with cures for the many disorders and diseases of the nervous system. We can always improve things later when we know more. I told them in the first lecture of the semester that most of the things they will learn in my class will be proven wrong at some point. Science advances by disproving one hypothesis after another. What mattered is that what they learned in my class could be used now, and in the near future, to solve real-world problems and to allow people to live happier and longer.

There are very few drugs that are completely understood. Most drugs were discovered by a lucky accident and we have little or no idea why or how they work. Viagra was supposedly discovered when nursing staff noticed persistent erections caused by the heart medication their patients were taking. Even some ancient drugs like aspirin, which came from willow bark, are still in debate regarding their mechanisms.

My teaching philosophy, that all truths are provisional, allows me to de-emphasize textbooks. Traditionally, students have to memorize every part of their textbooks if they want to get top marks. My students kept asking me, "Which parts of the textbook do we need to know for the test?" I would say, "Just think of the textbook as a guide to flesh out some of the things we covered in class. It is a convenient source of background material to help you make associations. Already, much of it has been proven wrong, and I will try to point out those things in lecture." Some of them are upset by this, wondering why they spent the money to buy it if it is not the gospel truth. This is a good lesson for them, to be skeptical of anything they read, even if it is in a textbook.

```
"I really liked your personal philosophy of
momentary truth and applying it to better our lives
and others. I believe it carries on to other fields
as well and I will be carrying it to whatever field
I may end up in. Thank you for the great semester!"
- IntroNeuro student Alvin Lee
```

Expect Respect

After a few years teaching at Georgia Tech, I discovered it was helpful to make it clear to students what level of respect to expect or even demand. Yes, demand — It helps them to know what you expect. If you are firm about being respected, you will be respected. Although I called them by their first names, if they used my first name, I corrected them, saying politely, "You may call me Professor Potter or Doctor Potter." Students will test your boundaries sometimes. If you respectfully stick to them, they learn to behave well.

It is actually demotivating for children (and presumably young adults) to be unsure about the relative power they have with people they interact with. Thus, it is important to make it clear to students that you are in charge of what goes on in your class. Self-deprecating stories are usually good for establishing a relationship with your students, as long as the stories don't undermine their confidence in you. Don't admit too many weaknesses or personal foibles. You want to make a personal connection so students feel comfortable with you, but not so comfortable that they walk all over you or write you off as fluffy. I learned this from several high school teachers I had who tried so hard to be cool that we just dismissed them. You are not there to be the students' friend, or the funniest stand-up comedian, but their teacher.

If you don't reciprocate a demand for respect with respect towards your students, you will lose face. It must be mutual. I used the syllabus to set the tone early on for how I feel about these issues, and I had very few problems. But most of my students were college seniors. If I were teaching junior high school, I might have had to work even harder at this tricky bit of social engineering.

***

Although this chapter may have seemed like a hodgepodge of advice about teaching, it was all aimed at turning a lecture-style class from a boring requirement into something that your students will be excited to attend. The recurring theme is to **motivate students by making lecture time more active and interactive.** If you heed my suggestions, I predict that your students will become more involved in the learning process, and become self-motivated to make the most of their time in class. Perhaps, as I often observed with my students, they will carry what they learned in class home with them and make it part of their lives in ways that are meaningful and rewarding.

CHAPTER 8

Creative Extra Credit

Students are motivated by being in control of how to excel. I allowed my students to earn up to 15% of their grade as extra credit, to make up for other aspects of the course they did not get full marks on. From an anonymous end-of-semester survey question, *"What was the best aspect of Introduction to Neuroscience?"* one IntroNeuro student responded:

```
"The ability to show effort and learning through
iterative projects and extra credit opportunities."
```

Different students learn differently. And the assessments that we use to grade them work well for some students but not others. For example, for some students, anxiety gets in the way of their thought process during tests or oral presentations. Some students may not enjoy participating in classroom discussions because they are shy or don't speak English well. I encouraged them to propose their own ideas for Extra Credit projects or assignments, and they came up with some creative ideas, which I will mention below.

Extra Credit Lecture Write-ups

```
"I liked that we were able to attend seminars and
write responses to them for extra credit. I got more
out of that than I expected." - alumnus Richard
Hartnet
```

I was lucky to be teaching neuroscience in a big city (Atlanta, Georgia) with a large number neuro-related departments at Georgia Tech, Emory University, Georgia State University, and Moorehouse School of Medicine. There were many public lectures with a neuro theme being given at these universities. My students were encouraged to attend and write a short review of them, for extra credit. They had to take notes (or record the talks) and write a full page, with some coherent structure, that summarized the speaker's main points, for up to one percent of extra credit. I actually compiled all the write-ups at the end of the semester into one giant PDF and gave it to all the students as a gift, and made it available to subsequent years' classes.

If you don't teach in a big city, fear not! As more and more such public lectures began to be posted on the Internet (on YouTube or on departmental or conference websites), I allowed students to watch those and do write-ups of them, too. That saved them from having to travel to a talk and be there at a certain time, and allowed them to rewind and play back parts they didn't understand the first time. The talks had to be at least 45 minutes long (so no 15-minute TED talks) and given during the semester, to be sure they were getting the most current science, and to eliminate the possibility of plagiarizing from previous semester's write-ups. I made sure to announce all the upcoming talks, whether in-person or online, to the entire class so that everyone had the same opportunities for extra credit.

> "I wanted to thank you for everything you taught us this semester, and the way you taught it. It really was great and is part of the reason I've chosen to pursue a related field. So I thought I should share that with you! I truly enjoyed all of it, especially the unique things like **the guest lectures and extra credit talks we attended as an added learning. It really exposed us to the real world** as you said. I will probably never have a class like this again." - Amit Parekh, 2010 IntroNeuro student

And a few years later, Amit responded to my alumni survey:

> "The most memorable thing was using a lot of my time during finals watching extra credit videos. More so than work, I found them to be more like stress relievers and that's when I really decided I want a career with something to do with the brain."

8. Creative Extra Credit

2006 Neuroscience Conference Windfall

Due to the disaster of Hurricane Katrina, the annual meeting of the Society for Neuroscience (SFN) in 2006 was relocated from New Orleans to Atlanta. That was a big windfall for my students. I managed to procure funding from our local chapter of the SFN for as many who wanted to go, to attend the conference for free. For extra credit, the students could write a report of what they learned at the conference. This is a 5-day conference with over 30,000 neuroscientists from around the world attending. The schedule is packed with talks and poster sessions going on in dozens of rooms in parallel, so it is not possible to see even half of all that is going on there.

The venues for the SFN Annual Meeting are huge. It was sometimes impossible to get across the conference center in time for the next talk on my itinerary. I would often wear my rollerblades to get around. In 1999 when the SFN was in Miami, I popped into a Sharper Image store of high-tech, high-priced inventions and bought a truly amazing mobility-enhancing gadget, a folding aluminum scooter called a "Razor." It was great for zooming around the convention center. My scientist friends were in awe and all wanted one, until I told them how much it cost. Little did I know that within 5 years, the price went down substantially and every single kid under age 10 in the US would have one.

SFN was a good chance for those of my students who attended to meet with potential advisors if they were headed for grad school, or to connect with companies exhibiting neuro-related products. I had my students present and discuss the highlights of what they saw at SFN in class after it was over.

In another year when the SFN meeting was far away and I was scheduled to give a talk there about my lab's research, I came up with a novel assignment for my IntroNeuro students called "The Remote-Controlled Professor." Because there are so many posters and talks at SFN's Annual Meeting, the SFN created software that attendees can use to search for keywords or certain researchers among the tens of thousands of abstracts, and tag the ones they wish to attend. Then the software creates an itinerary, and alerts them to conflicts where they wanted to be in two or more places at the same time, so they could make a tough decision about which one to attend. I would usually spend a day or two before the conference reading many abstracts and working on my SFN Itinerary.

For my RC Professor assignment, I taught my IntroNeuro students how to use the SFN's Abstract Browser, and asked each one to submit to me an abstract of a poster or talk that they wished they could see if they were at the SFN. Instead of making my itinerary from keywords related to my own research, I used my student's chosen abstracts. It was a remarkable experience!

143

I got to see and hear about many neuro topics I never would have thought to go to, some about things I had never heard of. I took notes for my students as I skated from poster to poster and talk to talk. When I returned to Atlanta after 5 exhausting days, I spent an entire lecture period reporting back to the class what I had learned, thanks to their excellent choices. These days, this idea could be made even more engaging by live-streaming highlights from the conference. That year, I relied on the grad students in my own research lab to go to the posters and talks related to my group's research and educate me with *their* post-conference write-ups.

YouTube Video Creation

The primary literature in scientific journals is full of jargon and heavily dependent on other papers. It is virtually impossible for most lay people to read and interpret it. As an extra credit assignment, I challenged my students to create a YouTube video that would highlight a scientific paper they had read in a way that could be appreciated by the lay person. This sort of distilling and explanation of complex topics is exactly what is needed to write a good Wikipedia article (see Chapter 10). Thus, to carry out this assignment was a great help to those who chose to do it, in writing their own Wikipedia articles.

Some used this opportunity to learn a bit of marketing. By creating an engaging or humorous video,[75] they could direct traffic to their Wikipedia article. Because YouTube was only getting started at the time, and because students didn't have smartphones with excellent video cameras in them, it was technically tricky just to record, edit, and upload a video to YouTube. Our library had a Media Creation Room for producing videos. This assignment worked better when it was done in pairs or small groups than individually. Students kept a log of what each group member had done to help produce the video, making grading easier.

YouTube and modern smartphones have made it so much easier now to produce and upload quality videos! Much younger students are doing similar video projects these days. We devoted a class period to watching the most interesting YouTube videos that my students created, and a YouTube playlist allowed them to watch any of them whenever they wished.

---

75. Here is an especially creative one by my student Austin Bennett, https://b.gatech.edu/2SXmGmK

Students' Extra Credit Ideas

I regularly mined my students for good ideas. I encouraged them to come up with their own assignments for extra credit. If I thought a student's idea was a good one, I would announce it to the whole class as a new opportunity for everyone to get a point or two of extra credit. The most popular idea had a great real-world connection: to attend charity walks for charities related to neurological disorders, including Alzheimer's Disease, Parkinson's Disease, Amyotrophic Lateral Sclerosis (motor neuron disease), and autism (Fig. 19). Usually at these walks, there were many booths where my students could ask questions about the nervous system and how it goes wrong. There were opportunities to meet people afflicted by disorders they had learned about in class. And by walking five kilometers with other students and random strangers, they probably talked about experiences with relatives who suffer from the disorder that was being funded by the walkers' donations and registration fees. They also walked to raise awareness of suicide, and they did gardening for the Jacob's Ladder neurodevelopmental school.

I hoped that these walks might encourage some of them to pursue a career in curing the disorders. Or perhaps, they would work on ways to reduce suffering in those who have it, their carers, and loved ones. Even just to raise awareness of the research is a worthy enough goal, however. I imagine the T-shirts they took home and proudly wore spurred on yet more conversations where they would have a chance to re-teach what they had learned.

Another good EC idea came from Savannah Cookson. She thought it would be fun and relevant to IntroNeuro for her classmates to go through a brain training course for extra credit if they wished. She liaised with the *Scientific Learning Corporation* to get a site license for their *Fast ForWord* program,[76] which has a variety of metrics that students and teachers can use to study how much improvement they are making in verbal fluency and other key language skills.

Having a wide selection of possible ways to earn extra credit was an effective way for me to allow my students to tailor their learning experience to the way they learn best. By allowing them to come up with their own ideas for extra credit, and letting them decide which, if any, extra credit opportunities to take part in, I provided my students with the motivation that comes with being

---

76. As their name suggests, this is a much more scientifically-based brain training program than most others out there, and has resulted in many peer-reviewed papers showing substantial benefits for dyslexic students. The company was created by the father of the cochlear implant, Dr. Michael Merzenich. https://www.scilearn.com/program/

in control of their learning. The ideas I described above are obviously specific to the courses and subject matter I taught. Have your students help you come up with your own ideas for how to make learning relevant and interesting to them, and **well-differentiated**, to accommodate different learning styles.

8. Creative Extra Credit

Figure 19. Georgia Tech students walking for extra credit and learning about neurological disorders in the Real World. At the Alzheimer's benefits, walkers were encouraged to write the names of loved ones with the disease on big flower pinwheels they carried in their honor.

CHAPTER 9

Clear Rules

The Syllabus

There are many ways to take advantage of the fact that agency, or a feeling of being in control of their educational experience, is highly motivating for students. I handed my students a detailed syllabus and schedule at the beginning of the first lecture, so they knew what to expect from the course. This allowed them to take control of their time, rather than having to deal with assignments foisted on them at random. It included not only the overall goals of the course and my policies, but a detailed schedule with every lecture topic and assignment listed in a calendar. Especially for college students, it is important for them to plan their time spent on each of their courses studying for tests, doing projects, having meetings with peers, etc. They sometimes also have a busy extracurricular schedule to integrate into this calendar, e.g., if they are on an intercollegiate sports team. This was difficult for me to accomplish in time for the beginning of the semester because I usually had about a dozen guest lecturers each semester and I had to have those all invited and confirmed before I could print the schedule. To write a good syllabus, I made changes each semester based on the feedback my previous students had suggested, and based on the observations by my teaching assistants and me about how things went last time.

With all the structure that a detailed schedule has, it may sound like the students had no agency at all. Many of the details I left up to them, so they still felt in control. I watched out for things that might cause problems for the students, and tried to fix them by tweaking the structure of the course as we went along. For example, if they found that a certain assignment was much more work than they had anticipated, I would create a lead-up assignment that would help them with the big one. Or have two rounds of assessment and improvement instead of just one chance to get it right. Many of my colleagues used only the simplest of syllabi, with not much detail in the schedule because then the teacher can "wing it" and be flexible during the semester in terms of what they have the class do and when. I recall how annoying that was for me when I was a student because it was impossible to plan my semester or to anticipate what was coming next.

The syllabus was a contract between my students and me. Because mine were elective courses, all of my students were free to drop the course — no one was being compelled to take it. If they stayed with it, they were agreeing to all the expectations I had set out in the syllabus. I tried to keep my rules positive and explain why I did unusual things like taking roll every lecture and subtracting points for being absent. I emphasized how my classes were very much focused on what happens in the lecture hall, and much less about what is in the textbook. Discussions with the students, or presentations by them, were valuable learning experiences that required them to participate actively in order to benefit.

I also thought about various problems I had had with students, such as them disputing their grades, cheating, procrastinating, being upset by certain subjects I lectured on, or having special needs because of a disability. I tried to forestall as many of these potential problems with clear policies and reassuring words in the syllabus. I repeatedly exhorted them to come see me after class or other office hours if they had any problems or if they needed extra help to get the grade they wanted. Many of them did, and learned that I was on their side, trying to help them make the most of their time, fees and tuition.[77]

My Grading

Perhaps one of the biggest surprises my students came across in my syllabi was my approach to grading. It was based on the heretical notion that **Everyone in the class can get an A**. I graded on a straight scale of points, and all the points were spelled out in the syllabus. My exams amounted to a much smaller proportion of their grade than in most college courses. Instead, tangible results of their projects were weighted heavily. If my students did all the things listed and did them well, they would get an A. They were in complete control of their grade, perhaps for the first time in their schooling.

---

[77]. I reminded my students how much they were paying for each class session, nearly $100 for Georgia Tech's out-of-state tuition & fees. *"Education is one of the few things a person is willing to pay for and not get."* — William Lowe Bryan

Even when I was a TA in grad school, I intuited that grading according to a bell curve was wrong. I got in trouble at that time when I gave out too many As to my psychobiology lab class. My fellow grad TAs said something like,

> *You are ruining the curve by giving out too many As! We expect each TA to have a few low grades, a few As and mostly Bs and Cs. Your class was over half As! No bad grades and only a few Bs. Obviously you are being far too easy on your students, and our students might feel like they have been treated unfairly, receiving too low grades from us, by comparison.*

To regain my credibility as a teacher, I showed them my syllabus, and they were shocked how much work I expected from my students. I was assigning my students WAY more work than they were assigning to theirs. I graded on a straight scale: If you do all the assigned work well, you get an A, regardless of what other students do. After my fellow TAs read my syllabus, they realized that I was definitely NOT being too easy on my students. Each one of those "too many" students had done a huge amount of work to earn an A from me.

For that psychobiology lab class I taught in grad school, I stuck with my system of grading on a straight scale. However, because of the controversy I caused, we also instituted a single department-wide final exam that every psychobiology lab student had to take, so we could see whether each TA was doing his or her job of getting the students to learn the important stuff. We could use those final exam scores to "normalize" a TA's grades if we felt an adjustment was needed to keep things fair across all the TAs' classes. In agreement with the grades I was giving, my students' scores on this final showed they had learned the material well.

Why did my students do so well? Why did so many of them put in the hours needed to meet my high expectations and get and A? Something (or things) I did motivated them far beyond everyone's expectations, mine, theirs, and my fellow TAs.

I strongly feel that grading on a curve is demotivating. To expect the distribution of any class's grades to form a bell curve is the enemy of the whole idea of a Growth Mindset, that any student can excel. And for such a small class as this lab class (~30 students) it makes no sense to use a bell curve. The "law of large numbers," that all things tend toward a normal distribution or bell-shaped curve, only applies if you actually have LARGE NUMBERS! It is quite possible to end up with a class that skews the average grade tendency one way or the other. But most importantly, I believe that each student, no matter what type of student they may be, has the potential to learn and do well in a class, to move themselves over to the right side of the distribution. **The only requirement for doing well is motivation** and everyone who is still alive has the potential to be motivated somehow. Here is evidence that my unusual grading practices helped to motivate my students:

> "Loved the setup of the course. I am not a strong test taker and I felt as though the assignments were much more beneficial and helpful. One of the best classes I have taken at Tech!" - anonymous IntroNeuro student

> "Dr. Potter … is straightforward and fair in his grading, and we can tell that he wants us to succeed. **All of these things make me put in more effort.**" - anonymous NeuroEng. Fun. student

Step one in motivating students is to NOT demotivate them. Take away the depressing prospect of grading on a curve: that a certain number of students in the class are GUARANTEED to get a bad grade, and only a very few will get an A. "Why should I bother trying? I certainly won't be one of those few As. I am not an A student," many students will say to themselves. If you grade on a straight scale, meaning that each student's grade is independent of all the others' grades, then every student has the empowering potential to get whatever grade they decide to earn. I handed out the scale in great detail at the beginning of the semester. All the assignments, due dates and exams were listed, so the students could psych themselves up for whatever grade they wished to get. They might have decided, on seeing the huge list of assignments, that they would only try for a C. With each course I taught, the majority of such students got so interested in the material and excited about the class that they kept upping their own expectations of what they would accomplish for the course.

> "It was definitely a love/hate relationship. At the beginning of that semester, the number and type of tasks that you presented on the syllabus were daunting; however, it turned out to be one of my favorite classes while at Tech. It was one of the toughest yet most rewarding classes I have ever taken." - alumnus Jared Ivey, writing about IntroNeuro

Attendance

I was unusual among my fellow professors in requiring my students to attend lectures. As I mentioned above, I felt that the lectures and discussions were the primary way they would learn, and that the textbook was only there to support what they learned in class. I took roll with an electronic student response system as described in the **Embrace Technology** section (Chapter 14, p. 208). I would ask one or two easy questions based on the previous lecture, and I collected their responses via their registered clickers. Taking roll only took three minutes no matter how large the class was. It helped that I had learned all of their names and faces. That deterred potential cheaters.

Their enthusiasm for the material they were learning soon got my students coming to the lectures on time, every session. A few complained about my required attendance policy, but it was necessary to send a clear message at the beginning of the course about how important the class meetings and discussions were for the goals of the course. I wanted to get my students engaged and to focus on material they found interesting. If they thought they could do well by just reading the textbook, they might not have come to class or paid attention. By making the reasons for my attendance policy clear, they would not be surprised later to find that my exams often included material brought up by students during class discussions.

I found that having a well-organized and well-justified set of rules and expectations for my students really helped things go more smoothly. Although some may have felt I was stricter than what they were used to from other college courses, everyone appreciated how following the syllabus carefully made the learning more fair and efficient. I always encouraged students to come talk to me if they felt they could not follow the rules for some reason, and I was open minded about bending or changing rules based on these discussions if necessary, such as excusing unavoidable absences.

As with most aspects of my teaching, the details of which rules were necessary were only worked out after years of having to deal with difficult or uncomfortable situations with my students. Therefore, I suggest to be sensitive to any issues that come up, and immediately make a note of them and refer to those notes when devising the next season's course and syllabus. If your students are too young for a syllabus, a poster on the wall with the class rules might suffice.

CHAPTER 10

Wikipedia Writing and Other Authentic Projects

One of the most successful aspects of IntroNeuro, in terms of student motivation, was a real-world project of writing articles for Wikipedia. I didn't expect that this assignment would have such lasting benefits for my students. Jenny Kim responded to my alumni survey:

> "I LOVED THE WIKIPEDIA ASSIGNMENT! I still go back
> to my wiki page and look at all the changes that
> people, doctors, scientists and professionals have
> made to my site. Knowing that someone studying a
> particular neuro-degenerative disease/illness can go
> to Google, type in the name and possibly end up at
> my Wikipedia page is really rewarding."

> "My current area of thesis graduate research
> (Auditory neurophysiology/neuroengineering) was
> largely inspired by the Wikipedia article and

> *YouTube video that we were required to complete."*
> *– alumnus Nishant Zachariah*

At the beginning of the semester, each student had to search Wikipedia for a neuro-related topic of interest to them that was not there yet, or was represented only by a **stub** (very brief and insufficient article). By the end of the semester, they would become an expert in their chosen topic and write a solid, detailed article on Wikipedia about it. When I began this idea in 2006, Wikipedia was not very highly regarded by academics. Many teachers forbade their students from even using it. I predicted that it would soon become a legitimate, useful and trusted source of information. My students have helped to make that happen! There are hundreds of neuroscience articles on Wikipedia whose first substantial versions were written by them.[78]

This assignment was a daunting task, made easier by breaking it down into a variety of sub-tasks and lead-up assignments, as described below. They built up their expertise gradually by doing extensive reading of the primary literature (peer-reviewed articles), secondary literature (books, mostly) and other sources.

The lead-up assignments (worth 21% of semester grade) were spread across the whole semester and included:

- Search for a potential Wikipedia topic that is presently missing or a stub.
- Conduct a literature search on your proposed topic.
- Read and summarize a review paper on the chosen topic.
- Choose a neuro book to read.
- Schedule an interview with a topic Expert.
- Write a report of the oral Expert interview.
- Practice Wikipedia editing in the Sandbox.
- Create an outline of the Wikipedia article.
- Review peers' Wikipedia article drafts.

---

78. Here is a list of the students' Wikipedia articles from my 2010 class: https://potterlab.gatech.edu/wikipedia-article-assignment-for-introneuro/. You can see their contributions on the View History tab of each article, near the "oldest" revisions.

Although it was a ton of work, by the end of the course almost everyone had created something they could be proud of. I occasionally get emails from my former students telling me that they are still maintaining the Wikipedia article they created for my class and proudly showing it to their friends and colleagues. By choosing a topic that was personally relevant, it was easier for them to dive into the research.

In an email in which alumnus and former IntroNeuro student Nikhil Dewan told me the good news that he was hired to do research for the National Institute for Mental Health, he said,

> "PS: They were only further impressed when they saw my Wikipedia page and that we had to complete such an assignment."

Oral Interview Assignment

By speaking directly with experts, so much more information can be learned quickly than by reading papers and books. Once my students had read a few papers and become familiar with the experts in their chosen Wikipedia topic, one of their lead-up assignments was to conduct an oral interview of one of those authors. Most scientific papers include the email address of the primary author. I coached them on how to approach busy academics for an interview. I explained ways to sneak through the senior researchers' defenses to get their attention, such as calling them on their office phone.

My students had to make it beneficial to all parties involved by letting the famous scientists know that their favorite research subject would soon have an article on Wikipedia. The interview had to be oral, either in person, by phone or by video conference. Jerry Pine always said, "The phone is the most valuable piece of equipment in the lab." He continually urged me to ring someone up if I had a question he could not answer.

Students got pointers not just from me, but from each other. After the interviews, I solicited advice from each student, directed to future students. I compiled the advice into a PDF book for subsequent classes. As the years went on, this became a great resource for them to learn the meta-skills of interviewing, scheduling interviews, asking good questions, keeping on track with scientists who might want to wander off topic, following up on leads, and taking notes.

> "I would suggest that all students wishing to get an interview with a clinician (MD or MD/PhD) to not waste their time with emails and to directly call them. Every email got ignored, including the person

> *I'm interviewing with, until I phoned them."* -Chris Giardina

I tried to explain to my students that the quick back-and-forth of an oral interview allows much more useful information to be conveyed, because each party can adjust what they are saying to match the other person's level. For example, if the Esteemed Scientist says something the student doesn't understand, the student can immediately ask for clarification. An email interview, by contrast, can easily go off-topic or be aimed too high for the student to digest. Sometimes, important information can be learned during an oral interview that the Expert is not willing to put in writing, such as the relative trustworthiness of other papers the student may have come across, or even shortcomings of the Expert's own work.

One student suggested, *"Keep asking where that is published."* Originally it was enough to cite an interview with an expert to substantiate a "fact" they wrote on Wikipedia. But after a few years, other editors on Wikipedia would call out such "Oral Interview" references with a "Needs citation" tag. My students then learned to ask the Expert to point them to key peer-reviewed papers or books where they might find the facts they mentioned. Here are more meta-skills learned:

> *"Some advice I would give next year students for conducting their interviews would be to not be intimidated. I was very intimidated to interview an expert in a field I knew very little about, but it turned out that Dr. Rorden was excited to share his knowledge of this topic and point me to places where I could learn more. Also, I would advise to make the list of questions beforehand and send them to the expert so that both he and you are prepared for the interview. Finally, I believe that one reason the interview was so beneficial was because it was done face to face. Try to find an expert in the area that you can interview face to face. It is easier to show your interest in the topic in person than over the phone."* - Jennifer Carlson

> *"This process proved that persistence is key when trying to contact an expert, and was good practice for contacting graduate school professors and research companies."* - Savannah Cookson

10. Wikipedia Writing and Other Authentic Projects

Becoming Wikipedians

I watched Wikipedia grow tremendously across my years teaching IntroNeuro. At first, I was one of very few teachers who were incorporating the editing of Wikipedia articles into their curriculum. There were no guides about how to go about this, for students or instructors. The best practices for creating and editing Wikipedia articles were not yet figured out. Anyone can easily hit the Edit tab and begin to edit Wikipedia. But because the whole world is watching, my students were motivated to do it well. The basic mechanics of Wikipedia editing are not very difficult to learn. However, the etiquette, style, citation requirements, and ways of interacting with other editors are subtle and complicated.

At some point, the Wikimedia Foundation began a system of training Wikipedia Ambassadors, whose job it is to help people edit Wikipedia. I asked my librarian, Lori Critz, if she would become one. She instantly agreed and she and two others at the Georgia Tech library took the course and became Ambassadors. This was a great help for me. I was always in catch-up mode when it came to teaching Wikipedia editing, so my students greatly benefited from having those Ambassadors to help them with learning the latest Best Practices.

After a while, the Wikimedia Foundation also set up a system for instructors doing Wikipedia editing assignments to set up a Course Page where students could keep tabs on which topics others had already chosen to work on, and other logistical aspects of making new Wikipedia articles. This idea has been so successful at motivating students that the Wikimedia Foundation created the non-profit spin-off, Wiki Education. They created the *Wiki Education Dashboard*[79] to help students and instructors improve Wikipedia. I strongly encourage you to consider Wikipedia editing for part of your curriculum, and avail of their resources for teachers.

One key requirement for my students was to create a username and always to do their editing *after* logging in to Wikipedia. Then I could tell, by looking at the History tab of their article, exactly what they had contributed to their article and when. This was important because there was nothing keeping others who had nothing to do with my course from also editing the same page.

Interaction with Wikipedians (volunteer Wikipedia editors) was a great lesson for many of my students. They learned that they had to work constructively with other self-proclaimed experts out there in the Real World who would not let them get away with poor writing or a lack of citations. I had students coming to me in a panic saying, "My whole article got deleted! What

---

79. https://dashboard.wikiedu.org/

do I do? Am I going to fail the class?" I calmly told them how to befriend their "enemies" and learn why what they wrote was deleted. Thankfully, every single Wikipedia article has a Talk tab at the top where mature, calm discussions can take place between editors who disagree on something, and usually my students used it to help them fix any problems and create an article everyone was happy with.

A side benefit of becoming Wikipedia authors is that my students also learned the mechanics of editing any wiki. There are more and more such collaborative websites where any visitor can edit and contribute. A good example is GitHub, a cloud repository and version control system used for large open-source collaborative software projects.[80]

Students who use wikis get used to the idea of always writing with care because there is a change log, or revision history that remembers everything. And we teachers can make good use of the *diff* function to highlight exactly what is different between two revisions, before and after a student of ours contributed to it. In Wikipedia, this is called "compare selected revisions" in the History tab. The number of bytes a student contributed is easily calculated because the size of each revision is given in bytes. Because wikis retain this history of all revisions, potential employers or admissions officers can see what the student contributed, how much, and how well written or referenced it was. Thus, the students' work on any of these wikis becomes a valuable item in their portfolios.

The Wikipedia assignment was daunting, not because the articles were long, but because of all the research needed to write a credible article. For my IntroNeuro course, my students had to write, on their chosen topic, a Wikipedia article of 15,000 to 25,000 bytes. That is only approximately 1,500-3,000 words. If other editors were also working on it during the semester, or if they had started by adding to an existing stub, they were required to add that many bytes of text to the final version. I chose this size by looking at the sizes of existing articles that I found most useful. Sizes in bytes are easily found using a desktop computer browser in the *View history* tab of the Wikipedia article. An overly long article may be just as bad as one that is too short. It usually means that it is meandering or includes too much tenuously related material that would be better written about in separate Wikipedia articles. This is good training for my students to learn to write concisely, something I am still working on!

In the Real World, for example, when writing a grant application, there is almost always a size limit. As with many of my rules, I was flexible about

---

80. Since so many of its programmers used GitHub for in-house software development, Microsoft bought it in 2018 for over $7 billion; it is here to stay.

the number of bytes. My students were encouraged to come talk to me early if they felt for some reason that they had to make their article less than 15,000 bytes. This probably meant they chose an obscure topic and they could not find enough material out there to write about. I would usually encourage them to find a new topic. If they felt their final contribution would be more than 25,000 bytes, there had to be a very good justification. If the topic could be clearly broken down into more than one sub-topic, it sometimes made a good opportunity for another student in the class to adopt that sub-topic, and the two students could collaborate.

It was not uncommon for a student to realize that they needed to change topics. I created a number of assignments designed to make sure that the students liked their topic, that there was enough peer-reviewed literature out there on it, and that I felt it was a legitimate neuroscience topic. There are all sorts of quack ideas and pseudo-scientific topics that may be misinterpreted as neuroscience by the uninformed. I had to vet each topic chosen by using my experience as a neuroscientist, and sometimes, by reviewing the literature myself a bit. This was easy because one of the early assignments was for them to hand in a list of at least 10 peer-reviewed publications that deal with the chosen topic in some way.

Occasionally, a student didn't realize until putting some work into reading about a topic that they just didn't like it, or perhaps they found another topic they really loved better. I let them change topics. I reminded everyone at the beginning that the earlier they commit to a topic they love, the less work it will be in the end.

One of the more disastrous possibilities is that a chosen topic the student thought was missing from Wikipedia was actually already well covered, but under a different name. They might waste time and effort writing a page that was already there. It was crucial for the students to learn the terminology surrounding their topics and to do a thorough search on Wikipedia to be sure the topics they chose were missing or were stubs.

Doing literature searching to find out what has already been written about a subject is great training for any student who is headed for graduate school or any career in research. As one scientist friend of mine quipped, *"Six months of research in the lab can save you an afternoon in the library."* Of course, thanks to Google's autocomplete suggestions, and especially Google Scholar, discovering the important related keywords is easier than ever.

In the Real World, most great things are built in stages, not all in one go. Students are much more motivated to finish a big project if they get encouragement and feedback along the way. The grading of my students' Wikipedia articles was done in several stages. Initially, they worked in their own private online workspace, called the Wikipedia Sandbox. Here, novice editors can practice the mechanics of editing and inserting citations. I had them use the Sandbox to create a brief outline for their article very early on, based on the reading and interviews they had been doing. This was a good point for them and me to do a reality check that the topic was a good one and would be doable. Near the end of the semester, a couple of weeks before their final article was due, they created a draft version that was supposed to be nearly finished. This was published in the public space, not in the sandbox. They could set flags in their public draft articles to mark them as a "work in progress." By making this draft public, they may have gotten helpful input from other more experienced Wikipedians. I graded it using the same rubric (see box below) as the final version, so they knew exactly where they would miss points and what to focus on improving.

My Wikipedia Article Grading Rubric

Two percent of IntroNeuro students' semester grade was allotted for each item below (20% total).

The article:

- incorporates factual and encyclopedic neurobiological information. It should have up-to-date content, with at least a couple refs in the last three years.

- is 15,000–25,000 bytes total, except by prior agreement with Prof. Potter.

- is readable by lay people and jargon is defined (WP:NOTJOURNAL)[81] and/or hyperlinked: see WP:OVERLINK vs. WP:UNDERLINK.

- has at least 10 peer-reviewed journal article references. This includes review papers. Cite recent reviews instead of older research, if possible, and follow WP:MEDRS for biomedical information.

- is linked to/from other Wikipedia articles where possible (so it's not a WP:ORPHAN) and uses red links (WP:RED) for needed pages.

---

81. If you put "WP:" before a keyword in Wikipedia's search box, you can access pages about how Wikipedia is run and organized.

- responds to the Talk page comments.
- is well formatted and follows Wikipedia style. It is tagged with appropriate WikiProject templates and course banner template to the article's Talk page. It has good organization, including a table of contents with headings (as per WP:HEADING) and follows WP:REFSPACE for formatting the references.
- is well written. It is neutral (WP:NPOV), with no unpublished original research (WP:OR). It is verifiable (WP:V). It has good grammar with no typos and is readable.
- has the student's Real Name or username in the History page and is listed on our course page.
- is Outstanding in some way, such as, it includes original media, or is very well referenced, creative, became a Featured Article, etc.

I think it is a good idea for **every assignment to include the opportunity for students to go beyond what is expected, in their own personal way.** The last item in the rubric was to encourage my students to be creative with their articles. They were given the chance to point out to me what they felt was outstanding about their article, in case I missed it.

For students to create a useful, lasting public artifact proved to be highly motivating and a great opportunity for learning many life skills. Years later, my alumni reported their Wikipedia articles as being important in their careers.

> "The Wikipedia assignment was unlike any other assignment I have ever had. It is really a smart idea because for most papers, students use Wikipedia to gather basic information without having to read through confusing, high level published papers. Since we were writing the Wiki page for our topic, there was no Wiki site to reference. For this assignment, I contacted a professor and researcher at a northern university and conducted an hour long phone interview. I read countless papers and synthesized all of the information into a Wikipedia

> *article written at a level that could be understood by the general population."* - alumna Sarah Wetherington

To Take Credit for Your Work is a Strong Motivator

I am a big believer that people should take responsibility for their actions. They should be proud of the good things they have done, and make amends for the bad ones. There are a few — very few — cases where being anonymous is a useful mechanism to protect someone. But in the science world, we sign our real names to every article we write because readers need to know where the information is coming from, whether it can be trusted, and whom to talk to if they have any additional questions about it. It helps readers trust the authors. For this reason, I strongly encouraged my students to make it possible to trace any edits they made on Wikipedia back to their real identity. Every editor on Wikipedia who has created a username has a User Page. This can be used to mention their real name, and perhaps where they are going to school and the name of the course in which they were assigned to work on Wikipedia. Their User Page has its own Talk page, where others can leave messages for them. Their usernames were also listed on our Course Page, which lists me as the instructor in case someone needed to get hold of me to tell me, for example, that I or my students were not following Wikipedia protocol. This did happen a few times as I blundered ahead, not always understanding Wikipedia etiquette myself.

The motivation that comes from putting your work out there in the Real World can be both positive and negative:

> *"The process of gathering information, publishing it in a public venue and taking credit/responsibility for the content of the writing was almost an entirely unique concept to me as an undergraduate. To that point my classes had required a significant writing component, however, there was never a requirement to put my name on the line and make my writing available to the public. To my surprise, that actually significantly altered the way I approached the writing and substantially improved the quality of my final product.* **The assignments motivated me to become engaged in the topic and do an excellent job because I wanted to represent myself well.** *This is the same process that I am now going through as a graduate student because all my*

> work will be published, thus representing myself, my lab and my school." – alumnus Mike Weiler

> "The prospect of being publicly shamed is a powerful impetus to produce acceptable work. The thought of other students (especially my friends) in this class scrutinizing, perhaps even laughing at my work is unbearable." – alumnus Mohan Natrajan.

Mohan created the Wikipedia article on *Neuroplastic effects of pollution*. It was excellent, so I presume his imagined shaming was effective for motivating him.

Your students do not need to create Wikipedia articles from scratch. There are many tasks on Wikipedia that need help from motivated and curious students. These can be as simple or as elaborate as your class time allows. Head over to the *Wiki Education Dashboard* to get started! Just make sure your students create their own User page so they can continue to take credit for their efforts, and perhaps, continue editing Wikipedia long after they finish the assignment.

I learned a number of important things by evolving my Wikipedia assignment. Eventually, it became the most influential, memorable thing my alumni mentioned about my course. I learned how to break a large assignment down into smaller ones, each an important step up the staircase toward the final product. I learned the importance of giving my students detailed feedback along the way, to reassure us both that they were on the right track and moving forward. I learned how influential it can be to have real people in the Real World comment on a student's work in progress. Most importantly, I saw many students of all sorts — including students who were previously unmotivated — rise to the challenge and create work to be proud of for years to come.

Many of the problems we ran into are a thing of the past, thanks to Wikipedia having a much more mature set of rules and etiquette, and to all of the instructor resources at the *Wiki Education Dashboard*. Some of the problems we had were unique to the field of biomedical engineering, such as worries about accidentally giving bad medical advice in an article that may end up causing serious harm to a reader. In later years, we depended heavily on input from the seasoned Wikipedia editors across the globe who specialize in biomedicine, making many authoring projects more collaborative than my students expected.

> "The assignments were well designed. Everyone I told about the Amazon book reviews and the Wikipedia

```
            articles commented on what a great idea they
            were." - anonymous IntroNeuro student
```

Amazon Book Reviews

I love books. I am an especially avid reader of non-fiction books about the brain, cognition, consciousness, neurophilosophy, and neuroengineering. Most of my students initially felt they were too busy to read books for their own enjoyment, especially non-fiction books that are often perceived as a chore. I successfully got them to read at least one book by making it a required part of the curriculum for my IntroNeuro class. An important control-related motivator was that they got to choose their book. The only requirement was that it be somehow related to neuroscience and at least potentially educational. They could even choose a fiction book, but there are not many neuro-fiction books out there. Many students chose a book that was related to their Wikipedia topic, but that was not a requirement. Once they read the book, they were graded *by each other* based on a structured, detailed book review they had to write for Amazon.com.

Amazon Book Review Instructions to Students

Your review should be at least 1000 words (about two pages at 12 point), well organized, well written, and should include:

- An informative title.
- Your Real Name™.
- A rating from 1-5 stars.
- A brief summary of the point of your review in the first sentence or two.
- Your overall opinion of the book.
- A synopsis of the parts of the book.
- An explanation of the style and structure of the book.
- Your opinions on specific parts or aspects of the book. This is the meat of your review, and should be easy to scan: headers, separate paragraphs, etc.

- Some useful or interesting quotes from the book.
- A summary of your opinions/review.
- A recommendation for potential readers: whether to get it, how to read it, or anything else you want to say straight to them.
- Anything else you want to put in there that you feel is appropriate and useful for a book review.

Note: No copying from other reviews — all text must be in your own words (except book quotes, obviously, which should be marked as such with quotation marks). Feel free to slam the book if you unfortunately chose a bad book. Keep your language civil and informative.

We devoted one or two class sessions to oral book reports. Students were randomly chosen to present their book review to the whole class. Every student had to come to class on those days ready to be chosen at any moment. There was only enough time for a few of my students to present their reviews. I had everyone's names written on small slips of paper and had a student in front reach into my "inflatable brain" bag to pick the next presenter. This kept them on their toes. There was a buzz of excitement in the room on presentation days. For the chosen book reviewers, I projected their live book review that was up on Amazon.com onto the screen behind them while they summarized it orally. Students knew that the topic of tomorrow's daily quiz would be something chosen from what the presenters had said, so they were motivated to pay attention to each other, and even to take notes.

Many presenters were very excited about the book they had read. I was pleasantly surprised how many students were disappointed when the session was over and they did not get to present their book. Sometimes by popular demand, we extended the book reports to two class sessions.

Peer assessment

Students got to learn about 5-8 neuro books from their peers during those book report days. But they got even more exposure to classmates' books during the *peer grading assignment*. I had each student read 5 other book reviews created by their classmates on Amazon. They had to rank them, according to how well they fulfilled the structure requirements above. They often complained that it was very difficult and unfair to give a rank of 4 or 5 to a review, as most were top quality. (Note that a rank scale is opposite from a "number of stars" scale with a rank of 1 being the best, and a rank of 5, the least-best. A student's grade on their own review was based on the mean peer ranking.) I explained to them that this is what happens when we submit grants to fund our research. Grants get ranked by peers. I have sat on many of those review panels and even though almost every proposal was written with great care and had great ideas proposed, we still had to rank them. Any grant proposals ranked 3, 4 or 5 didn't get funded. I have felt the pain of having been one of those low-ranked grant proposers who did not get funded. The NIH has only so much money to fund research. Real life may not always seem fair.

Graders of reviews had to justify their rankings, as scientists do when reviewing grant proposals. I gave everyone full marks for the *peer grading assignment* if they gave constructive feedback according to the instructions below. Some students took that feedback on board and improved their book review, because even though the grade for the *book review assignment* was already determined, the book review is out there in the Real World being read by many people. Many of my students' book reviews were voted as "Most Helpful Reviews" by visitors to Amazon.com thanks to the care with which they wrote them.

Merit Criteria for Peer Ranking of Neuro Book Reviews on Amazon:

As you are reading the book reviews, jot down notes that might help you rank them. Ask yourself,

- Does this review help me understand what this book is about and help me decide whether it is worth getting and reading?
- After reading the review, do I know the tone of the book, or level of technicality?
- Does the review indicate the target audience or for whom the book would be most useful?
- Is it well written? Do they use good grammar, spelling, and paragraphs that make sense?
- Does the writing flow? Is it exciting, creative, or thought-provoking?
- Is it easy to find information quickly, with separate sections and

10. Wikipedia Writing and Other Authentic Projects

headings?

- Are all the parts there? Parts I asked for were:

1. Real Name

2. Informative Title

3. A brief summary

4. Overall opinion and recommendation

5. Synopsis of the content and structure of the book

6. Useful or interesting quotes

7. Submission to the Assignment tool BEFORE due date

A side benefit of these assignments was that some students learned about another book from a classmate and read it just for fun. With this real-world Amazon Book Review assignment, I helped them break through the barrier of thinking that non-fiction books are a chore and not worth their time. When you get to choose books yourself based on your own interests, they can be one of the best entertainment values for the money around. Many of the students reported that their books were influential to their thinking and may change the course of their careers.

I note that I required my students to use their Real Name™ (now called a *verified profile* badge) on their book reviews. This was another lesson in being held accountable for one's opinions. As I mentioned in the Wikipedia assignment section, I feel that to sign one's name to one's work is an important aspect of establishing trust in authors and judging the merits of their ideas.

Amazon requires book reviewers to have bought something with a credit card in their name to verify their profile. Therefore, this requirement may not be feasible for minors. For the few of my students who complained that they did not have a credit card, I reminded them that they were now adults and should begin thinking of establishing a credit history with a card in their name. That was a lesson I did not expect to be teaching in IntroNeuro! How to establish trust online is a fascinating new and ever-changing topic that you could build an entire project around.

Years after graduating, alumni endorsed this real-world project-based course and explained how they benefited from it.

> "In addition to publicly displaying my work, the assignments helped to expose me to the types of

169

> *activities I now find myself doing on a regular basis in graduate school. The Amazon book review assignment helped me to think critically about the writing of others and be able to compose a thorough and thoughtful review of the main points. This skill has become invaluable as I assess journal articles for my research. The Wikipedia article was also extremely unique and was actually my favorite element of the class. That was my first exposure to truly 'publishing' scientific information. I still read the Wikipedia entry occasionally to this day, and I'm very proud of the work I put into that article. The experience has helped me to write journal articles of my research and I now have two published papers." – alumnus Mike Weiler*

Library Research

How to find and digest scientific papers are skills that I taught in all of my courses. They are central to being a successful scientist or engineer. I feel every biomedical engineering student needs to get good at the art of doing research with the peer-reviewed literature. Of course, this applies to many other academic and professional domains, too.

Books, whether monographs, edited volumes of manuscripts, or textbooks, are helpful in learning the relevant terminology and which topics are important in a field. But books tend to be out of date because their publication is a slow process, and they may not be carefully peer-reviewed by other scientists. These are usually referred to as *tertiary* sources.

News articles and science magazines (mostly referred to as *secondary* sources) are even more fraught with errors, misconceptions, or bias. For these reasons, there is no substitute for reading peer-reviewed papers (articles) published in reputable journals, known as the *primary literature*.

Students doing research in fields that are not normally considered science or engineering, such as social studies, linguistics, etc., will also benefit from learning how to find, read and analyze peer-reviewed journal articles in their topic of interest. However, such fields may rely more on material published in books (or other media) rather than periodicals.

The tools and resources available for doing literature searches keep changing and improving. Therefore, to help my students find journal articles, I enlisted the help of our librarian, Lori Critz, who specializes in biomedical engineering. She led workshops for my students, in a library room full of computers. They learned how to use our electronic databases of scholarly publications to build a customized bibliography with *Web of Science*. They also learned how to find and download papers using external search tools such as *Google Scholar*.

Once they became familiar with these tools, students could easily log in to the library server from their own computer to do their research. These days it is not actually necessary to visit a library to do excellent library research. A student can graduate never having pulled a heavy volume of scientific papers off the shelf. It is all PDFs now. I have always loved libraries, so I am sad about their waning relevance in the modern digital world. I miss the browsing experience of finding books and articles I was not expecting to find on the shelves, as more and more library holdings are put into off-site storage or closed stacks. But my sadness and nostalgia are balanced by the amazing fact that so much more knowledge is readily available to so many more people around the world than before the Web. Thank you, Sir Tim Berners-Lee.

Interpreting and Learning from Journal Articles

Finding good articles is only the first step in doing library research. Lori focused mainly on the mechanics of doing thorough literature searches and building a customized bibliography. Next, my students needed pointers on how to read and interpret the articles they found.

I based my paper-reading lessons in my classes on my experiences in the Real World of academic scientific research. I gave my students pointers on how to be skeptical of what they read, how to glean what is important from a dense technical paper, how to interpret graphs, charts, and statistical tests of significance, and how to interpret what is not written "between the lines" in a paper. I also taught them how science, like any academic endeavor, is done by real people subject to social influences. Scientists exhibit the same posturing, fighting for dominance, and grooming that Robert Sapolsky studies in tribes of baboons.

My students got lessons about scientific ethics and etiquette, for example, how to be grateful to the relevant foundational thinkers by giving credit where it is due and citing their work. Some of this instruction was done in the context of a **Journal Club**, a weekly tradition for my research group, and for many scientists. This is where everyone in the research group (or class) reads the same paper and meets to discuss, debate, and sometimes metaphorically destroy the paper.

It helps motivate the discussion if the paper's topic is current and of great interest to the students. I would often let students suggest which paper we ought to discuss, after having them do some literature searching.

Some papers we chose were more seminal than current: ones that were frequently cited by other papers we read. In that way, I highlighted the importance of knowing the history of a particular field.

I strived to get everyone involved in the discussion during a Journal Club. Some students might have been inclined to scan the paper superficially beforehand if they knew they would not be the main one presenting the paper that day. They might have hoped they could remain silent and passively absorb information. For that reason, I would often choose the presenter at random, at the beginning of the Journal Club meeting, to lead the discussion of the paper. Everyone was much more engaged and discussions were much more in-depth when everyone had read the paper well beforehand. The possibility of being chosen to present the paper was a good motivation to read it carefully ahead of time, to form some opinions, and to take some notes.

The details of what my students learned in their literature searches and Journal Clubs were less important than the meta-skills they learned, such as the courage to dive head-first into an unfamiliar topic. I have repeatedly observed that **deep exposure to a field of study transforms a student from apathetic to really excited about that topic**. Then learning becomes easy for them.

> "The interest that your class sparked was extremely valuable in my first year of medical school. We have an entire quarter dedicated to neurology – neuroscience and neuroanatomy. This quarter is generally dreaded, and most of my classmates were miserable, trying to rote memorize the complex pathways and anatomy of the nervous system. Although I still had a lot of learning to do, I found myself genuinely enjoying it. I really think that enjoyment was directly attributable to my experiences in BMED 4752." - alumna Audrey Southard

***

There are many ways to assess how much students are learning. Schools impose standardized exams, which often fail to test the types of learning that will really matter years later. Standardized exams seldom serve as effective sources of motivation for students. Much better assessments are those that are directly tied in to the Real World. These could include feedback from invited experts who watch student presentations, as we did with our Problem-Based Learning course. They may be comments by strangers who see students' work on the internet. They could be compliments from parents and the general public invited to an exhibit, performance, open house, or other culminating public event at the end of a project. In the Real World, grown-ups seldom find out how they are doing by taking a test. They get feedback directly from the people they are trying to help.

Try to make your assessments more like these highly motivating real-world ones, with the goal not of ranking and comparing students, but of truly assessing them and giving them feedback on the value of what they have accomplished.

Part IV

More Real-World Teaching and Learning

In this Part, I will show how it may be helpful not only for students, but also for teachers, to dissolve the usual barriers between what is going on in class and out there in the Real World. The success of the highly motivating real-world aspects of IntroNeuro encouraged me to take it to the next level with my other courses. In Problem-Based Learning class, and even more so in NeuroEngineering Fundamentals, I tried to emulate what it is like to do real research as a scientist/engineer, by having my students actually do real, publishable research in small groups. This approach helps address the fourth and fifth most important characteristics of successful teams (p. 95) at Google:
- Meaning: Finding a sense of purpose in either the work itself or the output.
- Impact: The results of one's work, the subjective judgment that your work is making a difference.

CHAPTER 11

Lab Class Without a Cookbook

My lab+lecture course called *Neuroengineering Fundamentals*, abbreviated "Neuroeng. Fun." started as *Hybrid Neural Microsystems* (HNM), when I was one of 4 professors who created and led the course. Prof. Steve DeWeerth got a grant from the National Science Foundation to create a graduate level course in neuroengineering, or *applied neuroscience*.[82] The course packed three modules into one semester, a cellular one (Prof. Rob Butera's), a network one (my module), and a human one (Prof. Lena Ting's). Each of us chose grad students from our research labs to serve as TAs who did most of the mentoring in the lab, while we gave lectures and led discussions about a wide range of current neuroengineering topics. As my graduate advisor did with me when I taught the lab part of his graduate neurochemistry course, I entrusted my TAs to lead the labs as they saw fit.

One key to the success of those labs was making myself always available to answer questions or to help solve problems. Particularly at the beginning of the semester, I spent much of my time in the teaching labs with my students, doing hands-on instruction the way Scott Fraser and Jerry Pine had done for me when I was a postdoc and needed to learn a new technique. I

---

82. I describe recent trends and the future of neuroengineering in my TEDx talk, *"NeuroEngineering: Neuroscience — APPLIED"* https://youtu.be/j4SSQcHt220

actually encouraged my students to phone me if they needed my input when I was not in the lab. They seldom did call on me, but knowing I cared about them and their experiments that much made a difference in their motivation.

I had a rule that they were not allowed to give up on something without convincing me first that what they were doing would never work. I was trying to build stick-to-itiveness or grit in them, as well as the kind of responsibility expected in the Real World:

> "The lab work in Neuroengineering was a fantastic prelude to graduate student work and bench research in general. One of the few courses to remind us that real world experiments stand behind what we read in textbooks, and positively reinforce that we can DO those experiments!" - alumnus Alex Stroh

> "Neuroengineering Fund allowed us to learn how to teach ourselves. Help was always available but it was really up to the student how deep we wanted to go into our projects or how adventurous we wanted to be with learning new skills. Not many other classes allow that kind of freedom, or demand that kind of responsibility, however taking that kind of initiative is expected in the real world. I believe it is an incredibly valuable experience to have while still having the safety net of being in school." - alumna Ashleigh Burns

One of the innovative ideas of this course was that NSF Graduate Fellows in the HNM program would take the course twice, once as first-years, and again when they were more experienced, as third-year grad students. Near the end of the HNM program in 2009, I opened the course to undergraduates and expanded the entire semester to be about the module I taught, in-vitro neural networks.

My philosophy about the course was to make it a microcosm of grad school. As much as was possible in one semester, I wanted the Neuroeng. Fun. students to do all the things that grad students do in biomedical engineering, such as come up with their own research projects and make their own equipment. I wanted to give the Neuroeng. Fun. students as much autonomy as I gave the grad students in my research lab.

Pre-made cookbook experiments, like we did in all the lab classes I took in school and college, are of little benefit to students. They were only a small step up from the Santa Claus candy jars my third-grade teacher had us mindlessly assemble. Self-designed experiments motivate students because they have chosen to research something they care about, and consequently, they feel a great sense of ownership and pride in the whole process.

Goals of the NeuroEng. Fun. Lab Course:

- Learn about the research tools available in the lab. This took place both in the lecture hall with slides and discussion, and in the lab with hands-on demonstrations and discussion.
- Learn about the model system we used all semester in the laboratory part of the course: networks of rat neurons growing in Petri dishes ("*in vitro*") wired with arrays of electrodes to computers. This was the same system we used in my research lab.
- Learn about neurotechnology and neuroengineering in general from me and several guest lecturers.
- Read about current research related to in-vitro neural networks.
- In student-chosen groups of three or four students, come up with a proposal for an experiment that will extend the state of the field into unknown territory.
- Discuss written proposals with me, the TAs and the rest of the class and refine them until feasible, across multiple class sessions.
- Learn to grow living neurons in the micro-electrode arrays. This required learning immaculate sterile technique, which will be useful for many biological research or surgical careers.
- Build any new equipment needed to carry out the groups' proposed experiments.
- Carry out experiments. Usually team members would take on specific roles for the group to divide up the work.
- Write code needed to collect or process data.
- Write everything down in an enduring lab notebook. Originally

> these were paper notebooks, but then became Google Docs for easy sharing and collaboration.
> - Crunch, process and interpret experimental data.
> - Improve things in the lab that aren't working well and repeat steps as needed.
> - Present the group's work to the class and sometimes, to invited experts.
> - Leave lab notebooks for future generations of students to learn from.

The first 3 items on this list usually fell under the category of scaffolding or things I taught explicitly, both in lectures and in the lab. However, I think the majority of the useful things learned by students in this class were by way of their own self-directed learning, doing, failing, and re-doing.

Neuroengineering in the Real World

Across the semester, as with my IntroNeuro class, I would invite guests to speak to the class about aspects of neuroengineering they were involved with. One favorite recurring guest was my friend, the author Michael Chorost. He is not a scientist, but a user of neuroengineering. He wrote the book, *"Rebuilt: How becoming part computer made me more human."* He is completely deaf, yet hears well thanks to neuroengineering: he uses cochlear implants. In his riveting book, and in his guest lectures to my class, he told the very personal story of growing up with impaired hearing, then losing hearing completely at age 40. He described having to adapt to the strange sounds his new implanted hearing technology gave him as technicians, programmers, and neuroengineers tweaked the software and auditory nerve stimulation.

Mike gave us many insights into how an end-user of neuro-tech feels and deals with the difficulties of learning to hear again. I had my students read excerpts from his book in advance of his visit and prepare questions to ask him. That they were well prepared promoted a lively discussion. For the first couple of years, Mike phoned in from far away. It is an amazing tribute to the success of neuroengineering that he was able to hear and understand my students asking their questions via speakerphone. Many students went on to read Mike's entire book because they had been hooked.

Whether material was from a guest speaker or from one of my own lectures, I always tried to tie the neurotechnology we were learning about to the Real World, and how it benefits real people. Here is an example: I managed to get funding to fly Mike out to give a public seminar in addition to giving a guest lecture for my class (Fig. 20). On one of Mike's visits, I brought him to meet two clinician/researchers we were both interested in. We went to a talk at Emory University by Dr. Karl Deisseroth, who is developing genetic tools to treat mental disorders with light. We also visited my friend, Dr. Phil Kennedy, who developed neural interfaces for locked-in patients, to enable completely paralyzed people to speak by just thinking of speaking. Phil gave us the grand tour of his company in Alpharetta (Neural Signals, Inc.) and we even got to watch him collecting neural signals from a patient's brain.

Those experiences were influential to Mike — he ended up writing about them in his excellent book, *"World Wide Mind: The Coming Integration of Humanity, Machines, and the Internet."* He probably would not have had those opportunities if it were not for my recruiting him as a guest lecturer for my class. This experience shows the benefits that can come from dissolving the boundaries that separate the class from the Real World.

Figure 20. Two deaf people conversing. Mike Chorost is chatting orally with another deaf person after his lecture, neither one needing to use their hands for signing, thanks to their cochlear implants.

My Neuroeng. Fun. students and I also had field trips to put the neuroengineering tools we discussed in class into a real-world context. One popular field trip was to walk across campus to the Center for Advanced Brain Imaging (CABI) where the students got to scan their own brains with the functional magnetic resonance imaging (fMRI) machine. fMRI shows which brain areas are active during a given task. Students got to choose which tasks they wanted to do.

11. Lab Class Without a Cookbook

Another field trip was to visit Prof. Melody Moore-Jackson's lab, where her research group develops brain interfaces for disabled or locked-in people, such as thought-controlled wheelchairs. Students measured their own EEG (electroencephalogram) and did their own self-designed experiments to see how their brainwaves changed under different conditions.

I hoped that some of the field trip experiments my students did would give new ideas to researchers at CABI or Moore-Jackson's lab. Thus, the field trips were not a fun day off, but possibly an opportunity for my students to launch a new research program. Whether they did or not, that possibility was a good motivator for my students.

Lab Notebooks and Group Work

> *"If you don't write it down, it didn't happen."* -Jerry Pine, the inventor of the micro-electrode array culture dish.

No matter what sorts of projects your students may be working on, for them to keep a detailed notebook of their process is beneficial in many ways. It keeps them on task. It ensures they don't forget important things that happened, both good and bad. It is a place to jot down data as they are collected, and then to write up any analysis of those data. It is perhaps the most useful resource instructors have for evaluating and grading students involved in free-form projects. Most of my experience with lab notebooks is in the context of doing scientific research. But I have also kept detailed Maker Notebooks for all of my own projects for years. I frequently go back to these, to remind myself what I learned at the *Jerome Pine School of Hard Knocks*, instead of making the same mistakes again on a similar project.

Science advances by the communication and combination of research findings and technological developments made by groups of people. Ideally, what gets written down carefully in a lab notebook eventually makes it into a peer-reviewed journal article. In my experience, only about 10% of experiments carried out in a research lab are successful and end up getting published. The rest could be called failures, but I prefer the term "learning experiences." **Every so-called failure teaches us something.** Therefore it was crucial for my Neuroeng. Fun. students to learn not to cover up their "failures" but to take copious notes about them, analyze them, and write down any lessons learned in their lab notebooks. This helped their group's (and perhaps others') experiments work better next time.

Originally my students kept paper notebooks, but now Google Docs (and other collaborative documentation systems such as Slack or GitHub) allow groups to create shared notebooks in which each person's contribution is clear, and the version history is automatically saved. Although having a digital notebook makes searching for keywords easier, I urged my students to put a Table of Contents at the front of each notebook, with page numbers and all the key words or phrases they thought they might use in the future to look for certain pieces of information buried within.

There are software packages specifically designed for documenting what goes on in the lab, but those usually cost money and may be overkill for the average lab class, such as including digital signing certificates and encryption. Those become more important when the research is potentially patentable, or must be kept hidden from competitors.

I recommend Google's excellent, free platform for documenting and sharing collaborative efforts in the classroom, even at the elementary school level. Students can collaboratively use Google Docs, in combination with Google Sheets for tables of data, and Google Slides for presentations. Google Calendars can keep teams on task to meet deadlines. Google has lumped all of these tools together, with many other useful apps for teachers and students, in *G Suite for Education* and *Classroom*.[83]

In his *"How to Make (almost) Anything"* course, Neil Gershenfeld encourages his students to create lasting tutorials on how to use certain equipment. He writes, *"Once students mastered a new capability, such as water-jet cutting or microcontroller programming, they had a near-evangelical interest in showing others how to use it."* [84]

This highly self-motivated drive to share knowledge between peers has resulted in a number of excellent websites full of maker tutorials. My favorite is Instructables.com, because it is completely free and is well-organized. Another good one for children is diy.org, which has nice badges to help motivate kids to level up by learning new skills. Subscriptions do cost money, but that helps keep the trolls away and makes diy.org a safe online environment. Contributing to one of these websites can be an excellent real-world project for your students.[85]

My student's grades were based to a large degree on how well they demonstrated learning in their lab notebooks. Although I pushed them to get

---

83. The paid Enterprise Edition of G Suite includes additional functionality, such as security tools, live customer support, large scale live streaming, and the ability to scan the internet for identical text to catch or avoid plagiarism. This FAQ is a good place to start if you are not familiar with Google's tools: https://support.google.com/edu/classroom/answer/6025224
84. Gershenfeld's book, *FAB*, p. 7
85. You can see Instructables I created about my own projects at https://www.instructables.com/howto/stevempotter/

good data that was potentially publishable, I did not grade them down if they did not get good data. I had to keep reminding them that failure is OK, as long as you write about it and learn from it.

If I read in their lab notebooks at the end of the semester that they had worked unsuccessfully on one small impossible task for a whole week and then gave up, I felt regret. I should have noticed that they were spinning their wheels and helped them. I tried to prevent such regrets with frequent oral check-ins and admonishments to call me or the TA over if they need help. I reiterated my rule: *"You are not allowed to give up on something unless I OK it."*

Students are used to competing against one another for grades because most teachers grade on a curve. Mine had to make large shifts in their attitude about sharing and openness in my courses. In the Real World, collaboration and group work, rather than competition and individual work, are the norm. I repeatedly had to remind my students to include relevant material from their teammates in their lab notebooks, with the appropriate acknowledgment of who did what.

Scientific journal articles are almost always a group effort, with author lists of about three to ten "authors." The journals have started requiring a paragraph stating explicitly what each author was responsible for in completing the work described. Writing such paragraphs, and deciding the order of the author list, are both easier when each researcher has carefully noted who did what in their lab notebooks.

Neuroeng. Fun. students would ask if including data collected, or analysis, by another member of their group in their notebook was plagiarism. I said, "It is not cheating as long as what each student did to advance the group's goals is clearly noted in your notebook." This served another purpose during grading. By comparing the notebooks of each member of a team, and seeing the same material presented in different ways by each member, I could get a very good idea of what the team actually accomplished, and what each person's role was. If one student in a group was not holding up their end of the project, it became clear in their teammate's notebooks, and during peer evaluations, where we discussed how effectively the team worked (See **Feedback between students: Lab Notebooks and Peer Evaluations**, p. 211).

Peer Pressure is a Strong Motivator

Group work is not to be feared by teachers or students. It is the norm in the Real World, whether in corporations or research labs. Why are groups not the norm in school? The reasons why students seldom work in groups probably have to do with grading, or classroom management. It may be more difficult to grade individuals on group projects. Teachers may fear they will lose control over a class when groups cause an escalation of noise and energy levels. When I see classes that are engaged in many simultaneous discussions, I feel it is a good thing.

How to deal with advanced students feeling weighed down by underperforming group members? Encourage them to help you raise those students up to their level with constructive feedback and advice. Peer mentoring is crucial in any group activity. In a lab class where complex experiments comprise many tasks that must be delegated to different people in the group, there is strong peer pressure on each team member to do their share. My students' lab notebooks often included compliments to those students who worked extra-hard to make the group's experiment a success. They also included notes about lagging team members and what they did to address that. I kept a close ear on intra-group communication. If it was not being done effectively and respectfully, I had a private or group discussion with the students involved to understand the problems and explain my perspectives on how things ought to work — just as I would if communication problems cropped up in my own research lab. Recurring problems were noted and resulted in discussions about etiquette with the whole class, or an amendment to the syllabus.

For example, "Don't be flaky!" became a part of the course etiquette. I urged students to let teammates know if they will be late or absent for a group activity. As with all aspects of the course, group dynamics were inspired by and modeled after what goes on in the research lab with undergrads, grad students, and postdocs often working together in small groups on a certain project. In both the classroom lab and the research lab, I have seen peer pressure serve as an effective motivator. **With good, constructive communication, each member of a group or project strives to become an important team player.**

Lab Class vs. Real Research

Getting experience in a lab doing real research can be a fantastic motivator. When I was a senior at UCSD, I worked in Prof. Ian Creese's lab a couple of days a week, for research course credit, not for pay. This was one of the most educational things I did at UCSD. I had a *mostly* supportive lab group. There was the Lab Manager, who was always extremely friendly and helpful to everyone in the lab, and even outside the lab: I learned a lot about how to treat vendors from whom we buy equipment and supplies by overhearing his phone conversations. He was always getting free stuff and special deals by being friendly to them. There were two lab technicians who taught me all the routine jobs of the lab and how to dissect rat brains. There was my easygoing Irish postdoc mentor, Dr. Tony Molloy, who directed which experiment I would do next according to his research goals.

Tony was a behavioral neuroscientist, and I was a biochemist. He watched how rats behave under the influence of certain drugs. He knew enough biochemistry to set me to work on various biochemical assays that would be helpful in understanding the effects of the drugs he was studying. However, it was up to me to figure out how to do the assays.

My research was about how the neurotransmitters dopamine and acetylcholine interact in the brain. I was homogenizing brain tissue and measuring enzyme activity of the rat striatum, part of the brain implicated in the etiology of Parkinson's Disease. A grad student in the lab, Ellen, was close to finishing up her PhD work. She routinely did the same assays that I needed to do, but refused to help me or even let me use any of her equipment or supplies. "You are NOT allowed to touch any of this, this or this!" she sternly warned me, "And I am too busy to help you." Six years later, when I was finishing my own PhD research, I realized that when you are near the end of your dissertation work, you don't want any distractions and you certainly don't want any clueless undergrads to mess up the things you are depending on to finish your PhD. I forgave her.[86] Because she gave me no help with the assays, I had to get all the equipment and supplies to duplicate Ellen's assay rig and learn the methods all by myself by scrutinizing the scientific papers.

Some of those assays were a grueling 12-hour process. I would come in after my morning classes and leave the lab after midnight. From others in the lab and from the literature, I learned to do what I had to do to get the job done. Dr. Creese was the Chair of the Neuroscience Department at that time, so I very seldom saw him. At the end of my time in his lab, he read my lab notebook with many charts of data from assays on *"The interactions between dopaminergic and cholinergic systems in the rat striatum,"* and commented, "This is better than Tony's notebook." My job at Kelco trained me to document my research well. As a "clueless undergrad" in the Creese lab, I managed to contribute something to the field's understanding of how the striatum works.

Now contrast that very rich educational and rewarding real-world work experience with what I was doing around the same time in my lab classes at UCSD. They were pretty much worthless. For example, in Organic Chemistry Lab, we were given an unknown chemical from a list of 5 or so, and had to do

---

86. Coincidentally, many years later, long after I had forgiven Ellen Hess for being preoccupied with graduating from Ian Creese's lab, I learned she had been hired as a professor at Emory University. We had both ended up at the same school in Atlanta! (My BME department is shared with Emory.) She does great research and was one of the favorite guest lecturers for my IntroNeuro class.

various tests to determine which chemical it was. I have never needed to do any of those tests since then. If I want to know which chemical I have, I just read the label on the chemical reagent's container!

In Physical Chemistry lab class, we used a "bomb calorimeter" to measure how much energy was in a small sample of food. Again, just read the label! It was all precisely scripted according to the lab class's cookbook. There was no expectation, or even possibility, of exploring new things. It was not allowed. As I write this, I am trying hard and I can't actually recall anything useful I learned in the various lab classes I had. They were too far removed from the Real World.

My work in the Creese lab, however, I remember clearly. Many times later in my own lab, I used techniques I learned during my undergrad research experience. My other undergrad research jobs (described in Ch. 4) working for Prof. Jack Roberts at Caltech (summer after second year) and working at Kelco R & D (summer after third year) also taught me many scientific and engineering skills, techniques and intuitions I still use today. **The Real World and the intrinsic motivations that it provides are just a *much* better teacher than any cookbook lab class.**

Since those days, I have had many Caltech, Georgia Tech, and Emory University undergrads work as researchers in my lab. We even had high school students doing research in the lab occasionally. My bar to accept new researchers was very low. They really only had to demonstrate that they were highly motivated to do actual research, not just wash dishes to have something to put on their résumé. I warned them that I would only write a letter of recommendation if they proved to be outstanding in some way. Just to put in time was not enough. If they had read our papers and came to me with some insightful questions, they were in.

I favor **intrinsic motivation** over **extrinsic motivation**. Like I did at UCSD, my lab's undergrad researchers worked for research credit, not for pay. (Occasionally, through their own initiative, they won a fellowship or research award that gave them some extra spending money, or allowed them to buy special equipment and supplies.)

Having good role models is important. Unlike with my UCSD research experience, I was careful to pair up undergrad researchers in my lab with someone else who wanted to mentor a "clueless undergrad" and get them up to speed. Many of those undergrads became crucial to our research. (Six of the Potter Lab members in the group photo on p. 257 were undergrad researchers.) They presented their work at conferences and got their names on papers. They added new life and fresh perspectives to the lab. The only extrinsic reward I can recall giving them was to buy pizza for our lab meetings. They were intrinsically motivated, knowing they were doing a valuable bit of real-world research to help advance our lab's goals and increase understanding of the brain's inner workings.

Student-designed Experiments

In devising the lab part of Neuroeng. Fun., I drew from all my experiences with lab research in the Real World, in my lab and the other labs I have worked in. Most importantly, I was determined NOT to hand the students the dreaded cookbook of experiments to do, as my former lab class teachers had done to me. My students had to write their own cookbooks as they went along, which were their lab notebooks. These included their evaluation of the course:

> *"Overall this class will challenge you and make you think critically about your ideas and experiments. It will make you a better experimental designer as well as more trusting in yourself since you have more freedom in this class than you will in any other class in the Biomedical Engineering field. I am happy I took this class and had my team for the class as well. Out of all the projects I did in BME with group work, this was by far my favorite and the one I learned the most in." - Neuroeng. Fun. student Kathryn Thomas*

In the research lab, the most educational experiences I had were doing real, self-driven research, not being told every detail of what to do. I was quite successful in duplicating that experience — for the first time for any lab class in my department — by creating a very open-ended lab for Neuroeng. Fun (Fig. 21). It was my job to make sure they had, or could make, the tools they needed to carry out the experiments they designed. As we discussed and refined their experiment ideas, I tried to be careful to shepherd them toward an experiment that was doable but quite challenging. Those would lead to the most intrinsic reward, compared to one that was too easy (boring) or too hard (frustrating).

If they had to buy new equipment or supplies, I found the money for it. In one case, I established a fruitful partnership with a Georgia Tech spinoff company, Axion Biosciences, that agreed to provide deluxe micro-electrode electrophysiology systems at a large discount in exchange for feedback from my students, who served as their beta testers. They were testing both hardware and software developed by Axion. Student feedback had real-world impact by improving the design of Axion's products.

Figure 21. Students in Neuroengineering Fundamentals lab class, thoroughly engaged in their custom-made lab research projects.

Good TAs ensured that my students learned the lab techniques they would need to do their experiments. I carefully chose experienced TAs who were good at those techniques, such as neural cell culturing. I enjoyed visiting the teaching lab for experiment debugging sessions and hands-on instruction and scaffolding for things I knew how to do well, such as microscopy, data interpretation and electronics fabrication.

> ```
> "Your availability during the lab sessions in Intro
> to Neuroengineering was essential for our group; I
> think without your assistance we never would have
> been able to get any data out of that lab course."
> - alumnus Cody Stone
> ```

Because my students were braving unknown territory in carrying out experiments of their own design in Neuroeng. Fun. lab, and because of their lack of experience, it was not uncommon for them to set out doing something I was pretty sure was impossible. Usually, I would point this out to them when we were discussing experimental design as a group. It might make a good learning experience for them to understand which limitations they were up against by giving it a go. One of my mottos is, *"The person who says it cannot be done should get out of the way of the person doing it!"* I love to be proven wrong when I say something is impossible. But if the students decide to give it a go, I would have to be on the lookout for signs of frustration.

When students are facing a seemingly impossible task, usually, a better approach is to change how the student feels about the task. For example, I said to my Neuroeng. Fun. students, "Your goal is to get great data and publish it in a peer-reviewed journal." I knew this was impossible, if for no other reason than that the process of writing a paper, submitting it and getting it published almost always takes longer than one semester. It often takes over a year. Thus, I told them it was probably impossible, but because we were trying to emulate the grad school experience, it makes an appropriate goal to shoot for. I made sure that they understood that every incremental step toward that goal would be an important accomplishment in itself, including the failures and setbacks.

As I mentioned when describing my first computer programming class at UCSD, learning to code gave me this valuable nugget: Almost any seemingly impossible task becomes doable when you break it down into a sequence of smaller tasks. "Poco a poco, se pasa el mar," was a saying I learned in seventh-grade Spanish class (Little by little, you can cross the sea). Another related saying even very young students can understand is, "Even the longest journey begins with a single step."

If the Big Picture Task ends up being impossible, like publishing a paper in one semester, the learning process of working on the small tasks that lead up to it make an incremental effort a very worthwhile endeavor. Teach your students how to break a big job down into sub-tasks, until this becomes a habit whenever they feel overwhelmed.

I gave the students autonomy by letting them decide when to ask the TAs or me for assistance. We mostly let the groups work independently, even if we noticed they were making a mistake, because the TAs and I remembered that was how we learned to get it right: get it wrong first and diagnose the problem, then fix it. If you always tell students the correct way to do things the first time, they may never understand why we do it that way.

One instructional technique I used is to break things or fail on purpose, as mentioned on page 33. For example, when soldering electrical connections, it is important to heat up both of the things you are trying to connect until they are hot enough to melt the solder. If you only heat up one, you end up with what's called a "cold solder joint." These may work for a while, but are very likely to fail soon. I would have students solder a few connections and then wiggle, tug or bang on them until they stopped conducting electricity to see how robust they were.

If you break things on purpose, under controlled conditions while being observant, you can acquire an intuitive understanding of the limits of the materials and tools you are working with. That will be remembered far longer than a textbook explanation of how to solder, because with hands-on learning, information is coming in through all of the student's senses. There is an intrinsic motivation to accomplish the task at hand, and this keeps students focused and paying attention.

There were plenty of things about neuroengineering I hoped my students learned by actually doing it. But years later, unless they become neuroengineers themselves, it is the meta-learning that will benefit them the most. Some of the meta-goals of Neuroeng. Fun. lab were to learn how to diagnose problems, how to fix equipment that is malfunctioning or connected incorrectly, how to make sure they used a large enough sample to believe that their results are statistically significant, how to keep the lab tidy, how to maintain a sterile environment, how to share things in high demand, how to work in groups, and how to record what goes on in the lab. Of course, I hoped they would all want to become neuroengineers!

> *"Neuroengineering Fund. improved my approach to problem solving and record keeping (lab notebooks) which will undoubtedly be of value in the future."*
> *- alumna Ashleigh Burns*

CHAPTER 12

Problem-Based Learning

Sometimes called *problem-driven learning*, the Problem-Based Learning approach to structuring learning involved having the students work in groups of 8 or so to "solve" large open-ended problems for several weeks per problem. I say "solve" because the problems had no clear solution and in many ways were "unGoogleable." An anonymous student in one of my Problem-Based Learning sections wrote,

> "Problem-Based Learning works. I looked up stuff because I wanted to solve the problem, and after each presentation I felt accomplished and I also felt that I had failed abjectly. I remember wishing, after the first presentation, that I could go back in time and talk to myself for five minutes and the project could have been 'done right.' There was a lot of freedom and I felt like I had opportunities to utilize my creative strengths. Besides that, the group work was very instructive and taught me exactly what I need to work on to avoid pissing off everyone when/if I ever get a job that requires human interaction."

This story refers to a common experience, that a group who thought they were doing well on their problem felt completely upstaged when they saw the presentation by another group who had clearly done a much better job. Equalizing quality and effort across facilitators and groups was always difficult. Having three problems across the semester helped, as well as post-problem debriefing sessions that reinforced the meta-skills learned.

Problems were chosen from current topics to highlight certain techniques we felt that BME students should learn, such as how to create a mathematical model of the spread of a contagious disease, or how to test a biomedical instrument for accuracy. As mentioned in Ch. 3 (Fig. 3, p. 21), Problem-Based Learning class meetings were in small rooms whose walls were entirely made of writable whiteboard. This allowed easy sharing of notes, creative brainstorming, teaching, and debating by everyone in the group. One faculty member sat in on each entire session (three hours total per week) as a "Facilitator" not as an instructor. I served as Facilitator for Problem-Based Learning courses every year I was at Georgia Tech, usually with two groups to facilitate per semester.

Facilitators were there to guide the students' inquiry process, and to teach only the meta-skills: how to work well as a group, how to find the needed information, how to plan the work, etc. (See the **Problem-Based Learning Assessment Rubric**, Fig. 22, p. 197) We tried as much as possible not to lead them in any particular direction, and not to serve as a source of facts or background on the specific problem, unless it happened to be our own area of expertise, in which case the students were allowed to interview us.

The day we began on a new Problem, we followed a set sequence to get started. I handed out the Problem Description, usually about a half page, which they read and jotted notes on in silence for about 15 minutes. Then one student would be chosen as the Scribe to write on the walls lists of *What we know*, *What we think*, and *What we should find out*, as suggested by the whole team. Often, because the problems cover completely unfamiliar territory, the *Know* column only had a few items taken directly from the Problem Description. As the Facilitator, I had to keep them skeptical, in case a confident student seemed to know something about the problem domain. Most such things had to end up being verified in the *What we should find out* or *Inquiry* section. Students would usually spend over an hour creating this initial list, really trying hard to put up any related ideas they think might be relevant. Before leaving class that first day, all of the Inquiry Items were divided up among the students to go find out before our next meeting. They would often work in pairs to do this in front of a computer outside of class. I would give them pointers on how to find things out, during almost every class meeting (sometimes with help from the librarians). Finding and then digesting technical information (p. 170) is a complex and useful skill that will benefit them throughout life.

For most problems, after the students had done a bit of inquiry and seemed to have some clue about the scope of the Problem, it was helpful for them to create Mind Maps, where all the relevant aspects of a Problem are connected with lines, often labeled with a verb (see Fig. 18, p. 105). I found it most helpful when each student drew their own Mind Map independently. Then at the next meeting, they would pass them around and create a group Mind Map on the wall, and photograph it when they were all happy that it represented their understanding of the problem. This served the purpose of making it graphically clear where the gaps in their knowledge were, and what steps were needed to fill them.

Because the problem topics were constantly changing from semester to semester, and because they ranged across the entire field of biomedical engineering, it was unlikely that any given faculty Facilitator would know much more about the specific problem topic than the students would. It was up to the students to become the experts by doing the needed research. By breaking a tricky Problem down in this organized way, and delegating parts to individuals or pairs to work on, any Problem that seemed scary at first could be tamed.

Problem-Based Learning was originally developed for medical schools, where med students tackle certain surgical approaches or how to treat a specific disease. My department at Georgia Tech, Biomedical Engineering, is shared with Emory University School of Medicine, so many of our faculty are deeply immersed in the clinical world. Wendy Newstetter adapted this idea from med school to a first-year BME undergrad course before I began there in 2002. Our students usually spent five to six weeks diving quite deeply into each problem, with a group-written report and presentation at the end.

There were a few things about our implementation of Problem-Based Learning that could have been improved to help make the students more motivated. I learned a lot by facilitating Problem-Based Learning, and I tried to address these issues in designing my other courses (Introduction to Neuroscience and Neuroengineering Fundamentals).

Students may feel completely lost at the beginning and get discouraged. It helped to have the Experts in the Field give a lecture or two on the problem topic at the beginning to orient the students toward the big unanswered questions. I often have this clueless and overwhelmed feeling when starting a new research project, so I felt it was a good lesson for students to get used to the feeling and to embrace it.

The problem topics were chosen by the course administrators, and may or may not have been ones that especially interested any given student. Administrators did not always succeed in coming up with engaging problems. Students might have taken ownership of a problem sooner and with more enthusiasm if it had been one that they themselves devised, as proven by my Neuroeng. Fun. lab classes.

All Problem-Based Learning groups of 8 students (about a dozen groups for our incoming class) would tackle the same problem at the same time. This sometimes created a sort of informal competition between groups who wanted to show that their solution to a problem was the best, though we Facilitators did not encourage competitive behavior.

Sometimes, having over 100 students all working on the same problem caused a shortage of some scarce resource, such as a key book in the library, or a key expert who might get annoyed at too many requests for interviews by students. However, having them all work on the same problem did make it easier to compare and grade the students, and ensure that the workload was about the same across groups.

At the end of each 5-week problem, after the report was written and presented, the 8 students and I spent an entire meeting period unpacking and reflecting on our experiences with the problem. This included discussing self- and peer-assessments that the students had written and brought in with them. They were instructed to use the same rubric (Fig. 22) that we Facilitators used to grade them at the end of the semester. We expected these first-year students to be pretty poor in most of these learning goals at first. Consequently, when grading, we put much more weight on their performance at the end of the semester, on their third problem.

A learning goal for the peer-assessment discussion itself was how to deliver criticism of a teammate's performance in a constructive way. As a facilitator, I tried to reduce the number of arguments and tears shed in class by enforcing a "constructive comments only" rule and reminding my students that we are all learning and improving.

I invited them to be equally critical of my facilitating, the course structure, or the choice of problem. I would take their advice about my performance on board and I would feed back to the course administrators constructive advice on the course and problem.

Thus, with constant feedback and readjusting, I saw many, many students become outstanding at the important meta-learning goals of the Problem-Based Learning course. Those included written and oral communication, doing literature searching, brainstorming, working in groups, presenting one's ideas, and being skeptical. I did not care much if they remembered little about pancreatic cancer or how a sphygmomanometer works after the course was over. In that sense the problem topics were merely a vehicle for teaching important meta-skills.

1300 PBL ASSESSMENT RUBRIC

	EXCEPTIONAL (A)	PROFICIENT (B)	FAIR (C)	POOR (D)
INQUIRY SKILLS	• Actively looks for and recognizes inadequacies of existing knowledge • Consistently seeks and asks probing questions • Identifies learning needs & sets learning objectives • Utilizes advanced search strategies • Always evaluates inquiry by assessing reliability and appropriateness of sources	• Recognizes inadequacies of existing knowledge • Generally asks probing questions • Utilizes appropriate search strategies • Mostly evaluates inquiry by assessing reliability and appropriateness of sources • Utilizes effective search strategies	• Occasionally claims areas of inquiry but mostly takes what's left • Occasionally asks questions • Uses search engines like Google to find easily available information of questionable reliability/appropriateness	• Takes whatever is left for inquiry • Rarely, if ever, asks questions • Fails to recognize limits of understanding/knowledge • Fails to assess the reliability or appropriateness of sources • Demonstrates unsystematic search strategies
KNOWLEDGE BUILDING	• Thoroughly digests findings and communicates effectively to self and others • Consistently identifies deep principles for organizing knowledge as evidenced in research notebook • Constructs an extensive and thorough knowledge base in all problem aspects • Continually asks probing questions	• Digest findings and communicates to self and others • Identifies deep principles for organizing knowledge • Constructs a thorough knowledge base in most problem aspects • Asks probing questions	• Reads inquiry results to group without thorough understanding of material • Learns own area of inquiry but not those of others • Occasionally asks questions	• Fails to understand or be able to communicate inquiry findings • Rarely if ever asks questions • Fails to use the problem to develop/enhance BME knowledge
PROBLEM SOLVING	• Repeatedly explores the problem statement to identify critical features • Defines/redefines the problem and identifies problem goals • Breaks problem down into appropriate parts • Identifies and defines appropriate criteria • Frequently uses white boards to assist in problem solving • Consistently applies inquiry results to problem • Develops models and hypotheses	• Explores the problem statement to identify critical features • Seeks to understand problem goals • Identifies criteria • Uses inquiry in problem solving • Uses white boards to assist in problem-solving • Occasionally develops models/hypotheses	• Relies on group to identify critical features • Lets group identify problem goals and then follows along • Sometimes applies inquiry to problem solving	• Fails to define problem • Articulates no problem goals • Never uses the white boards • Fails to apply inquiry to problem • Never suggests a plan of attack • Fails to develop analytic framework
TEAM SKILLS	• Actively listens to and encourages team members • Willingly foregoes personal goals for group goals • Always avoids contributing excessive or irrelevant information • Expresses disappointment or disagreement directly to team members when warranted • Finds ways to gives emotional support to others on the team • Clearly demonstrates enthusiasm and involvement • Monitors group progress and facilitates interaction with other members • Facilitates a distributed leadership among team members	• Supports group goals • Avoids contributing irrelevant information • Expresses disagreement directly • Gives emotional support to others • Demonstrates enthusiasm and involvement • Facilitates interaction with other members • Completes tasks on time	• Goes along with the group • Follows but does not lead • Avoids confrontation even when angry or frustrate • Engages in limited interaction with other members • Occasionally comes unprepared with no explanation • Leads but has trouble giving leadership to others in the group	• Does not help in developing team skills • Gives no emotional or intellectual support to team • Lets group down by failing to complete tasks • Observes silently contributing little to process • Shows little or no enthusiasm or involvement • Talks over others and fails to relinquish the floor • Takes on too many responsibilities thereby disenfranchising other team members

Figure 22. Problem-Based Learning rubric, created by Wendy Newstetter. Problem-Based Learning students used this to calibrate their peer- and self-assessments, and we facilitators used it to determine their final grades.

The main shortcoming of our first-year Problem-Based Learning course, in my opinion, was the fact that students knew they were not actually expected to change the world for the better. Though we had taken ideas from the current literature or even current events, such as a recent outbreak of H1N1 virus, once the students wrote their report and gave their presentation, all their effort was wasted; reports were discarded and forgotten.

To help connect their work to the Real World, we invited actual experts in the disciplines related to the problem to give a lecture at the beginning of a problem, or to watch the final presentations and give their feedback to the students. It was hoped that the students' findings and ideas about how to "solve" the problem would actually be beneficial to practitioners and researchers in the field. In a few cases, Problem-Based Learning groups got along so well, and felt they had come up with such a clever solution, they started their own startup companies. However, this was the exception and not a stated goal of the course. More often, the specifics of a Problem-Based Learning problem were forgotten soon after the semester was over.

To have students carry out cookbook-style experiments, do scripted projects, or work on toy problems is a lot like putting training wheels on a child's bike. It is one way to ease into something new and difficult. It may help them learn safely, preventing painful mishaps. If you (or your students or administrators) are doubtful or anxious about implementing Project-Based Learning in your classroom, these non-ideal approaches may be just what you need to become comfortable doing projects instead of drills. Eventually, all good parents (or wise children) take off the training wheels. Kids enjoy the thrill of really leaning into the turns while riding their bikes, and many would learn better and faster (as I did) with no training wheels in the first place. Yes, there may be crashes and scrapes, but that is real life.

Senior Design

The first-years' Problem-Based Learning course's shortcoming of not being closely tied to the Real World was addressed in a similar course BME majors took as seniors, Capstone (Senior) Design. This course was created and taught by Professors of the Practice, Franklin Bost and James Rains. The training wheels were off! Each group had to find a client, who might be a clinician at Emory (or elsewhere in Atlanta), or perhaps they might be a research lab head tackling a biomedical problem. Students spent time with the client, including shadowing them at work, to identify a process or device that needed improving. Then they worked as a group for the rest of the semester going through several design-build-test-improve cycles.

The hope and expectation for this course was for the client actually to benefit from their work, and for the students to present their work as a poster or paper at a relevant conference. I was a client a few times for teams of Senior Design students, who built devices for my research lab. Because college seniors are so busy, I found that many of the students on teams working in my research lab put in very little effort and their delivered products were disappointing to me and them. I was not at all involved in the teaching side of Senior Design, but if I were, I would have done some early assessments and course corrections to address the seniors' flagging motivation or distraction due to too many demands on their time.

One big motivator for budding engineers was the *Capstone Design Expo* held at the end of the school year in Georgia Tech's huge basketball stadium. Senior Design groups from BME and quite a few other departments exhibit their inventions, methods, and ideas to the public, including many recruiters from industry. Awards are given out to groups with the most clever or well-developed and tested ideas. A well-presented project might result in funds from an angel investor to start a company or to license and manufacture the design. High-paying jobs are offered on the spot.

Another highly motivating real-world event that some of my students took part in was the *InVenture Prize*. Groups of students from across the university might have developed a promising invention in their Senior Design class. Or perhaps it was a side project they worked on in the Invention Studio or their dorms. If they definitely wanted to commercialize it, they could present their work on a TV show that was broadcast on Georgia Public Television. This big annual competition has been called "American Idol for nerds," but is more like the *Shark Tank* or *Dragon's Den*, as winners are awarded substantial startup funding. Quite a few interdisciplinary student groups from the *InVenture Prize* or the *Capstone Design Expo* have gone on to become successful companies.[87] These are great ways to motivate students by encouraging them to come up with ideas that are useful in the Real World, and to allow them to hit the ground running once they graduate.

***

I hope that the examples I described in **Part IV** inspire you to try similar things at your school, even if the details may not be applicable. The excitement and motivation that happens when students get to devise projects that somehow improve the world can transform them from apathetic to exceptional in a matter of weeks. The powerful social motivation that always happens when students work as part of a well-integrated team gives these excited students meta-skills and lessons they will carry with them throughout their lives.

---

87. See https://innovation.cae.gatech.edu/startups-page

Part V

Feedback for Continual Improvement

Hopefully, you are reading this book because you want to try out some new ideas for teaching and learning that will enhance your students' motivation. But which new ideas should you try? How should you implement them? Probably, the way to get started is just to forge ahead and try out something that grabs you and feels like fun. Don't worry too much if it seems that you may not have planned it well. The route to success in teaching is not always well mapped. I have an approach that is guaranteed to work, sooner or later: keep soliciting feedback and keep adjusting what you do in ways that address whatever problems may come up in your initial attempts. Don't give up, adapt!

CHAPTER 13

Too much effort?

You might think you don't have time to add even one little extra thing to your long list of teaching duties. Don't feel like the ideas I am advocating are something extra you must do. Instead, think of them as new teaching methods that will eventually replace the old ones. As I mentioned at the outset, I promote an evolutionary, rather than revolutionary, approach to improving student motivation. I did not include all the pitfalls, nor emphasize the slow process of getting to a point where I saw nearly all of my students accomplish great things because they were highly motivated. I wrote this book to help you speed up that process, but you are bound to encounter pitfalls unique to your own situation. Expect them and don't get discouraged. If it seems like implementing real-world Project-Based Learning is a huge burden and you are wondering whether it is worth the effort, you are asking the wrong question. The key secret to keep in mind is that **nothing is a huge burden when you are highly motivated**. This goes for teachers as well as students. So the question to ask is, "Where do I get the motivation to do this?" Answer: Everywhere you can!

As anyone who has a workout buddy will tell you, having a partner who is committed to the same goals as you are really helps to motivate you. Don't develop a new approach to teaching in isolation. Ideally, get your colleagues on board and work on it as a pair or group. I was lucky to have great co-teachers and mentors at Georgia Tech. But we were always so busy running our research labs that to meet and talk about how we should teach required a conscious effort. It was always worth it.

I encourage you to get your administrators on your side, too. You will probably need additional resources and permissions to implement real-world projects. It is certainly possible for students to do a wide range of projects for little or no money, so you might gravitate towards those until things are running smoothly, before asking for a fully kitted-out makerspace for your school.

There are many success stories out there that you can show to your bosses or school board to win their support. Edutopia.org is a great place to start. When you feel ready for a Big Ask, I recommend considering a grant from the National Science Foundation. The NSF requires inclusive educational aspects in all of their grants, and it is very open-minded about funding novel and innovative ideas in teaching. Even if you feel you don't deal with science in your teaching, that is OK. You can always turn a new teaching method into a scientific study if you get the right collaborators on board.

If you are afraid that setting students loose on projects will result in chaos in the classroom, don't worry. When students become engaged, they behave well and self-regulate. It actually becomes *less* work for you if you previously had to spend much time and effort keeping your class under control. You will probably find that previously hyperactive and misbehaving students become quietly focused when they are really into their projects.

Good helpers can be motivating. Let anyone who helps you do your teaching know how important they are, and treat them well. This could include administrative support, maintenance and custodial staff, teaching assistants, co-teachers and even your students. If, when you ask for help, your helpers eagerly join you to solve problems because they know how appreciated they are, you will multiply your capabilities and amplify your enthusiasm.

Cards, thank-you notes, and compliments go a long way in winning your helpers' loyalty. My wife hand-makes lovely cards which I often use to give sincere thanks to those who have gone out of their way to be helpful. I have noticed them displayed proudly in my helpers' offices years after giving them.

Don't expect miracles early on in moving toward more real-world Project-Based Learning. Move forward one step at a time. Break big tasks down into doable chunks. Pause to bask in every little success, and learn from every little or big failure to keep improving. Do it with friends. Ask for help and respect your helpers. Getting good, useful feedback from your students can be one of the most motivating things you can do to encourage you to keep improving.

CHAPTER 14

How to Get Feedback

At the beginning of my courses, I made it clear to my TAs and my students that the course was always a "work in progress" and that I was open to suggestions and ideas about how to improve any aspect of it.

At Georgia Tech, each course has a voluntary, anonymous survey given online in the last few days of the course (before the final exam), called CIOS (Course and Instructor Opinion Survey). You have seen some of my students' CIOS anonymous comments quoted throughout this book. For many of my colleagues, this was the only feedback they would get about their teaching. They did not bother to solicit, or were afraid of soliciting, additional feedback. Remember, as I said in Part I, we professors at research universities are incentivized toward getting grants funded and papers published, not toward teaching.

The statistics and comments from CIOS were useful in helping to improve the course next year. But unfortunately the feedback came too late to do anything to address shortcomings of the current semester's course. Results became available only after grades were submitted, just as we headed off for winter or summer break, and it was all too easy just to forget them. It took some amount of self-discipline and effort to remember to download and analyze the CIOS results, and revisit them a few weeks or months later, when planning the next iteration of the course. My hands-off Department Chairs never sought to meet with me to discuss my teaching. They probably did not ever look at my CIOS results themselves, unless I brought those to their attention. I may have been the only person who regularly read my own courses' CIOS results, for all I know.

Another big problem with CIOS is that it is voluntary for the students. In the run-up to finals, students are so busy that filling out a 10-minute CIOS form may not be at the top of their to-do list. Although faculty could not see their CIOS results until after all the finals were graded and grades submitted, we were able to monitor the response rate continuously. To get a reasonable and useful number of responses, most professors had to bribe their students with some perk, such as a reduction in the overall workload if the response rate reaches a certain threshold. Then peer pressure would kick in as students asked each other if they had filled out the CIOS form yet, so everyone could receive the perk.

Disappointed by the shortcomings of CIOS, I got feedback from my students through a variety of additional means. An important message that I put in the syllabus, and repeated throughout the semester was, "Your input and suggestions are always appreciated." Every semester and every class of students is different and presents new issues and problems to deal with.

The most useful and reliable feedback was to add a survey question or two to each midterm exam, quiz, and final exam. For example, I might ask, "What are the best and worst things about this course so far?" or, "What advice would you give to future students about how to do well in this course?" I might also use exam questions to understand the students' perceptions and attitudes about certain assignments, or solicit their suggestions for improving them next year.

I graded these survey questions in a binary way: If the student provided any useful information and put a modicum of thought into their answer, they got full credit. If they blew off the question or were so vague as to be unhelpful, they got a zero for that question. Of course, I made it clear that there was no penalty for being critical of me or the course. In fact, well thought-out critical answers were encouraged. As with all interactions in the classroom, I encouraged students to be respectful and constructive.

Students feel greatly respected and empowered when they are asked how they feel about a course, especially if they see me improve my teaching as a result of something they suggested. Because of that, I often would point to aspects of the course that previous years' students had helped to shape and improve by giving me useful feedback. For example, I thought that making an assignment due the day before Thanksgiving would allow them to enjoy the holiday without having to do homework. But I failed to realize that many of them needed to travel for a day to get home. When they explained this to me, I adjusted the due dates to what worked for them, and canceled class for the Wednesday before Thanksgiving.

After I had been teaching the same course for a few years to BME seniors, I reached out to former students, with help from Georgia Tech's Alumni Association, to ask them how my courses may have influenced them. I created a survey using Google Forms,[88] and the answers to their questions were sent to a spreadsheet where I could sort and arrange them in various ways. I was surprised how many former students, now busy in grad school, med school, or working in industry, were willing to complete the survey. Their comments were among the most useful feedback I have solicited because the alumni were now in a position to look objectively at the merits of all their college courses in comparison.

The idea of making a useful or positive difference in someone's life is a great goal for teachers to strive for. What came up repeatedly in the responses was that they got a lot more out of the real-world learning experiences than they expected. Some of the benefits of my courses were not appreciated until years later, say, when the alumni began giving more talks or making cold calls as part of their job. Activities in my classes helped them to become more relaxed and skillful in these situations.

Some of the most useful feedback I got was not specifically solicited. Perhaps because I trained my students to speak up in class and ask as many questions as they wanted, they also felt comfortable sending me emails with both complimentary and critical feedback. My "suggestion box" was always open.

Complimentary feedback can be very helpful to let you know what you are doing right, or what gets your students excited. Of course, you have to be wary of students trying to influence your grading or otherwise gain an unfair advantage over their peers. I would consciously distance myself from any positive or negative emotions such feedback might evoke in me, especially during grading. Positive student comments can be leveraged for support from administrators to pursue a new idea or to keep an experimental teaching program funded.

Some students may want to leave anonymous feedback about touchy issues. I let them know they could slip a note under my office door or speak to one of my TAs when I was not around, who would relay their comments anonymously to me.

Comments and suggestions that originated from the TAs themselves were also often helpful, as they usually had already taken the course, and now got to see it from a different perspective.

Thanks to all the positive comments about my courses from my students, solicited and especially unsolicited, I was encouraged to write this book. With their input, the courses got better each year. Now that I am no longer teaching in the university setting, I hope that by sharing what worked and what didn't, I am passing my baton to you to explore new terrain, and

---

88. https://docs.google.com/forms

spark excitement about real-world teaching in the minds of other teachers and administrators.

Embrace Technology

I worked at one of the top engineering-focused public universities in the country. Georgia Tech students *love* technology. *I* love technology. But it was still tough to keep up with all the advances that students seem to have no trouble adopting. I was very lucky that we had a Center for Enhancement of Teaching and Learning that led workshops on all sorts of new technology that was available to us. Sometimes, it was forced on us, like a new course management system called T-square (based on Sakai)[89] that I eventually came to love. But usually it was optional, adopted first by the most technophilic profs.

One helpful tool to get feedback from my students was the so-called *clickers*, or student response system (SRS), small wifi-connected keypad remotes that each student bought at the bookstore if their course required them. If all of your students have mobile phones or tablets, perhaps they can use an app for SRS. I used clickers for in-class quizzes and polls. I found these were great for reinforcing one or two key concepts from the previous lecture. I would give a 5-minute quiz at the beginning of each class. As I mentioned in the **Attendance** section (p. 153), the clickers were also handy for automatically taking roll, and getting students to be on time and settle down quickly. Tardy students ran in with their clickers in hand ready to do the quiz before it vanished off the screen. The clickers were also capable of taking anonymous polls, which was helpful for questions that students might be embarrassed to answer with a show of hands.

I experimented with an online course meeting place called *Piazza*. This is a micro-social network where I created a forum just for my class. My students could ask questions and other students could try to answer them. Sometimes, I (or my TAs) would chime in on Piazza to answer a tricky question. But often, their fellow students were proud to show they knew the answer. Usually, if one student had a question, many other students were wondering the same thing. The Piazza forum made it very efficient to answer them all at the same time, rather than with many separate emails or office visits. Piazza was also useful for having live Q&A sessions on the night before a test.

Inspired by the MOOC (massive open online course) fad, I tried out a system that recorded the audio of my lectures and made a presentation that was synced with my slides. My students could replay this on their own as many

---

89. Sakai learning management system, https://www.sakailms.org/

times as they wanted, in case they were absent, not paying enough attention, or just a bit lost during class. I could tell that my students loved these recordings from all the reminders they gave me if I forgot to upload them promptly.

For another class, I enlisted our Distance Learning office to video my lectures. I made the videos available to my students, as well as to students at another university that I was collaborating with. These video recordings were met with mediocre enthusiasm by the remote school. I think that because my lectures were quite interactive, to watch recordings of them passively from a distance was not nearly as engaging. We did not manage to set up a reliable live two-way link where distant learners could ask questions and participate in discussions. I imagine that with live Q&A, the distance learning would have been much more successful. Thanks to COVID-19 and enforced physical distancing, there are increasingly many ways to stream video courses in real time with two-way interaction. I expect that many geographical barriers will soon become a thing of the past.

Many teachers are experimenting with a **flipped classroom** that relies on recorded videos of lectures, which students can watch on their own time. This frees up the time usually spent in class on lectures. This time can be spent instead on a free-form classroom experience in which the teacher roves from student to student, offering more personalized help. In a sense, the lectures are at home, and the homework is in school. One huge motivational advantage of this idea happens when teachers also encourage students to help each other learn. It can be very intrinsically rewarding when students know they are ahead of others, and then work to bring their classmates up to their level of understanding. It is also motivating for the slower student to get past a frustrating barrier with the help of a friend.

The flipped classroom may get us closer to Salman Khan's ideal where students spend however much time they need to accomplish a learning goal, before moving on to the next one. The structure of the flipped classroom tolerates students progressing at different rates better than when teachers use a traditional live lecture model. My NeuroEng. Fun. class was sort of like this, in the sense that the lab part was very much paced by each team's agreed-upon goals, not by any schedule I imposed. Except at the beginning of the semester, when I was giving needed orientation and scaffolding, the lab work did not depend on the lectures — the lecture topics were quite independent. And in the lab, team members would cooperate to make sure everyone on the team knew what they were doing.

The big disadvantage of a flipped-classroom model is the effort and planning teachers have to put into making the lectures ahead of time. This is becoming less of an issue as more lectures become available online that can be borrowed for this purpose. However, students will usually prefer to hear from their own instructor rather than a stranger found on YouTube.

More and more software tools are being created, such as *Screencast-O-Matic.com*, that make it easy for instructors at all levels to create more engaging recorded lectures that include voiceovers, animation, underlining, circling, highlighting, and other ways to keep students' attention while they are watching recorded material in a potentially distracting environment. These tools can also be used to personalize others' lectures, emphasizing the points you feel are most important for your students to learn.

An obvious disadvantage of pre-recorded material is that these lectures can't be genuinely interactive. As I emphasized earlier in Chapter 7: **to make lectures interactive is the most effective way to build student excitement, make sure the instruction is given at the correct level, maintain engagement, and ensure learning.** As with my clicker quizzes in class, recorded lectures can include short quizzes to encourage the students to pause and think about what they just learned for a few seconds. There are software tools, like *edpuzzle.com*, that allow instructors to tally responses to these embedded quizzes, to see how well students are understanding certain points. It is up to instructors to look at the tallies and then go back to that material with students who failed to get it, and try a new explanation. Hopefully, the lack of real-time interaction of recorded lectures will be compensated for by the individualized face-time that takes place in class.

Although I am advising progressive teachers to embrace technology, I was careful in my classes to allow students to use their computers, tablets and smartphones ONLY when it was appropriate. When I was lecturing and having discussions with them, I usually prohibited all screens and had them silence their phones. For this generation of students, there are many distracting alerts and notifications pulling their attention away from class. For them to stay focused on the material, remove as many distractions as possible. The social network will still be there when class is over.

The specific technology I recommend is only a jumping-off point. Educational technology is moving so fast, it is likely to be obsolete by the time you read this, replaced by the next great thing. Totally immersive 3D virtual reality? Wires plugged directly into students' brains? The take-home message here is to keep tabs on what's out there and experiment with new technology. This usually requires a few cycles of practice to become familiar with its quirks, so don't be discouraged if it does not seem to work for you right away. Read the instruction manuals and FAQs, and get help from those who have already mastered it.

Feedback Between Students: Lab Notebooks and Peer Evaluations

An important goal in NeuroEng. Fun. lab was for every student's lab notebook to be useful. I gave the students a clear explanation of how I would grade them, at the beginning of the semester, so they could work to include all the components I think are valuable in a lab notebook. I gave them leeway to come up with their own enhancements and organizing schemes. As with all my classes, there was no grading curve; everyone could get the grade they wanted, if they were willing to put in the effort. Grades in general are an extrinsic motivator. It is much better to get students to come up with their own intrinsic motivations for learning. My job was to convince them that making a useful notebook was a worthy goal in itself. I observed repeatedly that at some point in the semester, they would become intrinsically motivated to make their notebooks as useful as possible to future generations of Neuroeng. Fun. students. (They were urged to gift their notebooks to the course's growing library at the end of the year.)

To encourage excellence, I graded iteratively and continually gave and sought advice. I encouraged students to make sure everyone in their group was valuable. I had students turn in their notebooks at least a week before the final due date, for me to look them over carefully and give specific feedback on any shortcomings. They could also ask me to look over their notebooks at any time during the course to see how they were doing and give feedback, which I gladly did. This way, they were not hit by any surprises about their final grade. They could choose to ignore my advice about how to make their notebooks excellent, but most did not. They were highly motivated to get kudos from their peers, as evidenced by what teammates said in their notebooks about them. Almost every student in the end had created a well-organized and useful notebook that demonstrated what they learned in the lab part of the course. If they wished, they could also include their notes about the lecture part of the course.

An unusual aspect of my grading for Neuroeng. Fun. lab was that 10% of the students' grade depended on how well they filled out self and peer evaluations. I shared with the students our *Problem-Based Learning Assessment Rubric* (Fig. 22) to help them judge objectively how well they and their teammates promoted the success of the course's goals and Problem-Based Learning meta-skills. Below is part of the Peer Evaluation form that NeuroEng. Fun. students completed at the midpoint and end of the semester (Fig. 23). It also had sections for them to evaluate themselves, the TA, me and the course. They brought in these evaluations for a frank discussion with me and the rest of their group.

The mid-semester discussion was key to fixing any problems with poor team skills. Any bad feelings could be resolved and goals could be set for improving the group's performance. I expected these peer assessment discussions to be awkward and difficult. Surprisingly, because these BME seniors had done peer assessments in their first-year Problem-Based Learning class, they knew how to deliver constructive feedback and to give praise where it was due. As a result, they were more often uplifting for me and the students. Even the ones who weren't pulling their weight learned what to do to regain motivation and a feeling of belonging in the group.

The end-of-semester discussion was great for making students realize how much they had accomplished and grown, and to reinforce what they learned from mistakes they made or things that did not go as well as they could have.

BMED 4400 Spring 2013 – Prof. Potter

NEUROENGINEERING FUNDAMENTALS – PEER AND COURSE EVALUATIONS

4-24-13

Evaluator:____________________

Team's name:____________________

brains and machines

Evaluate your teammates, yourself, the TA, the instructor, and the course in an honest but constructive way. For your teammates and yourself, pay attention to the PBL Assessment criteria (see last page), including self-directed inquiry, problem solving, and group skills. Feel free to add any other items you think are appropriate. Bring this to lab for discussion. This Peer Evaluation is worth 5% of your grade, so put some thought into it.

1. Teammate:____________________
Evaluation:

Figure 23. Peer evaluation forms included space to write a detailed paragraph evaluating each team member, the TA, me, and the course. They also prompted the evaluators to assign suggested letter grades to each of those people and to the course. At the end was a copy of the Problem-Based Learning Assessment Criteria they had seen when they took Problem-Based Learning as first-years.

I took under consideration the suggested grades in the peer evaluations when it came time for me to issue the final semester grades. If they seemed to contradict what I had observed, that would trigger further discussion and investigation. However, for grading I depended more on the objective evidence found in their notebooks, and my own experience interpreting how well they fulfilled the items in the Rubric. Thus, the peer assessments were more a lesson in how to give constructive, critical feedback to one's teammates.

14. How to Get Feedback

The Teacher, TA and Course assessment items of the form provided a wealth of feedback I used continually to adjust and improve the mechanics of the course or my own lecturing and mentoring. For example, students requested more technical detail in lectures on certain topics that I had only given a broad overview of, such as neurally controlled limb prostheses. It is often hard to guess ahead of time how sophisticated the students' thinking will be on a given topic. The most effective approach is to keep asking them for feedback.

Allie Del Giorno's evaluation of the course is typical of the thoughtful and useful feedback my students provided:

> "The lab portion of this class was extremely valuable for learning teamwork and acquiring hands-on lab skills for studying the brain and potentially developing technology to interface with it. I found **the most valuable part to be learning how to do research in a team**; I have done many group projects, but asking questions and developing/performing experiments with a team of people is a totally different dynamic. I learned that the most effective teams seem to be people with different skill sets and a common goal. The lab also taught us **how to develop and refine our own ideas.** I do wish we had a little more guidance in the beginning on what to do. Getting stepped through a sample project to see how really good grad students have accomplished projects would be great."

Excellent advice! But this was tough to implement. I have noticed, after advising many grad students in my lab, that each one has her or his own way of progressing through grad school, of getting a project from idea to publication. But certainly, aspects of Allie's suggestion could be implemented with some actual case studies, even if they are idealized. Regarding the lecture part of the course, Allie said,

> "The lectures were useful for learning new approaches in neuroengineering. These were some of the best lectures I've had at Tech because they didn't teach us old concepts that don't get used anymore. They taught something I think is much more important: **how have people developed new techniques / new approaches to studying the brain?** I don't think there are many classes in the country that teach this way! At the same time, I'm not sure we

> learned enough modeling and data analysis tools during the lectures; **a day or two of covering how to apply data analysis to real neural data would be great. I think a lot more technical detail should be put into this course if possible;** even if you can't cover everything, giving an idea of what kinds of math / engineering tools are needed to actually solve these problems and turn the big ideas into tangible projects seems important to me."

Allie brought up a very important issue. She was also doing independent research in another professor's lab, so she had probably already seen how much time and effort real researchers have to put into analyzing their data, and how useful certain analytical tools are for that, such as simulations or statistical analysis. I decided that, because the types of data different groups acquired were so varied, I would coach teams individually on their data analysis on an ad hoc basis, as I did with each of the grad students in my research lab.

Feedback from the lab notebooks of NeuroEng. Fun. students shows that although this was an extremely challenging course, students got a lot out of it, especially skills related to working on a team:

> "Bitter sweet end to an amazing semester with amazing people. This class really showed me how to successfully design an experiment in a very demanding laboratory." - Rakshya Khatri

> "This class has been a huge learning experience. Being able to learn from your mistakes and adapt because of them made our project successful. This class may be one of my favorites I've taken at Georgia Tech and I'm glad that I stuck through it all." - Neal Klumb

> "I'm sad that this class has ended. I am unable to quantify how much I've learned about neuroscience, neurotechnology, and lab. More importantly, I had the privilege of working with a great team and I feel like we have all grown together." - Christine Dela Cerna

Lessons Learned From Critical Comments From My Students

Getting critical feedback sometimes requires developing a thick skin. Most people don't enjoy being told about their faults and shortcomings. It was painful to learn that I had failed a student in some way, or had made a serious mistake in running the class. I nevertheless took their comments on board and asked myself how I could change to do better in the future. The key is not to take things too personally, and to acknowledge that there is always room for improvement. In that light, constructive criticisms are valuable gifts that will help improve one's teaching and the course, and eventually, students' lives.

If a comment is painful to hear, it helps if you know each student as a unique person. Try to get into their mindset. Think about where those opinions came from. I have found that hurt feelings on both sides are usually repaired by more communication. When appropriate, talking privately with the student about a difficult or emotion-laden criticism can work wonders in turning bad feelings into a bold plan of action for how to prevent similar problems in the future. For those types of conversations, I highly recommend they be in person, not via email, to avoid misunderstandings and to benefit from the body language and intonation cues of face-to-face interaction.

Early on, I experimented with negative reinforcement to motivate my students. Being the extremely social animals that we are, the potential for embarrassment can be a strong motivator. However, humiliation in front of peers can be devastating and can backfire. At first, I did not see the harm in calling out students who needed to work on their class interaction points, or who breached classroom norms, but one of my students educated me:

> "... Dr.Potter chastised her in an email sent to the whole class, rather than having a private conversation. Suffice it to say a lot of people felt this was very unprofessional. I also felt that reading off names of the people with the lowest participation grades was very disrespectful and unprofessional."

From this criticism I learned that negative reinforcement can be demotivating, and thus should be avoided. After that, I tried to keep all my feedback positive, and if I felt a student was falling short of my expectations or violating class norms, I would communicate privately about it in a constructive way. For example, I could try to understand a chronically sleepy student in a dialog, "Are you having a hard time sleeping at night? Or is it a matter of not having enough time to get the sleep you need? Is there anything I can do to liven up the lectures?"

From this CIOS evaluation by a NeuroEng. Fun. student from 2006 I clearly needed an attitude adjustment:

> "Potter's teaching style can be summed up mostly as distant and critical. He demands a lot from his students, and is noticeably disappointed in his students a lot. This is not a very motivating environment to foster learning, when your main motivator is to not disappoint the professor constantly."

I learned how important it is to curb my judgmental nature (I am an xNTJ)[90] and be more positive when my students' accomplishments are less than I expected. I learned that it helps to get into the details with a student about what they think might have gone wrong. Often, I found out that it was something out of their control, such as an equipment failure, or infection of the cultures they were growing. By employing the "Value of learning from failures" strategy, I became less "distant and critical."

The comment below, and other similar anonymous comments from students in the combined Hybrid Neural Microsystems/NeuroEng. Fun. course helped me adjust the way I gave the lectures for this course. Many grad students (HNM Fellows) and some undergrads like Allie felt the lectures were too rudimentary and wanted to go more in-depth into the topics I brought up. Meanwhile, other undergrads felt I went over their heads at times. Thus, I learned to spend more time probing the students' understanding, and teaching at a number of levels of detail. When the NSF-funded HNM project had finished, I chose to teach it as a course only for undergrads.

> "Functionally, combining a graduate and undergraduate level course was a mistake. The instructor's teaching style was at times more catered to one group or another, and ultimately this hurt the cohesiveness of the course material. I consistently learned a great deal in lab and working on projects, but lecture sessions were more hit-or-miss." - anonymous HNM student

---

90. In the Myers-Briggs personality types, that's Introvert/Extrovert mix, Intuitive, Thinking, Judgmental.

There were also many comments from the first couple of years of HNM/Neuroeng. Fun. complaining that we had tried to put too many topics into one semester. These rang true, because we always had to skip planned activities to get on to the next module in time. As a result, I decided to omit the cellular and human modules, and spend the entire semester on the networks module. This was the closest module to what was going on in my own research lab, so I had plenty of material and equipment to scaffold the students and help them come up with really good, long network research projects for NeuroEng. Fun.

> "HNM is both great and awful. Often it consumes far too much time and effort (relative to other courses), but the rewards of concentrated lab work can be (and has been) well worth it, in my opinion."
> - anonymous HNM student

> "This class was unique in that I learned a great deal of PRACTICAL information regarding general lab techniques. It definitely helped to build my can-do attitude about certain things, like building hardware and fixing software. It was, however, an extremely intensive course, and I feel this was somewhat detrimental to my progress in research/other courses. I'd suggest doing just one module, and alternating the 'scope' of the course (cell culture scale versus human scale) from year to year." - anonymous HNM student

Some students got extra motivation by knowing that the equipment and techniques that they developed in lab class would be put to use in my own research lab. The students helped me and my research group do real-world research long after the semester was over.

***

Not only is it a good idea to instill a growth mindset in your students, but also to hold yourself to the same principles of continual improvement through directed effort. You will never be finished improving, if for no other reason than that students and educational technology keep changing. It takes constant, conscious effort to note deficiencies in how you teach and to address them. To keep soliciting feedback from your students (and from colleagues, parents, and administrators) will make it clear to you what needs the most attention. As you address teaching challenges, keep remembering that you are probably trying to solve problems that others have already solved. To heed their advice will greatly smooth the path forward. See the material I recommend at the end of the book in **Recommended Reading, Watching and Listening** if you are not sure where to find wise advice from teachers like you.

Part VI

Where Education is Headed

In this part, I will cover some of my overarching philosophies about teaching, and how they mesh with recent advances in real-world approaches to teaching. Many thoughtful teachers agree that traditional schooling often fails to prepare children to be effective, contented, motivated citizens in this rapidly changing, modern world. But where federal or state governments are involved, trying to change course is harder than turning an aircraft carrier with a small tugboat. Thankfully, many progressive educators have decided to disembark and head off in their own speedboats.

As I have said many times, I believe real-world project-based learning is the most effective way to motivate students to love learning. But it certainly is not the only way. It can be mixed well with other types of learning experiences. In this Part, I will get up on my soap box about teaching philosophies, and mention some of the good ideas I have recently learned about from other progressive educators and institutions.

In the Conclusion chapter, I will recap my most important points and suggestions. I will include a list of things I did differently than most of my colleagues, as a summary of the potentially useful, unusual approaches sprinkled elsewhere in the book.

CHAPTER 15

Rants and Suggestions for Change

Intelligences

Many teachers believe that a student comes into their class with a fixed label on them: Good Student or Bad Student, Clever or Slow, Quiet or Boisterous. They pigeonhole them and then treat them according to their presumed-permanent labels. In the education administration world they call this "tracking": putting the students into an AP (advanced placement) track or a remedial track of courses, for example. I believe this practice is very harmful. I am perhaps unusual in that I believe that **every single person is a genius doing some things, and pretty bad doing others, but can improve in any way with the right motivation**.

I was raised in an unfortunate environment in the 70s where second-graders were labeled with a number after taking an IQ test. This one number was all that most teachers and parents needed to know to decide how "smart" a student was. Becoming a neuroscientist and learning about how the brain works, I realized how simplistic or in fact, downright wrong this is. The brain is packed full of circuits that allow us to do an extremely wide array of amazing things. As one of my neuroscience professors, V. S. Ramachandran said, our brains evolved as a mass of kluges and hacks.[91] These got the job done for our ancestors, so those protohumans succeeded in surviving longer and making more offspring.

---

91. Gary Marcus, *Kluge: The Haphazard Construction of the Human Mind*, Houghton Miflin, 2008

The key hack that defines humanity is our unusual ability to learn new skills and the knowledge base needed to implement them. We excel at adapting to whatever environment we happen to find ourselves in. School is no exception. Students can learn new intelligences. You could think of many of the meta-skills I refer to in this book as different types of intelligence. They can all be improved with effort and the right motivation.

Let's take inventiveness, for example. I have long been fascinated by creative processes of all sorts, but especially by the way useful things get invented. Inventors all agree that a good invention seldom pops out of nowhere into the inventor's head. Usually there is a fertile intellectual landscape of similar things out there already. When Edison was "inventing" the light bulb, so were many other clever people elsewhere, all racing to get to market first. Then comes the hard work of just trying out many variations of the basic idea. Edison said, "Genius is 1% inspiration and 99% perspiration." He and his large team are said to have tested out hundreds of different ideas for a filament that would last before they found a good one.[92] This process requires persistence, a skill that can be learned.

It also requires getting good at "lateral thinking," an idea promoted by Edward de Bono, who wrote many books to teach and exercise this creativity skill. A more recent book by Steven M. Johnson,[93] *Have Fun Inventing: Learn to Think up Products and Imagine Future Inventions,* expands on and demonstrates de Bono's advice, as he describes how he makes his fantastic, detailed cartoons of possible inventions. Johnson has been perfecting the art of developing his cartoons by drawing many "extrapolations and permutations of objects" since he was a teenager. He even explains how "Empathy for your subject can improve your lateral thinking." Therefore, even this one type of intelligence, inventiveness, is actually based on many separate learnable skills, such as persistence, lateral thinking, and empathy. In Edison's case, it also included the ability to manage a large team.

You will need to fight the natural human tendency to stereotype people as you get to know your students. Any time you find yourself expecting that a student might do poorly because you think they "are not good at" something, ask yourself, "How can I motivate them to work on improving this particular intelligence?" Make them aware of how many intelligences they already possess, and of others that they can improve with focused effort.

---

92. In his engaging book, *How We Got to Now: Six Innovations That Made the Modern World,* Steven Johnson described Edison's process and said, "There was no light bulb moment in the story of the light bulb."
93. Not to be confused with Steven Johnson, the author mentioned in the previous footnote: Steven M. Johnson, *Have Fun Inventing: Learn to Think up Products and Imagine Future Inventions,* (2012) Patent Depending Press.

15. Rants and Suggestions for Change

Growth Mindset

Students fare much better in school if they have a "growth mindset." [94] Carol Dweck's term implies a belief that abilities are not fixed, but can be developed with effort. You may believe you are promoting a growth mindset in class, but ask yourself if you are actually and continuously implementing this idea that, with effort, *all* students can learn and improve. Or are you consciously or subconsciously labeling students as "good" or "bad"?

It may be difficult to give every student the individualized attention they need to succeed — **differentiated learning** — but it is not hard to let them know it is available. I have found that if students are motivated and excited about learning, and if they need something more to accomplish that, they will come to me and ask for help. Then I can either help them or find someone else who can. To make it easier for them to ask for help, I let them know I care, that I want them to succeed, and that it is OK to come talk to me about their special needs. If you truly adopt the growth mindset about your students, and keep emphasizing that they are in control of how much they improve and learn, they will adopt the growth mindset about themselves, taking charge of their education.

What Went Wrong With Schooling in the US?

Traditional schooling has gone from bad to worse, especially in the US. It has become the norm for students to be bored with school, to need cajoling to get out of bed and onto the school bus. How did we get into this mess? Ted Dintersmith and Salman Khan explain this in their excellent books on school reform.[95] In 1893, a *Committee of Ten* education leaders in the US got together and came up with a plan to transform schooling from rural one-room schoolhouses with all ages learning together to a factory model: huge schools full of classrooms, each covering a separate discipline, segregated by age, with pupils sitting attentively in rows, and commanded by bells. This would prepare them for the factory whistle. When the US had a manufacturing economy and

---

94. Carol Dweck, *Mindset: The New Psychology of Success,* (2006) Ballantine Books.
95. Each of these books has many great ideas about how to improve education, and inspiring stories of progressive teachers who are doing it: Salman Khan, *The One World School House: Education Reimagined,* (2012) Twelve, and Ted Dintersmith, *What School Could Be: Insights and Inspiration from Teachers Across America,* (2018) Princeton University Press.

employed hordes of docile factory workers, this might have made sense. This factory-style format made school BORING, and the lack of control by the students over their classroom life has been terribly demotivating. Why has it persisted nearly unchanged for over a century, despite factories playing a decreasing role in the American economy? Institutional inertia? Fear of change? I don't know.

Then in 2001 came the *No Child Left Behind Act* that compelled teachers to "teach to the test" for their school to receive federal funding. Sadly, most of the meta-skills and knowledge needed to be a good citizen and a productive, motivated worker in the modern world are not among the standard criteria being tested. Standardized tests cover mostly the same **Three Rs** and factoids chosen by the *Committee of Ten* in 1893.

Getting their students ready for the next standardized test has sapped teachers' time and motivation to improve schooling. The Federal Government's poor attempt at education reform, the *Every Student Succeeds Act* (2015) did little to change this, like putting inflatable tires on a horse-drawn buggy. The sad irony in the names of these initiatives is that they use population metrics, not individualized attention to students, to rank schools and incentivize them to teach better. Many, many children are being left behind and not succeeding. And federal legislators' idea of an "incentive" is to take away funding for poor-performing schools, the very ones that need the most resources to improve their statistics.

The other devastating thing that NCLB did, in combination with an obsessive over-emphasis of the importance of going to college, was to ring the death knell of shop classes in middle and high school. I learned many important and useful things in my shop classes, and think that to replace them with more rows of desks for test prep was a big mistake.

The Three Rs: RIP?

Do we need to learn "the basics" of reading, writing and arithmetic? How important is it for students to know their times tables in the age of ubiquitous calculators? Why should students learn how to spell when there are spell checkers that can fix bad spelling? More relevant to my own courses, why should my students learn the names of brain parts when they can be found easily now on Wikipedia or in a book? Here is why:

My opinion is that for now at least, we should not bury the basics to rest in peace. It is still important for students to have learning fundamentals in their own heads. This will allow them to interpret what they read and hear, and provide the ingredients that when mixed together, become their creative output. Someday, maybe our subconscious mind will be able to do Internet searches for what it does not know via the miracles of neuroengineering. Until

15. Rants and Suggestions for Change

then, we have to wait for a question to reach some level of interest in our conscious thoughts before we bother looking it up. And yet, most of our creative process is subconscious. I believe we would be hobbling human creativity and intuition (and ability to communicate and perceive) by not having the basics stored in our neural circuits, quickly and easily accessible to our subconscious mind. Clearly, reading and 'riting underlie all types of learning and should be learned early on, when children's brains are the most plastic.

Learning the basics and doing projects to learn should not be viewed as mutually exclusive or even at odds with each other. Although all students need to learn the three Rs, perhaps the way they learn the basics ought to change. Instead of learning times tables like a kind of long poem with little meaning, math could be learned in a much more hands-on, relevant way. It could be done in a more interdisciplinary and multisensory way that would result in a much richer network of connections between different concepts.

Kids could be given many problems and situations in which multiplying things matters, and then they might be more motivated to learn the times tables. For example, a cabinetmaker or printer needs to know times tables in deciding how many pieces can be produced from a big sheet of plywood or paper. When kids arrange collections of things in various rectangular grids, they can get an intuitive understanding of times tables, division and remainders. By computing volumes in different units (such as cubic meters or milliliters), three dimensional multiplication can be understood intuitively (volume = height x width x depth). This topic was never taught to me in school, but I have needed to use it often in the lab and workshop. In school, we only learned that a *cube root* was an esoteric possibility, not a way to understand how to pack boxes on a pallet.[96]

Paul France's third-grade "Millions Project"[97] allowed his students to get an intuitive understanding of *one million* by having them collect thousands of empty soda cans from home, each worth 250 points. Groups of cans were organized into rectangles by the students. They collected and grouped cans for months. As they saw the blocks of cans grow, they learned about increasingly larger powers of ten.

If the cans were collected by cleaning up litter, then I would say this math project could have significant real-world impact and extra motivation. I

---

96. For example, suppose you had 1728 cube-shaped boxes and wondered if they would fit on a 1 x 1 m pallet. The cube root of 1728 is 12, so you just need to see if 12 boxes fit in a meter; are they less than 8.3 cm on one side?
97. https://www.edutopia.org/article/what-does-million-look

often get a rush of satisfaction and pride after picking up litter for my local Tidy Towns club and seeing a mess transformed into a clean roadway.

Mr. Barnes' projects had us do comparison shopping and learn Unit Price Marketing, or draw the floor-plan of a house and calculate its total area. These were very helpful for becoming good at doing math on the fly, for things that are actually useful. I believe no kids need to fear math. If math were always taught in the context of accomplishing some part of a project, or solving a real-world problem, young students would soak it up. They would grow up knowing how useful it is.

Students need to be taught tricks for estimation. Estimation skills are seldom part of traditional 'rithmetic. It is useful even to be able to estimate merely what order of magnitude (factor of ten) a result should be — that is part of thinking critically. In many fields, you don't have access to the specific numbers, so estimating is crucial. If a politician says a tax increase on the richest 2% will add a trillion dollars to the budget, how big a change will that make to the nation's GDP? I recall that my Dad loved calculating rough figures in his head to try to answer my questions. Now, I can sometimes do that too; estimation is a set of skills I have finally picked up over the years. It is relevant to all subjects, not just math.

Like many useful skills, the ability to estimate requires that one has learned the basics well, to the point where one's subconscious mind can easily and quickly access them to help form intuitions and hunches. But I feel that learning the basics by rote memorization and repetition is a poor way to retain them, compared to learning them while being engaged in a project or solving a real-world problem.

Education Needs to Become Less Compartmentalized

A number of factors have conspired to make traditional education further and further removed from what matters in the Real World today. A big one is the dividing of material taught into isolated subjects. I think math is the worst victim of this. The vast majority of the mathematics I learned in math class had no obvious application to anything outside of school. I loved the bits that did seem applicable to the real world, the so-called *word problems*. But even these were often contrived scenarios like trains racing toward each other on the same track. If this were ever to happen, the last thing the train operators would do is say, "Uh-oh! We got us a problem here! Let's sit down calmly and do some algebra!"

The current system of having years of isolated math classes is ridiculous and guaranteed to bore and frustrate many kids. To learn math in isolation from its application leads to the assumption that math has no value other than for eggheads. It is quite possible that many of the math lessons kids are now studying in school *are* useless or out of date. Consider the quadratic equation, for example. How many times have I ever needed to know how to derive the quadratic equation in the course of my scientific career? Zero. And factoring it in math class did not explain to me what it was good for. I am pretty sure I never even needed to factor second-order polynomials to do my biomedical engineering job.

When I need to do serious math, I run computer programs and simulations. Matlab, Mathematica, the Photomath app, or just my calculator app can do 90% of the drudgery of math, leaving more of my brain power to interpret data, and to think of new ways to process it and to visualize it. It is useful to know the difference between a median and a mean, but I learned this much better in the context of trying to understand data that I myself collected and needed for something. By working with noisy microscopic images, I learned that a median filter is better than a mean filter for reducing noise while preserving fine detail.

After taking isolated (ungrounded in reality) math classes for about 15 years in school, I finally took a class that just *used* math, Physical Chemistry. We had to derive from first principles all the important chemistry equations that I had already learned by rote memorization, like $PV=nRT$, using the math I learned in high school. During that course, a light bulb suddenly lit up over my head, "Wow! Differential equations are actually useful for something!" For some reason, sadly, no teacher in the 15 years before Physical Chemistry class had ever been able to make me realize how useful math is — and I was a student who enjoyed my math classes. Imagine how little the students who say "I HATE math!" get out of their math classes. Although many mathematicians love the beauty of math, it was not originally created as a fine art form whose purpose is manipulating symbols because they are intrinsically beautiful. It was created to solve problems, to answer questions in the Real World.

Reading and writing should be part of every class, not isolated to English class. Students don't see them as a chore when they practice reading and writing as part of an exciting project. They see them as a means to learn and communicate well. I emphasized the importance of good, careful writing when grading all of my real-world assignments. And as I mentioned before, I coached reading skills in every course I taught, so that my students could easily digest the scientific literature.

The problem of isolated silos of learning is endemic in US education, at all levels, and will take a long time to fix. We can start by assigning our students to work on projects that require them to become proficient in a range of disciplines in order to complete them. For example, a simple robot project can be used to learn many things. Even for elementary school students, these could include:

- mechanical engineering and the math behind it
- electronics and the math behind it
- coding and the logical thought process it requires (such as breaking a big task into smaller jobs)
- social dynamics, if they work in groups

    As Salman Khan said, *"No subject is ever finished. No concept is sealed off from other concepts."* [98] When I built the 2-photon microscope for my lab, I needed to learn a lot about optics, ultrafast pulsed lasers, electronics, chemistry, robotics, programming, data crunching, image processing, solid-state physics, plumbing and fluid control, and thermal management. To successfully image living specimens without killing them, I had to learn their biology. When I wanted my grad students to understand the machine and do good science, I did not send them to take ten different courses. I just had them use the microscope as much as they could, ideally with me or another person who knew a lot about it already. I encouraged them to ask questions, and I referred them to relevant papers if I couldn't answer them myself.

    There is a place for lectures and book study. Each new tool has some background information that is helpful in using it, drawn from a variety of disciplines. If students need a certain tool to get an exciting project completed, then they will be much more motivated to put the effort into learning the background. They can be trusted to ask for scaffolding if they need it. Teachers can then just point them in the right direction, give a short demonstration, or give a full lecture, as appropriate. As students use the tool to make progress on their project, this background information gets reinforced in their memory, eventually becoming a set of subconscious intuitions that we call mastery or expertise.

    A fantastic example of combining what would usually be considered non-overlapping disciplines is portrayed in the documentary, *"Most Likely to Succeed."* [99] A group of students in a progressive project-oriented high school are followed across the semester as they devise and build clever mechanical mechanisms to represent how civilizations tend to rise and fall. They were being mentored by a history teacher and a physics teacher, and learned much more than "just" history and physics. The school makes the students' projects more meaningful by having a big open house event where all the projects are demonstrated to families, friends and the general public. More and more

---

98. Salman Khan, *The One World Schoolhouse: Education Reimagined* (2012) Twelve, p. 51.
99. https://teddintersmith.com/mltsfilm/

schools will adopt such discipline-spanning activities, and hire interdisciplinary teachers. The old system of keeping every subject isolated in separate classes and taught by separate departments will eventually die out. I hope you will advance this trend. Team up with your colleagues and devise ways to mix the material you like to teach with their favorite topics, to produce more engaging lessons.

We Are Wasting Children's Lives

Teaching should not just be an *exercise* to prepare students for something that *may* (or may not) happen when they are 18 or older. Why are we wasting students' abundant energy and creativity with rote memorization, toy problems and pointless exercises that benefit no one and often bore them? **Students can benefit the world continually during the learning process.** They can experience the motivation that happens when they realize they have created something useful and shared it with others who appreciate that. We are essentially giving all college-bound kids a 17-year prison sentence. For me, this was a 23-year sentence! It is unfortunate that I had to spend 23 years in school to finally "begin" my career.

We prevent kids from interacting with the Real World until they are "fully ready" and have "learned their Three Rs." By wrapping them up in cotton wool in the safe confines of the classroom walls, we are stunting their intellectual development. Children and young adults can and should be active members of society. Our appropriate aversion to the child exploitation of the Industrial Revolution has caused the way we deal with children to swing too far in the other direction: Isolate them from the Big Bad Real World.

With Project-Based Learning, the students are setting their own pace, often working on projects they choose, and ideally, only projects they are excited about. It is hard to see how that can be exploitative, in the sense that forcing them to mine coal or work on an assembly line was in the old days.

Why must we give every learner the same sets of knowledge and skills? Imagine a world in which science fairs are more popular than sporting events. Picture a future in which the million-dollar salaries get paid to the most clever makers and instructors instead of athletes and movie stars. No, really — Stop reading and imagine that for a minute.

We are beginning to see a few young YouTubers who have created such interesting and useful content that they have millions of followers and are making good money. What if the good ideas from science fairs get turned into useful products, methods, and technological advances, and the underage geniuses who came up with the ideas could profit from them? Real-world curriculum will help make this happen. Imagine a world in which students would rather keep working on their school project than watch TV or play video games. What does that take? Only motivation.

Things I Would Change About the Educational System if I Could Wave a Magic Wand and Make it So:

- Teachers would get the pay and respect they deserve.
- Most or all classes would be project-based. They would have much more hands-on, active learning than they do now.
- Subjects would be mixed together like they are in any real-world project.
- Projects would have real-world impacts, not be toy projects or solved problems.
- Every student would be motivated to do well. Really and truly, no child would be left behind.
- Teachers would keep exploring and trying new ways to teach better.
- Administrators would give teachers the resources they ask for. It should be easy and common to test or implement a new idea in teaching.
- Grades would be de-emphasized and tangible accomplishments emphasized.
- Perks and incentives would encourage teachers to be more involved in teaching, to take risks, and to innovate.

    Unfortunately, many of these changes will require a large shift in the way society views education. However, there is much cause for optimism, as suggested by innovations mentioned in the next chapter.

CHAPTER 16

Hope: Alternative Approaches to Teaching

Vocational Schools and Apprenticeships

Project-Based Learning is not the latest new thing. There are a number of colleges and universities that have emphasized Project-Based Learning for some time, such as Purdue, Olin College, Northeastern, Stanford, Waterloo, Worcester Polytechnic, and the Cal Poly schools. Graduates from their programs are highly sought after because employers know that they learned much more than just the textbook stuff. These schools' educational approaches and innovations need to be more widely adopted not only by other colleges, but also by K-12 schools.

Project-Based Learning is in fact a very old thing: apprenticeships and vocational training. Other countries depend on this, but in the US, trade schools became nearly extinct. For example, the Georgia Institute of Technology started out as a trade school in 1888, called the Georgia School of Technology. Students learned the methods and theory of engineering while making and selling engineered products to keep the school in the black. Across the middle of the 20th century, Georgia Tech became much more focused on academics and research, and less and less on hands-on training for industrial trades.

Notice the connotations evoked by the terms "Blue-collar," "Working class," and "Union workers." Those who did not get into college are stigmatized, let alone those who did not even graduate from high school. Trade schools are considered, sadly, even "lower" than community colleges, which are filled with those hopeful that they eventually will be accepted into a 4-year college degree program when they get enough general education requirements out of the way.

For contrast, look at Switzerland and Germany, where vocational training is common and highly regarded. To apprentice in a trade is the route taken by a large fraction of young adults, male and female. Switzerland's VET (vocational education and training) system is highly successful, with less than 4% youth unemployment. Their parents are proud. My Swiss nieces did clockmaking (horology), bookkeeping, hotel management and police psychology apprenticeships. The Swiss do not share our misguided belief that every student needs to attend college to be happy and successful.

I believe strongly that every single student can do well in school (and in society) when motivated, whether they go to college or not. But how best to make that happen? This needs to be actually and truly tailored to each unique student's personality, interests, and background.

Today's economy is very much an information and service-based one in which most jobs are highly specialized and ever-changing. Thanks to the boom in Artificial Intelligence (AI), many careers will cease to exist in the next decade, being replaced by new and more creative jobs that we can hardly imagine.[100] The students of today need, more than anything else, to learn how to be adaptable. Knowing factoids is of less and less value in a world where so many resources are just a tap away on our smartphones. Today's students need to be experts at the meta-skill of learning and critically analyzing new things, and at being self-motivated. It is to be expected that they will have to shift jobs due to a tumultuous economy and changing technology. It is up to them to retrain and move on to the next vocation, or become good at a variety of different part-time gigs.

Imagine a future in which children, college students, and learners of all sorts are so excited about school that they jump out of bed and rush through breakfast to begin a new day of learning. Have you ever had this experience with something? You fall asleep at night with thoughts of what you learned that day filling your head, and wake up eager to try out new ideas of how to approach learning challenges. It was probably a self-directed project, not a traditional school, that got you this motivated. Because of NCLB-based priorities and the stigma against vocational training, US K-12 education focuses on rote memorization of factoids and preparation for college. I would wager that very few students wake up excited that they will get to do more drills and tests today.

---

100. Kevin Kelly, *The Inevitable: Understanding the 12 Technological Forces That Will Shape Our Future* (2016), Viking.

True masters at any particular trade are a dying breed in America. Very few young people are willing to commit to years-long apprenticeships to work directly under their guidance. Masters are too busy being managers. Nowadays, graduates wait until they are 18 (or 22) to get a "real job" and they begin it being pretty clueless no matter what schooling they had. Everyone just expects that new employees will need at least 5 years, or maybe 10, before becoming a highly skilled worker who knows the trade. During that 5 years they finally get the real-world learning experience that they failed to get in school. But they usually don't get to work with the master at the firm. Instead, they work with a team of other newbies led by someone slightly less clueless.

The master may have been promoted to a desk job because that is what firms do. Good workers keep getting promoted until they are managers, no longer actually practicing their trade. I am speaking from my own experience. Pretty much all older professors I know, including me before I resigned, no longer work in the lab and no longer do hands-on mentoring of underlings in the lab. Just about the time we become masters at our trade (research in a specific field using specific research tools) we get tenure and spend the rest of our career managing a big lab and writing grants. We have to go on sabbatical to spend time in our own lab! All the direct mentoring is delegated to postdocs and grad students with varying levels of skill.

The new model for trade schools and apprenticeships is now Project-Based Learning and entrepreneurship, which can begin at any age. Much of this is happening in a self-directed way outside of school at makerspaces.

Others Doing Great Things With Real-World Teaching

Up to this point, this book was based mostly on my own teaching and learning experiences. I focused on what worked for me and my students. As I warned in Part I, I am not well read in the educational literature. I avoided reading books on educational topics until the later stages of writing this book; I wanted to write my perspectives without being too influenced by those of other teachers, learning scientists, and educational theorists.

When I did look into it, I was pleasantly surprised how much great material is out there, and how much of it echoes what I had already written, though perhaps with different terminology. If you are new to Project-Based Learning, I hope I have inspired you to shift more of your teaching in that direction. Below are just a few examples and resources I have come across recently that promote the approaches I have found to be highly motivating in my own teaching practice.

I highly recommend Ted Dintersmith's inspiring book, *"What School Could Be."* He describes traveling to all 50 states in America to meet with teachers and school administrators who are trying new things and succeeding. A good number of these approaches could be called Project-Based Learning, and some projects were tied to the Real World to enhance student motivation, like I did with my students.

Expeditionary Learning (EL)[101] schools follow a model created for Outward Bound, which has been doing outdoor education since 1941. According to Wikipedia, the EL schools "are exemplified by Project-Based Learning expeditions, where students engage in interdisciplinary, in-depth study of compelling topics, in groups and in their community, with assessment coming through cumulative products, public presentations, and portfolios." Great! Since 1993, EL has gone from 10 to 153 K-12 schools across the US. That seems like a pretty slow uptake to me, given the clear benefits and successes of the EL program.

Although I am excited about EL, I don't agree with its big-picture goal. ELeducation.org says, "Our goal for each student is college acceptance." I would argue that college is not the ideal goal for everyone, because higher education all too often fails to prepare young adults for the Real World. Furthermore, this goal ignores the benefits students get even while they are still students in grade school, and all the people who are helped when students do real-world projects.

Society needs to change its thinking about schooling from being a long preparation process to being a continuously enhancing and enabling process that can benefit students (and others outside of school) at every step of their schooling. As educators, we should ask ourselves, "How can my students benefit *now* from the things they are learning?" Project-Based Learning can easily make the connection in the students' minds between the effort of learning and its benefits. That depends, however, on choosing projects whose *why* is clear. If the students can point to where the results of their efforts and learning have benefited others, they receive a great intrinsic reward from the reward circuitry in their brains. That causes a big boost in motivation and learning.

Conversely, if students spend time and effort on a project whose purpose is not relevant to them or not clear, they will be demotivated by a feeling of having wasted their time, or of getting a bad grade, or by the scorn of teammates, teachers and parents who are disappointed by their lack of engagement.

---

101. See https://eleducation.org/. Not to be confused with the ASCD publication EL Magazine, where EL stands for Educational Leadership.

One way to ensure that a project will be engaging, interesting and relevant to your students is to have them collaborate with you in devising the project. Choosing real-world projects with benefits that are clear and motivating to your students will be difficult, but much less so if you include the students in the process. The catchphrase is to give them "voice and choice." Continually solicit their feedback as you provide the necessary background, context or scaffolding for a potential project area. If they feel a sense of agency in project creation, they will be more motivated and inclined to take ownership of the project and their own learning goals.

For example, a middle school Spanish teacher in Ohio, Becky Searls, had her class investigate how they could help students in Puerto Rico after Hurricane Maria devastated the island. Her students practiced their Spanish by communicating with other students and teachers in Puerto Rico. They learned of an urgent need for school supplies, so they decided to organize a Service Learning Project[102] to gather donated school supplies and ship them to Puerto Rico. Such an interdisciplinary and beneficial real-world project taught her students much more than just Spanish and was probably highly rewarding not only for her students, but for herself, too. They learned social skills, the politics of US Territories, the science of meteorology, and media literacy, among other things. This knowledge was put to use immediately by her students, not just years later when they finally get a career job.

There are increasingly many excellent resources out there to help you and your students come up with good projects, including ideas and plans for specific projects of all types. *The Buck Institute for Education* (now called *PBLworks*, pblworks.org), specializes in Project-Based Learning. They have many such resources available for free, including videos and detailed project plans that are geared to address the learning goals and Common Core standards that are tested in standardized tests.

For example, in one called "The Ultimate Design Challenge," high school students set out to improve the design of a container of their choice, to result in less environmental impact, better usability, or cheaper production. They do mathematical modeling of the design and in the process learn many math skills intuitively, such as graphing and understanding derivatives (Common Core standards IF.B.4, IF.B.5, IF.B.6, RST.11-12.3). I wish my algebra and calculus classes had included such projects to help me understand why I was being taught all those equations. Creativity and communication meta-skills (which are two of the "21st Century Competencies") are

---

102. Becky Searls, *"How to Make the End of the School Year Meaningful!"* May 19, 2018. https://medium.com/@beckyjoy/how-to-make-the-end-of-the-school-year-meaningful-577177488dcb

emphasized through teamwork. To make it real-world motivated, teams present their final designs to practicing design engineers and to the community.

A project like this can also expose students to the more modern approaches to mathematics used by practicing scientists and engineers, namely, computer modeling, simulation and design tools. For example, my favorite computer-aided design (CAD) package, Fusion360, is available for free from Autodesk to teachers, makers and students. It is not a toy or entry-level app, but a highly sophisticated suite of design tools actually used in industry. It might seem overwhelming to most learners with no exposure to CAD, but there are so many tutorials and videos on the web about how to use Fusion360 that this is not a problem. Instead, it is an opportunity to teach how complex things can be understood by breaking them down into small steps.

This CAD package is also great for reinforcing the teaching approach: **learning is much easier and is better retained when it is carried out to get a specific job done.** For example, I have led workshops in makerspaces where in a few hours, I taught lay people who never used Fusion360 before to design a 3D model that they then carve out of wood using a computer-numeric-controlled (CNC) carver. Many carved their favorite sports team logos. Some of these learners were senior citizens who were not even familiar with computers! (Fig. 24)

If you want to get started with project-based teaching and learning but feel overwhelmed by all the possibilities, as I said before, just start by picking one or two things that seem like fun. Try them out and see how it goes by introspection and by collecting feedback. Then improve and build the curriculum iteratively. I have recently found some excellent resources with very specific suggestions and guidelines for those to whom this approach to teaching seems too chaotic or too different from traditional classroom teaching.

A fantastic resource from the folks at PBLworks is the book, *Setting the Standard for Project Based Learning.*[103] It explains a well thought-out set of "Gold Standards" for Project-Based Learning to help design new curricula and then to determine how effective it is. This will save teachers and school administrators from having to endure many of the hard knocks I and others did in the 2000s decade, as we blundered ahead with little guidance or background.

---

103. John Larmer, John Mergendoller & Suzie Boss, *Setting the Standard for Project Based Learning,* (2015) ASCD.

16. Hope: Alternative Approaches to Teaching

Figure 24. Project-Based Learning works for oldsters, too. I taught a computerized woodworking workshop at the Drogheda Men's Shed in Ireland. This was for retired men who learned enough CAD and CNC in one day to carve these nice crests of their favorite teams. Having them choose whatever they wanted to carve was highly motivating.

Any teacher who is hesitant to adopt project-based teaching and learning will feel confident and ready to begin trying out some projects after reading their book. "Teachers, you can do PBL (Project-Based Learning) with all students, in all grade levels and all subject areas," they say, and I would add, even at the university level. Larmer, Mergendoller and Boss are great cheerleaders for Project-Based Learning: "The more you can turn over to your students, the better….You'll be pleased and maybe even amazed by what your students can do!" I sure was.

Suzie Boss and John Larmer's book, *Project Based Teaching: How to Create Rigorous and Engaging Learning Experiences*[104] contains many

---

104. Suzie Boss and John Larmer, *Project Based Teaching: How to Create Rigorous and Engaging Learning Experiences,* (2018) ASCD.

practical and specific examples and tips to help teachers implement their Gold Standard principles of Project-Based Learning. PBLworks also holds workshops and conferences to allow the uninitiated to be mentored by those who know how to make Project-Based Learning successful.

Based on her experiences teaching teachers how to do Project-Based Learning in their classrooms, Jennifer Pieratt has written two workbooks, one aimed at elementary school teachers, and the other at high school teachers. They are both called *Keep it Real with PBL*,[105] and they link to many of her downloadable web resources to accompany and expand on what is in the books.

A. J. Juliani has written a book about his own successes with cultivating projects in collaboration with his students to make the world a better place. In *The PBL Playbook: A Step-by-Step Guide to Actually Doing Project-Based Learning*,[106] he described his own learning process about motivating his students, and gave many specific suggestions for how to make Project-Based Learning work for you. He also collected stories of many other successful teachers who have incorporated real-world learning projects into their curriculum.

There are many technology-driven advances available for teachers to modernize their curriculum. As mentioned in the **Embrace Technology** section (p. 208), flipped classrooms and massive open online courses are enabled by easy video recording of lectures. There are micro-social networks like Piazza. I think the most transformative technologies, in terms of motivating students to love learning, are the tools that make it easy for them to create lasting works that can be easily shared with the entire world. This can be via an existing platform like Wikipedia, YouTube, Instructables.com or DIY.org. Students can create their own web pages or entire blogs themselves. All of these options make it easy for both teachers and students to come up with and share exciting projects, regardless of which subjects are being covered.

Edge Future Learning is a progressive initiative in Great Britain to begin to fill the widening gap between what secondary school graduates are prepared for and what modern UK industry needs. The Edge Foundation is reforming education in England by focusing on three key principles:

- **Make learning relevant to real life.** Break down subject

---

105. Jennifer Pieratt, *Keep it Real with PBL: A Practical Guide for Planning Project-Based Learning,* Elementary and secondary school editions (2019, 2020) Corwin.
106. A. J. Juliani, *The PBL Playbook: A Step-by-Step Guide to Actually Doing Project-Based Learning,* (2019) Write Nerdy.

boundaries and teach through a real-world lens.

- **Develop transferable skills.** Equip young people with the skills they need for further study, life and work.
- **Involve employers and the community.** Engage local employers and the community in developing the future plan for the school or college and in curriculum delivery.

They have taken the best of what is working at progressive schools across the UK, Finland and the US, and partnered with Ford Next Generation Learning to implement a bold strategy for reforming schools and teaching. Member schools get funding to hire a full-time community/industry liaison to make sure the projects the students do are well connected to the Real World. The students and teachers report in YouTube videos[107] that it is working — they are excited and engaged, and remember what they learned while doing interdisciplinary real-world projects. I think it is a great idea to have a staff member whose sole job is to make the connections to the community and industry. However, I also feel that this task should be done at least in part by the students themselves. To put effort into establishing links to the Real World is a wonderful educational experience, and I have seen students get very excited and motivated by the connections they make themselves.

These few recommendations are limited to those I have come across recently, near the end of writing this book. We seem to have hit upon many of the same effective solutions for motivating students to love learning. I am sure there are many more good resources out there, and that more are being created all the time. To keep up to date, I find that listening to podcasts that focus on progressive teaching is helpful. I highly recommend the *Cult of Pedagogy* podcast[108] and blog, by Jennifer Gonzalez, the *Getting Smart* podcast and blog,[109] and the *Mind/Shift* podcast from Ki Sung and Katrina Schwartz at National Public Radio.[110]

---

107. Edge Future Learning at the Edge Foundation, North East region of England: https://www.youtube.com/watch?v=jhc1XeWTnSY
108. https://www.cultofpedagogy.com/category/podcast/
109. https://www.gettingsmart.com/categories/series/podcasts/
110. https://podcasts.apple.com/podcast/id1078765985

CHAPTER 17

Conclusion

Unfortunately, despite sharing Harry's surname, I don't have a magic wand. I am only a muggle. I was not as successful at motivating administrators and colleagues to change teaching as I was at motivating students to love learning. From reading about many successful advances in teaching approaches, as mentioned in the last section, it seems that effective change in education comes from the bottom up, one progressive and adventurous teacher at a time. When administrators and parents see teachers doing things that work, and children who are thriving, they take notice and are likely to provide the resources to spread new ideas and methods.

Each of us must not be bashful in letting others know about our successes. Spurred on by my students' positive comments, I gathered up my real-world curriculum in 2010 into a looseleaf binder for Georgia Tech's Center for Enhancement of Teaching and Learning. I met with the director, Dr. Donna Llewellyn, to explain to her what I had been doing in my classes, to give her the binder, and to ask how I could begin to share these ideas with my colleagues. She invited me to take part in some of their workshops, leading discussions about real-world teaching and how it motivates students.

I would like to say that my ideas spread like wildfire. Unfortunately, as mentioned at the beginning, there are few incentives at research universities for professors to improve their teaching. Teaching workshops are often voluntary and difficult for professors to squeeze into a busy schedule of mentoring grad students, writing grants, writing papers, going to conferences, sitting on various committees, and teaching classes. Even for those who love teaching like I do, it takes immense effort to postpone other responsibilities, tear yourself away from the daily routine and go to a teaching workshop.

Departmental retreats where I presented my ideas on teaching were better attended because they were mandatory. But again the uptake and implementation of my ideas were low because my colleagues believed it would require some extra effort added to an already hectic schedule. I failed to emphasize why this is the wrong way to view things (see **Chapter 13**, **Too much effort?**, p. 203).

Since then, the education landscape has changed substantially for the better. More and more progressive teachers are getting the message and trying out new ideas to enhance student engagement and learning. At my BME department, Prof. Joe Le Doux won funding from the Kern Family Foundation to develop an **entrepreneurial mindset** curriculum whose goal is to empower students to become "agents of change." The program includes story-driven learning. Students are taught how to put their ideas, goals and accomplishments into understandable, brief stories. These stories could be used to build public support or to solicit funding from investors, for example, if they want to start a new enterprise.

My friend and colleague in Georgia Tech's Mechanical Engineering department, Prof. Craig Forest, has been instrumental in bringing students into the Real World in a number of ways. He was integral in getting the *Invention Studio* started (the student-run makerspace, p. 12), as well as the *InVenture Prize* TV contest (p. 199) for potential entrepreneurs at Georgia Tech. Craig has helped to catalyze the creation of many new startup companies by students with CREATE-X, an initiative backed by an anonymous donation of $35M. He leads the initiative's *Make* section, geared toward developing prototyping skills, in a *Learn-Make-Launch* sequence of entrepreneurial programs. The CREATE-X Startup Launch summer accelerator program[111] is a follow-on from the *Capstone Design Expo* described in Senior Design (p. 198). Design teams of recently graduated students who are accepted into the program are given resources, coaching, and legal advice to form a startup company. This eases their transition from being university students with a good idea, to being successful businesses poised to change the world for the better.

***

This is not the end of the story, but just the beginning! Progressive and creative teachers like you can transform learning at all levels into something that students love and look forward to. Imagine schools full of highly motivated students who can't wait to get to work on their projects, and who continually improve the Real World. Imagine a world where all young people are valued as capable contributors to society.

---

111. https://create-x.gatech.edu/about

Things I Did Differently Than Most Professors

- **Solicited student feedback continually throughout the year, not just at the end:**
  - Asked, "How am I doing? What is most interesting to you?"
  - Asked for brainstorming lists during the lecture.
  - Gave many raise-your-hand-if surveys.
  - Asked a student by name to answer a speculative question.
  - Used clicker quizzes as surveys, too.
  - Collected non-anonymous course feedback via exam questions.
- **Continually improved:**
  - My courses were a Work-in-Progress — all suggestions for improvement were taken seriously.
- **Used many examples and analogies:**
  - Tailored lectures to students' interests (as suggested by the index cards from the first day, or questions they asked).
- **Learned every single student's name, even in classes of over 100 students:**
  - Filmed each student saying their name and something they are interested in or why they took this class, to get to know them. Collected index cards with their profile and interests.
- **Encouraged frequent questions and discussions. "No question is too dumb to ask" policy:**
  - Held Q&A "office hours" right after class.
  - Moved it out of the lecture hall to a more comfortable area,

like the atrium or outside.

- **Taught that Science is not about Truth:**
  - Science is to get some job done.
  - In applied science, engineering and medicine, we go with something if it works, even with incomplete understanding.
- **De-emphasized the textbook and facts:**
  - In the future, you will instantly be able to look up any facts, so no need to memorize most of them. Plus, many "facts" will be overturned at some point.
  - Had students learn just enough facts to be critical, conversant and curious about a topic.
- **Tried to be humble about my area of expertise:**
  - We probably only know 2% of how the brain works. I know even less.
- **Required class attendance.**
- **Used clicker quizzes at the beginning of each lecture to encourage students to be on-time and to take roll.**
- **Did not grade on a curve. Every student can get an A.**
- **Had about a dozen guest lecturers per semester and attended those classes myself.**
- **Gave my students real-world assignments that left enduring benefits for the public. Students would:**
  - write an article for Wikipedia.
  - choose and read a book and write a review on Amazon.com.
  - interview an expert orally.
  - go to public lectures by scientists about their latest research.
  - design and carry out a cutting-edge experiment and collect potentially publishable data.
  - create a YouTube video to explain a scientific paper to lay

people.
- **Kept changing and updating the subject matter of lectures every single semester.**
- **Had students sometimes grade each other, or use the Real World to grade them:**
  - Wikipedia article editing.
  - Amazon book reviews.
- **Had students give written and oral feedback to each other.**
- **Made tests that were often evaluated by my students as "Fun" or "A learning experience."**
- **Didn't allow screens or other distractions in class.**
- **Created very detailed class schedules so students could plan their efforts with regard to other responsibilities.**
- **Gave students a variety of ways to do well in the class:**
  - De-emphasized exam scores.
  - Provided many extra credit opportunities.
- **Taught students that "The process is more important than the outcome."**
- **Included projects that involved making new things, software, data analyses, etc:**
  - Not well pretested by me or previous students.
  - High chance of failure is OK and is the norm in the Real World.
- **Encouraged learning from failure and did not grade them down if their experiments failed.**
- **Gave students plenty of scope for coming up with their own tasks:**
  - Choosing their own book, writing an article of their choice for Wikipedia, watching talks by scientists of their choosing, and coming up with new ideas for extra credit.

- **Encouraged group efforts:**
    - Many activities were done as a small, student-selected group, with them deciding on the separate responsibilities of each member.
- **Coached useful life skills unrelated to the specifics of the course material:**
    - Interviewing, reviewing, presenting, ranking peers, editing, reading scientific papers, etc.
- **Involved my students with scientific conferences in the Real World:**
    - Got funding for my students to attend a major scientific conference.
    - Had my students determine what I visited and saw at a major scientific conference.
- **Used peer pressure to keep every member of a team on-task:**
    - Their shared notebooks had to describe what they did and what their teammates did.
    - Students discussed self- and peer-evaluations in a group, several times per semester.

Take-home Messages

- *Motivation is at the root of all learning.*
- *To learn is intrinsically rewarding and should be fun.*
- *Understanding some of the brain mechanisms of motivation and learning is helpful for teachers.*
- *Student excitement in the medium-to-high range optimizes attention and learning.*
- *Social interactions are the strongest motivators.*
- *Real-world impact greatly enhances motivation.*
- *Children can and should be active contributors to society.*
- *Know your students. Let them know you.*
- *Control and ownership by the students are powerful motivators.*
- *Any difficult task can be made easier by breaking it down into sub-tasks.*
- *Make your rules and boundaries clear to your students and stick to them.*
- *Keep getting feedback and keep adjusting your methods and curricula.*
- *Keep giving feedback to students and let them help each other.*
- *Every single student is smart in some ways and can learn and improve the world if they are motivated.*

Epilogue

Education After Covid-19

As I write this (October 2020), the world is still reeling from the pandemic caused by the coronavirus, SARS-CoV-2. Most people are still getting used to a new pandemic life where interpersonal interactions must be carefully limited to prevent the spread of disease. Instruction at home by parents or remote teachers is the new norm. There is much discussion about how education will change as a result of this and other potential pandemics. We all hope effective vaccines and treatments will be developed so that we can all get back to our normal pre-COVID-19 lives.

I doubt things will ever quite go back to how they were, and that is not necessarily a bad thing. I see this pandemic as a good excuse to move toward the kinds of real-world learning experiences I advocate. Already, I have heard about many dedicated and creative teachers and parents taking up the challenge of doing all of their instruction online, and re-thinking what is important in education. New tools and open online resources are being created.[112] New ways to structure a learning experience are being tested out. Teachers and students are also quickly becoming adept at using pre-existing online tools. Many online tools and resources are international and freely available.

Therefore, I am very optimistic that this crisis will help modernize education and bring disparate cultures together in ways most students, teachers and parents would not have considered otherwise. Perhaps the COVID-19 pandemic will merely serve to accelerate trends in education that were already well in progress, such as the profusion of useful and free educational videos and courses on YouTube, and distance learning that gets students from faraway regions talking and working together on shared projects.

Many (but by no means all) of my favorite types of projects involve hands-on learning and group interactions. These will be more difficult to implement as long as we are worried about casual transmission of diseases. But not impossible! I spent my scientific career culturing neural cells in petri dishes. Neurons do not multiply *in vitro* as do other cell types, and they have little or no immune system. Therefore, it is extremely easy to kill them accidentally with just one bacterium or mold spore. Nevertheless, our lab

---

112. https://en.wikipedia.org/wiki/Open_educational_resources

managed to keep primary neural cell cultures alive for well over a year[113] by using the right equipment (masks, gloves, laminar flow hoods, sealed culture dishes, autoclaves, etc.) and strictly following sterility protocols. Surgeons do this all the time, too.

In my maker life, I routinely wear personal protective equipment for hours on end, to protect me from loud noises, sawdust, chemical vapors, sharp blades, and flying sparks. No one in the lab, the operating room or the makerspace complains about having to take all these precautions, we just do them because they are necessary. I expect that schools will go through a process of devising similar sets of equipment and safety protocols, and we will once again be able to work together in person on exciting and motivating hands-on projects that improve the Real World.

---

113. Potter, S.M., DeMarse, T. B. (2001) *"A new approach to neural cell culture for long-term studies."* J. Neurosci. Methods 110: 17-24.

Recommended Reading, Watching and Listening

- ***What School Could Be: Insights and Inspiration from Teachers Across America***, by Ted Dintersmith (2018) Princeton University Press.
- ***Most Likely to Succeed: Preparing Our Kids for the Innovation Era***, by Tony Wagner and Ted Dintersmith (2015) Scribner. This book accompanies a documentary they made with the same name that is a great example of breaking down disciplinary boundaries in a project-based high school. The film has won no fewer than 24 awards at film festivals. *https://teddintersmith.com/mltsfilm/*
- ***The One World Schoolhouse: Education Reimagined***, by Salman Khan (2012) Twelve.
- ***Setting the Standard for Project Based Learning: A Proven Approach to Rigorous Classroom Instruction***, by John Larmer, John Mergendoller, and Suzie Boss (2015) ASCD.
- ***Project Based Teaching: How to Create Rigorous and Engaging Learning Experiences***, by Suzie Boss with John Larmer (2018) ASCD.
- ***Free to Make: How the Maker Movement is Changing Our Schools, Our Jobs, and Our Minds***, by Dale Dougherty with Ariane Conrad (2016) North Atlantic Books.
- ***Invent to Learn: Making, Tinkering, and Engineering in the Classroom***, by Sylvia Libow Martinez and Gary Stager (2013) Constructing Modern Knowledge Press.
- ***Design, Make, Play: Growing the Next Generation of STEM Innovators***, edited by Margaret Honey and David E. Kanter (2013) Routledge.
- ***Reinvented*** magazine, aimed at getting more girls involved in

STEM fields, with maker projects and inspiring stories about successful women engineers and scientists.

- *HackSpace, Elektor, Servo, Nuts and Volts*, and *Make:* maker magazines full of projects with connected online content.

- *Keep it Real with PBL: A Practical Guide for Planning Project-Based Learning,* two workbooks by Jennifer Pieratt for either elementary or secondary school teachers with specific lesson plans and advice for implementing project-based learning (2019, 2020) Corwin.

- *The PBL Playbook: A Step-by-Step Guide to Actually Doing Project-Based Learning, a book by* A. J. Juliani that includes many inspiring examples of real-world projects (2019) Write Nerdy.

- *Brain Rules: 12 Principles for Surviving and Thriving at Work, Home, and School,* 2nd Edition by John Medina (2014) Pear Press.

- *FAB: The Coming Revolution on Your Desktop — From Personal Computers to Personal Fabrication,* describes the *How to Make (almost) Anything* course that started the FabLab movement, by Neil Gershenfeld (2005) Basic Books.

- *Cult of Pedagogy,* a website, blog and podcast by Jennifer Gonzalez, which have many useful resources for teachers, including a book that explains how to use technology to enhance teaching. *https://www.cultofpedagogy.com/*

- *GettingSmart.com* is committed to accelerating the future of teaching, leading and learning. They produce a wide-ranging podcast on new approaches to teaching. Their blog by the Getting Smart team, and many guest authors, is well organized by topic.

- *PBLworks.org*, formerly, The Buck Institute for Education, provides project-based learning workshops, curricula, and resources for K-12 teachers.

- *Edutopia.org*, website of the George Lucas Educational Foundation, shines a light on what works in K-12 education.

- *Stem Learning* *https://www.stem.org.uk/* and *Edge Future Learning* *https://www.edge.co.uk/edge-future-learning*, two initiatives to reform education in the UK to make it more relevant to and integrated with the modern world.

- ***The MindShift Podcast*** on National Public Radio. Ki Sung and Katrina Schwartz host interviews and discussions about innovations in education that are shaping how kids learn. *https://www.npr.org/podcasts/464615685/mind-shift-podcast.*

Acknowledgments

Thanks to

Dad (Philip D. Potter), for teaching me how to be curious, for instilling in me a love for science, engineering, and making, and for always patiently answering my dumb questions.

Mom (Mary Spears), for teaching me how to be creative and rebellious.

My loving and supportive siblings, for always being my friends, teaching me many useful skills and sharing their wisdom.

Scott Eliason, for our enduring friendship and many stimulating conversations.

My teachers, especially Bob Barnes, for first exposing me to real-world teaching and learning.

UCSD (undergrad): Dana Wolinsky, for encouraging me to take up teaching; Barbara Sawrey, for my first and only course in teaching, How be a Chemistry TA.

UCI (grad school): My mentors and advisor: Brett Johnson, Joseph Najbauer, Cindy Woo, Dana Aswad.

Caltech mentors (postdoc): Jerry Pine and Scott Fraser.

Georgia Tech Problem-Based Learning leaders: Wendy Newstetter and Barbara Fasse.

Lori Critz and all the librarians at Georgia Tech.

Georgia Tech Center for Enhancement of Teaching and Learning (CETL): Joyce Weinsheimer and Donna Llewellyn.

My Georgia Tech and Emory colleagues: Nael McCarty, Steve DeWeerth, Rob Butera, Lena Ting, Ravi Bellamkonda, Michelle LaPlaca, Bob Lee, Chris Rozell, Garrett Stanley, Shawn Hochman, Richard Nichols, Joe Le Doux, Essi Behravesh, and

James Raines.

My collaborators, especially Bob Gross, Pete Wenner and Beth Buffalo, Emory professors who co-advised some of my grad students.

My many administrative assistants and support staff at Caltech and Georgia Tech.

My lab's funders, especially the Center for Behavioral Neuroscience, the Coulter Foundation, the National Institutes of Health, and the National Science Foundation.

My BME department chairs, Don Giddens, Larry McIntire, Ravi Bellamkonda, and Susan Margulies, for letting me do what I want and for their vision to make this department shared between Emory University and Georgia Tech into a truly great biomedical research and teaching machine.

The many students, technicians and postdocs who worked in my lab (Fig. 25).

My guest lecturers.

My TAs.

Readers of drafts of this book, especially Michael Chorost, Richard Pelletier, Scott Eliason, Richard Millwood and Nancy Pine.

My interviewees: Sandra Brown-Potter, Aidan Smyth, Becky Searls, Jennifer Reid, Sunny Bains, Joe Le Doux, Craig Forest, and Elyse Watkins.

My former students, for all the great feedback they gave me to help me improve.

My darling wife, Máiréad Reid, who supports me always and who helped edit this book.

My NaNoWriMo Municipal Liaison, Grace Tierney and writing friends.

Jimmy Wales for creating Wikipedia and the Wikimedia Foundation. Thanks also to the thousands of Wikipedians who have made it the most comprehensive and useful encyclopedia ever.

Tim Berners-Lee for inventing the World Wide Web, changing the Internet into something useful for everyone.

Sergey Brin and Larry Page, for striving to make all the world's information easily and freely accessible, and enabling anyone to be a teacher on YouTube.

Figure 25. Potter Lab research group, circa 2012. I thank my research group and everyone in the Laboratory for Neuroengineering at Georgia Tech & Emory University's Department of Biomedical Engineering. You can meet all my previous lab members and download our papers at my research website, https://potterlab.gatech.edu. Photo by Michelle Mancini.

INDEX

2
2-photon microscope x, 53-55, 55-56, 228
21st Century Skills (meta-skills) x, 12, 20, 22, 24, 27, 30, 34-37, 43, 47, 51, 57-58, 72, 90, 92, 157-58, 163, 169, 172, 192, 194, 196, 207, 222, 235, 246

3
3D molecular models 41-42

A
Absences 186
Academia 10
Accomplishments 73, 80, 84-85, 92-93, 212, 230
Active learning ix, 72, 72, 121, 123-40
Addictions 80-81, 91, 123
ADHD 75
Administrators 3, 203, 207, 230, 241
Adrenalin 64, 69
Advisor 44, 46-47
Agency ix-xii, 102, 149, 235
Alumni survey 16, 165, 169, 206-7
Amazon.com 92, 165-68, 244
Analog electronics 45-46
Analogies 51, 101, 133, 243
Anger 64, 69
Animal models 62
Anonymity 159, 163-64, 166, 169, 207-8
Antenna engineering 39
Ant-proof Candy Dish 13
Anxiety 71-72, 99, 141
Aphasia 101

Appendix material box:6, box:18-19, box:61, box:63-65, box:69-70, box:75-76, box:78-79, box:124-25, 138, 162, 166, box:168-69, box:179-80
Apple II 40-41
Apprenticeships 87, 89, 231-33
Arduino 40
Art 27, 222
Assessments 141, 172
Associations 24, 78, 118-19, 121, 133, 225
Asymptotic learning 88-89, 137
Atlanta 9, 13, 89-90, 142
Attendance 153, 244
Attention 26, 75, 77-81, 84, 112
Attention Deficit Hyperactivity Disorder 75
Audio-Visual (A/V) systems 130
Authentic project 46, 85-86, 108, 109, 145, 155, 163-65, 169, 178, 226, 238
Autonomy 54-55, 103, 178, 192. See also Control
Autos 33, 47-52
Awards 5, 93, 188
Axion Biosciences 189
Axon ix

B
Baja Bug 48, 50-51
Bakkum, Douglas 28
Barnes, Bob 33-34, 226, 255
Basal ganglia 78-79
Belford, Dr. Gary 132
Bell curve 98, 151

Belonging 94
Ben-Ary, Guy 28
Benkeser, Paul 22
Berners-Lee, Sir Tim 92, 171
Biochemistry 42, 47, 187
Biology 228
Biomedical Engineering 4, 165, 178, 195
Biomedical research 54
Bipolar disease 39
Blind spots 124
Blogs 238
Blushing 99
Bodily signals ix, 78, 80
Body language 100
Book reading 166, 170
Book reviews 166-67
Boredom 71, 84, 126, 129, 189, 223-24, 226
Boss, Suzie 236
Bost, Franklin 198
Boundaries 119
Bower, Prof. Jim 107
Brain-Computer Interfaces 5
Brain Damage 75
Brain mechanisms 247
Brains 17-26
Brainstorming 104, 133, 243
Brain training 145
Breaking down difficult tasks 40, 54, 74, 82, 156, 161, 165, 191, 195, 236, 247
Brosnan, Sarah 96
Brown-Potter, Sandra 34, 125, 255-56
Brumfield, John 21
Buck Institute for Education 235-36
Butera, Prof. Rob 177
Bytes 160

C

CAD and CAM 10-11, 237

Calculus 40
California Institute of Technology 9, 41, 52, 85, 103, 107
California Polytechnic State Universities 231
Calming 74
Caltech 9, 41, 52, 85, 103, 107
Caltech Pre-college Science Initiative 107
Capstone Design Expo 199, 242
Caratti, John 38
Caring about students 117-18, 178, 215, 247
Car repairs 48-52
Cars 33, 47-52
Center for Advanced Brain Imaging 182
Center for Behavioral Neuroscience 55
Center for Enhancement of Teaching and Learning 25, 208, 241
Cerebellum 78-79
CETL 25, 208, 241
Charity walks 145, 147
Cheating 95, 97, 142, 150, 185, 207
Checkpoints 80. See also Monitoring progress
Chemistry 42, 228
Children as contributors to society 86, 235, 247
Chorost, Dr. Michael 180, 256
Chromatography 43-44
Circuit 43-44
Clarity of rules or structure 96, 119, 139, 149, 153, 247
Classroom 229
Classroom lighting 131
Clickers (student response system) 153, 208
Client 86, 198

Clueless and overwhelmed feeling 80, 192, 195, 236
Cochlear implants 116, 180, 182
Coding 10-11, 38, 40, 57, 179, 191
Cognitive Science 62
Collaboration 81, 92, 94, 106, 144, 183, 185-86, 194-95, 198, 203, 235, 246
College-bound 84-85, 232, 234
Comfort zone, out of one's 34, 37, 122
Committee of Ten 223
Common Core standards 235
Communication 100, 129, 186, 215, 235
Community college 232
Community engagement 86, 239
Community/industry liaison 239
Comparing 97. See also Peer pressure
Competition 90, 98, 185, 195
Compliments 85, 91, 94-95, 186, 204, 207, 211
Computer-Aided Design (CAD) 236
Computer-Numeric-Controlled (CNC) 236
Computers 38, 40, 209
Computer support 132
Conferences 143, 246
Confidence 24, 29, 34, 48-49, 80-81, 85, 90, 98-100, 127
Confocal microscope 54
Conformity 102
Connections 24, 78, 118-19, 121, 133, 225
Conscious processing 77-79
Constructive Comments Only rule 196, 212
Control 102, 146, 150, 166, 171, 189, 195, 224, 239, 247. See also Autonomy

Conversations 90, 244
Cookbook lab 47, 177-78, 187, 189, 198. See also Toy project or problem
Cortex ix, 63, 101
Course and Instructor Opinion Survey (CIOS) 205
Courses I taught 15-26
Covering the material 120
COVID-19 249
Crafts 30
CREATE-X 242
Creativity 28, 30, 104, 163, 222, 225
Creese, Prof. Ian 186
Crista Smyth 28, 255
Critical feedback 215
Critical thinking 90, 171
Critz, Lori 159, 170, 255
Csíkszentmihályi, Mihály 80
Cult of Pedagogy 239
Cultural transmission of knowledge 101
Curiosity 112, 121, 136, 165

D

Dad 29-30, 33, 38-41, 51-52, 121, 226
Data analysis 180, 214
de Bono, Edward 222
Debriefing 92, 194, 211. See also Reinforcement, reflecting & reviewing to remember
Deep Brain Stimulation 137
Deep Space Network 39
Deisseroth, Dr. Karl 181
Del Giorno, Allie 213
Delinquents 35
DeMarse, Dr. Thomas 28
Demotivators 96, 102, 140, 151, 215, 224, 234
Dependability 96
Depression 39

Descartes 61
Design of experiments and projects 179, 189, 191, 214, 235, 244-45. See also Control
de Waal, Frans 96
DeWeerth, Prof. Steve 177, 255
Dewey Decimal System 135
Differentiated learning ix, 223
Difficulty 73
Digital electronics 45-46
Dintersmith, Ted 223, 234
Disability services 102
Discussion-oriented lectures 113, 120-22, 124, 150, 172
Disgust 136
Disruptive behaviors 72
Dissertation 43-44, 47, 187
Distractions 72, 75, 77, 80, 84, 93, 106, 130, 199, 210, 245
Dolphin brain 62
Dopamine ix, 63, 65, 68, 76-77, 85, 91, 187
Doubts about Project-Based Learning 26
Dougherty, Dale 11
Driftwood art 28
Driving 79, 131
Drugs 137, 139
Dualism 61
Duncan, Dr. Dan 40
Dweck, Carol 223
Dyslexia 145

E

Echos and reverberation 132
Edge Future Learning 238
Editing 160
Educational technology 210
Edutopia.org 204
EEG x, 183
Effort 6, 79-80, 93-94, 117, 203, 209

Electroencephalogram x, 183. See also EEG
Electronics 10, 43, 228
Elephant brain 62
Eliason, Scott 33, 83, 255
Embarrassment 94, 97, 99, 215
Embodied Cultured Networks 28
Emory University 4, 25, 142, 181, 195
Emotional content 135
Empathy 222
Empowering 206
Endorphins xi, 64-65, 91
Enduring digital artifacts 92
Engagement 95, 112, 117, 129, 131, 144, 164, 190, 204, 210
Enthusiasm 54, 68, 104, 112, 129
Entrepreneurship 233, 242
Epinephrine 64, 69
Episodic memories 135
Estimation 226
Ethics 116, 171
Etiquette 75, 93, 159, 164-65, 171, 186, 215
Every Student Succeeds Act 224
Evolutionary approach to improve schooling 4-5, 92, 165, 203, 236
Evolution of neural circuits 101
Excitement 41, 68-70, 73, 82, 93, 99, 122, 131, 167, 172, 229, 232, 247
Executive functions ix, 63, 75, 77
Expeditionary Learning (EL) 234
Exploratorium 126
Explorer One 39
Extra credit 141, 245
Extrinsic rewards ix, 188, 211
Extroversion 36, 38
Eye contact 100

F

FabLab 11

Face-to-face communication 101, 215
Facilitation in PBL 90, 193-94, 196
Factoids 109, 112, 224, 232, 244
Failure 33, 45, 108, 180, 183, 185, 191-92, 193, 198, 203-4, 212, 214, 216, 245
Fairness 95-96
Fasse, Dr. Barbara 21, 255
Father 29-30, 33, 38-41, 51-52, 121, 226
Fear 64, 99, 136
Fear of missing out 95
Feedback from students 5, 128, 196, 201, 204, 205-6, 208, 213, 217, 243, 247
Feedback to students 58, 79-80, 82, 86, 161, 165, 168, 172, 186, 209, 211, 247
Field trips 182
Fight or flight system xii, 64, 99, 136
Final exam 151-52, 206
Flash cards 117, 243
Flexible schedules 89-90, 149, 206
Flipped classrooms ix, 209, 238
Flow 79-80, 82-84
Flowers, Mary 132
Focused attention 77, 82, 192
Ford Next Generation Learning 239
Forest, Prof. Craig 12, 242
Fraser, Prof. Scott E. 53, 53, 85, 132, 177, 255
Frontal lobes 63, 75
Frustration 80, 82, 189, 191, 226
Fun 108, 122-23
Functional art 29-30, 32
Functional Magnetic Resonance Imaging 182
Furniture 130, 132
Fusion360 236

G

Gage, Phineas 75
Gamblen, Phil 28
Gap year 37-38
Gaze direction 100
Gear, Alice "Mamie" (grandmother) 34, 48
Georgia Institute of Technology 4, 9, 9, 25, 142, 195, 208, 231, 241, 257
Georgia Tech 4, 9, 9, 25, 142, 195, 208, 231, 241, 257
Germany 232
Gershenfeld, Prof. Neil 11, 184
Getting-to-know-you exercise 95, 117
Github 183
Glossary ix, 25
Goldilocks Tasks 79
Gold Standards 236, 238
Gonzalez, Jennifer 239
Google 95, 134, 175, 184
Google Docs 183
Google News 134
Google Scholar 161, 171
Gordon Prize 22-23
Grading 84, 97, 150, 152, 162, 167, 183, 185, 211, 230, 244-45
Grad School 46, 178, 191
Graduate (Grad) students 55, 115, 132, 178, 186
Grandmother 34, 48
Green Fluorescent Protein 54
Grit 178, 185, 222
Grocery store 34, 37
Group-mates 94, 96-97
Group activities 81, 92, 94, 106, 144, 183, 185-86, 194-95, 198, 203, 235, 246
Growth mindset 26, 217, 223, 247
G Suite 184

Guest lecturers 113, 149, 180, 195, 198, 244
Gumby's train 5

H
Habits 79
Hackathons 71-72
Hands-on learning 47, 191-92, 213, 225, 228, 250
Hang gliding 33, 50, 82-83
Happiness 84-85
Harry Potter 241
Helpers 204
Helping others 94
Hess, Prof. Ellen 187
High-Performance Liquid Chromatography 43-44
High-bandwidth interaction 101, 133
Hippocampus 133, 135
Hiring 54
HM 134
Hofstadter, Prof. Douglas 133
HP-9000 41
HPLC 43-44
Human brain 62, 65
Human uniqueness 62, 65, 78, 100-101, 222
Humiliation 94, 215
Humor 122, 144
Hybrid Neural Microsystems. See NeuroEngineering Fundamentals
Hybrots 28
Hyperactivity 75, 204

I
Illiteracy 36
Imagining 106
Impossible tasks 80, 104, 191
Impulsive behavior 75, 77
Incentives 230
Incremental assessment 86
Index cards 117, 243
Industry job 43

Innate skills 62-63, 93, 101, 106
Inquiry-based teaching and learning 107, 194
Insecurity 81
Instincts 62-63, 93, 101, 106
Intelligences 221-22
Interaction 92, 95, 113, 122, 210
Interactive museums 126
Interdisciplinary learning 4, 225, 227-28, 235, 238
Interoception ix, 78, 80
Interviews 73-74, 86, 156-57, 244
Intrinsic rewards & motivation ix, 24, 41, 80, 85, 106, 188, 192, 211, 247
Introduction to Neuroscience 15-26, 109
Invention Studio 12, 12, 199, 242
Inventiveness 222
InVenture Prize 199, 242
IQ test 221
Ireland 10, 237
Isolated silos of learning 227
Iterative refinement 179, 213

J
Jalopies 47-49
Jet Propulsion Laboratory 38-39
Johnson, Dr. Brett 46, 255
Johnson, Steven 222
Johnson, Steven M. 222
Josephson, Prof. Bob 43
Journal articles 129, 156, 170-71, 187, 195
Journal clubs 171
JPL 38-39
Juliani, A. J. 238
Juvenile delinquents 35

K
Kelco R&D 42
Kennedy, Dr. Phil 181
Khan, Salman 89, 223, 228

Khan Academy 89
Kinesthesia 78
Kudos 85, 91, 94-95, 186, 204, 207, 211

L
Lab benches 132
Labeling of students 221
Lab notebooks 179, 183, 185-87, 211, 246
Laboratory for Neuroengineering 9, 19, 257
Larmer, John 236
Lasers 55, 228
Lateral thinking 222
Leadership 94
Learning circuitry 63
Learning curve x, 72, 73, 87-88
Learning from failure 33, 45, 108, 180, 183, 185, 191-92, 193, 198, 203-4, 212, 214, 216, 245
Lecture halls 131
Lectures 111
Le Doux, Prof. Joe 22, 242, 255
LeMoncheck, John 40
Levitating Candy Dish 13
Librarians 159, 170, 255
Library 133, 135, 170
Library research 86
Lighting 131
Links 24, 118, 133
Literature searching 161, 171
Llewellyn, Dr. Donna 241, 255
Locus coeruleus 64

M
Macintosh 38, 41
Magic wand 230
Maker Faire 11-14
Maker magazines 133
Maker Movement x, 10
Maker sabbatical 14
Makerspaces x, 11-14, 132-33, 236

Making 10
Mamelak, Dr. Adam 55
Mamie (Alice Gear) 34, 48
Manic depression 39
Mastery x, 89, 233
Materialism 61-62
Mathematics 225-26, 235
Mating instincts xii, 35-36, 65, 93, 123
McCarty, Prof. Nael 15, 115, 255
MEA 52, 179
MEART 28
Median vs. mean filters 227
Medical school 115
Medina, John 136
Memory 133
Mentors 53, 85, 103, 107, 177, 186, 188, 228, 233
Mergendoller, Dr. John 236
Merzenich, Dr. Michael 145
Meta-skills x, 12, 20, 22, 24, 27, 30, 34-37, 43, 47, 51, 57-58, 72, 90, 92, 157-58, 163, 169, 172, 192, 194, 196, 207, 222, 235, 246
Micro-Electrode Arrays 52, 179
Microprocessors 40
Microscopes 52-54
Mind maps 104-5, 194
Mindshift 239
Mnemonics 24, 118, 133. See also Associations
Moldable xi, 65, 77, 225
Molloy, Dr. Tony 187
Mom 27
Money 37, 84-85, 97-98, 150. See also Extrinsic rewards
Monitoring progress 79-80, 82, 185, 209
Monkeys 96
MOOCs 208, 238
Moore-Jackson, Prof. Melody 183

Mother 27
Motivation 5, 67-69, 72, 73, 93-94, 96, 102, 108, 113, 145, 151, 164, 183, 186, 203, 228-29, 239, 247
Movement 72, 125. See also Active learning
MPLSM x, 53-55, 55-56, 228
Multi-Electrode Array 52, 179
Multiphoton Laser-Scanning Microscope x, 53-55, 55, 228. See also 2-photon microscope
Myers-Briggs personality types 216
Myths 137-38

N

Name learning 117, 153, 243
NASA 38-39
National Science Foundation 177-78, 204
NCLB 11, 224, 230, 232
Negative reinforcement 215
Nervous breakdown 39
Nervousness 99
Neural engineering 18
Neural interfaces 181
Neurobiology 61, 67
Neuroeng. Fun. 18, 55, 57, 104, 177-78, 183, 185, 189-92, 211, 216-17
Neuroengineering 18, 116, 180, 213
NeuroEngineering Fundamentals 18, 55, 57, 104, 177-78, 183, 185, 189-92, 211, 216-17
Neuroethics 116
Neuromodulators 68, 74, 77, 85, 91-92
Neuron x
Neuroscience 116
Neurotransmitters x, 63, 68, 187
Newsetter, Dr. Wendy 21, 195, 197, 255

No Child Left Behind 11, 224, 230, 232
Noise 132, 186
Nonverbal cues 100
No Question Is Too Dumb To Ask 121-22, 243
Noradrenalin xi, 64-65, 76-77, 136
Noradrenergic system xi, 64
Norepinephrine xi, 64-65, 76-77, 136
Norms 75, 93, 159, 164-65, 171, 186, 215
Northeastern University 231
No Screens Allowed policy 130, 245
Notebooks 179, 183, 185-87, 211, 246
NQITDTA 121-22, 243
Nucleus accumbens 63

O

Office hours 150, 243
Olin College 231
Online learning 89, 249
Online research 86, 171
Opiate system xi, 64-65, 91
Optimal performance 70, 74
Oral interviews 73-74, 86, 156-57, 244
Organizing systems 132
Orienting and protective responses 78
Outward Bound 234
Ownership 54, 102, 179, 235, 247
Oxytocin 65

P

Parasympathetic Nervous System xi, 99
Parents 3, 84-85, 241
Parker, Prof. Ian 43
Parkinson's Disease 137
Pasadena 9
Pascal programming 38

Passion 113, 129
Pawley, Prof. Jim 116
PBL (Problem-Based Learning) xi, 20, 90, 104, 172-73, 193-95, 197-98
PBLworks 235-36
Peer evaluation 212, 245-46
Peer pressure 185-86, 206, 246
Peer review 80, 156, 167, 185, 196, 211, 245
Peers 94, 96-97
Peer-to-peer learning 12, 20-21, 133, 184, 186, 194-95, 208-9, 211
Pep talk 80
Peptides 43-44, 47
Performance 71, 82, 99
Personal connection 120, 140
Personal experiences 29, 120, 140
Personal Protective Equipment 250
PhD thesis 43-44, 47, 187
Phrenology 137
Physical chemistry 227
Physical skills 78
Physics 40
Piazza 208
Pieratt, Jennifer 238
Pine, Prof. Jerome "Jerry" iii, 52, 53, 85, 107-8, 157, 177, 183, 255
Pineal gland 61
Piston, Dr. Dave 128
Plagiarism 142, 184-85
Plasticity xi, 65, 77, 225
Play 79, 106
Podcasts 133, 239
Political correctness 123
Post-doctoral 9, 53, 55
  Postdoc 9, 53, 55
Post-Traumatic Stress Disorder xi, 64
Postural feedback 100
Potter, Harry 241

Potter, Philip D. 29-30, 33, 38-41, 51-52, 121, 226, 255
Potter, Scott 33, 48-49, 255
Potter Lab research 9, 28, 57, 86, 179, 217
Power posing 100
Prefrontal cortex 63, 75-76, 78, 85
Presentation skills 127, 193
Pretending 101, 106
Pride 104
Primary literature 144, 156, 170-71, 187, 195
Problem-Based Learning xi, 20, 90, 104, 172-73, 193-95, 197-98
Problems in PBL class 194
Procrastination 74, 150
Professors 9-10, 38, 46, 117, 137, 205, 233, 241, 243-47
Programming 10-11, 38, 40, 57, 179, 191
Project-Based Learning xi, 26, 58, 103, 132, 183, 227, 231, 234, 236, 238
Proprioception 78
Provisional truths 138-39
Prozac 137
Psychobiology 47, 62, 126, 151
Psychology 61
PTSD xi, 64
Public presentation 172, 198-99, 228, 234, 236, 244
Public speaking 94, 99, 127, 150
Publish or perish 10, 205
Punishment 106
Purdue University 231

Q

Q-bert 40
Quiet students 34, 74, 116, 122
Quizzes 102, 153, 167, 206, 208, 210, 244

R

Radioactivity 44
Rains, James 198, 256
Ramachandran, Prof. V. S. 221
Rankings 168
Rants 221
Rapid Eye Movement sleep 76
Reading, writing and arithmetic 224, 227
Reading papers 129, 156, 170-71, 187, 195
Real World xi, 17, 26
  Real-world curricula 23-24, 34, 46, 85-86, 90, 108, 109, 143, 145, 155, 163-65, 168-69, 178, 181, 203, 226, 238, 244
  Real-world impact 24, 86, 92, 98, 133, 145, 155, 163, 165, 169, 187-88, 190, 198-99, 207, 211, 217, 225, 229, 234-35, 242, 247
  Real-world projects 46, 85-86, 108, 109, 145, 155, 163-65, 169, 178, 226, 238
Recording lectures 208-10
Recursion 39
Reductionism 49, 62
Reflect and review 92, 194, 211. See also Reinforcement, reflecting & reviewing to remember
Reflexive responses 78
Reid, Máiréad 10, 204, 256
Reinforcement, reflecting & reviewing to remember 83, 120, 135, 196
Relaxation 74, 99
REM 76
Remembering names 117, 153, 243
Repetition 83, 120-21, 135, 196
Replay of memories 136
Research by the Potter Lab 9, 28, 57, 86, 179, 217

Research report 86
Respect 94, 119, 122, 139, 206, 230
Responsibility 94-95, 178
Reward system ix, 85
  Reward circuits ix, 68, 85, 234
  Reward nuclei ix, 63, 85
Roberts, Prof. John D. (Jack) 41
Robotics 98, 227
Robotron: 2084 80-81
Rolston, Dr. John 81
Roving nomad 38, 49
Rubric xi, 97, 162, 196-97, 211
Rules 119, 132, 139, 150, 153. See also Clarity of rules or structure

S

Sabbatical 10, 233
Safety 95
Sandbox 161-62
Sandra Brown-Potter 34, 125, 255-56
Scaffolding xi, 58, 68, 103-4, 180, 189, 191, 194, 209, 217, 235
Scarf Lady 37
Schooling 223
Schwartz, Katrina 239
Science 137, 139, 244
Science, Technology, Engineering and Math xi, 126
Science fairs 29-30, 229
Science museums 126
Scientific Learning Corporation 145
Scientific method 47, 51
Scotoma 124
Scott Potter 33, 48-49, 255
Scripted projects 47, 177-78, 187, 189, 198
Searls, Becky 235, 256
Selective Serotonin Re-uptake Inhibitor 137
Self-confidence 24, 29, 34, 48-49, 80-81, 85, 90, 98-100, 127

Self image 81
Self-paced learning 80, 89-90, 209, 229
Senior Design 86, 198-99, 242
Setting expectations 118, 153
Sex xii, 35-36, 65, 93, 123
SFN 143
Shaded Boxes (appendices) box:6, box:18-19, box:61, box:63-65, box:69-70, box:75-76, box:78-79, box:124-25, 138, 162, 166, box:168-69, box:179-80
Shame 165
Shock 136
Shop classes 30, 224
Silent Barrage 28-29
Skadal, Dan 82
Ski Club 35
Slack 183
Slackers 186
Smartphones 77, 130, 144, 210
Smyth, Crista 28, 255
Social engineering 131
Social interactions 92-93, 106, 171, 247
Society for Neuroscience 143
Software 38, 184, 210, 227, 249
Soldering 192
Spacecraft 39
Spanish 235
Spears, Mary (mother) 27
Special needs 119
Spoken and written language 101
Spreadsheet 42
SSRI 137
Standardized testing 25, 120, 172
Stanford University 231
Startup companies 198-99, 229, 242
Status 93, 97, 100
STEAM 126
Steampunk xi, 12

Steep learning curve x, 88
STEM xi, 126
Stick-to-itiveness 178, 185, 222
Stories 29, 120, 140
Stress 71-72
Stubbornness 82
Stubs in Wikipedia xi, 156, 161
Student-driven learning 47
Stuttering 99
Sub-goals 40, 54, 74, 82, 156, 161, 165, 191, 195, 236, 247
Subconscious mental processes 224, 226, 228
Subcortical brain structures 79
Subroutines 40
Success 204
Suction 138
Summer projects 56-57, 82
Sung, Ki 239
Surprise 64, 74, 106, 121
Survey questions 206, 208, 243
Sweating 99
Switzerland 232
Syllabus 140, 149, 151, 245
SymbioticA 28
Sympathetic Nervous System xii, 64, 68-69, 99, 136
Symphony of Science 130
Synapse xii
Synthesizer 40-41, 45-46

T

TA xii, 47, 73-74, 121, 126-27, 151, 177, 185, 191-92, 207
Taking ownership 54, 102, 179, 235, 247
Taking roll 150, 208
Teaching assistant xii, 47, 73-74, 121, 126-27, 151, 177, 185, 191-92, 207
Teaching environment 130
Teaching philosophies 219

Teaching to the test 224
Teams 95-96, 132, 175, 185, 199, 212
Teamwork 81, 92, 94, 106, 144, 183, 185-86, 194-95, 198, 203, 213-14, 222, 236, 246
Technology 131, 208, 210
TED talks 96, 129, 142
Telephone, value of 157, 178, 180
Tests 151-52, 206
Textbooks 17, 139, 150, 153, 170, 244
Think-pair-share 116
Three Rs xii, 224
Threshold 72
Time management 149
Ting, Prof. Lena 177, 255
Tinkering 106, 108, 126
Toastmasters speaking clubs 121, 127
Tools 132
Topic choice 156, 161-62
Toy project or problem xii, 25-26, 198. See also Cookbook lab
TPLSM x, 53-55, 55, 228
Tracking students 221
Trade schools 231, 233
Traditional schooling 223
Trepanation 18
Truth 137, 139, 244
Two-way communication 113, 158, 160, 180, 209

U
UCI 4, 43, 62
UCSD 4, 25, 38, 127, 186-87
Unconscious circuits 78
Undergraduate research 114, 186, 188, 214
Universities emphasizing Project-Based Learning 231
University of California, Irvine 4, 43, 62
University of California, San Diego 4, 25, 38, 127, 186-87
Unschooling xii, 106
Usernames on Wikipedia 164. See also Anonymity

V
Vagabond 38, 49
Vasopressin 65
Ventral tegmental area 63
Vestibular senses 78
Videoconferencing 101, 133
Video games 80-81, 91, 123
Visualizing and imagining 47, 83, 85
Vocational schools 231, 233
Voice and choice xii, 103, 124, 132, 189, 235
VTA 63
VW Beetle 48, 50-51

W
Wasting children's lives 229
Waterloo, University of 231
Welding 30, 33
Wetware 29
Whiteboards 133
  Whiteboard rooms 20-21
White matter 63
Why? 3, 22, 24, 84, 112, 120, 175, 234
Wife 10, 204, 256
Wikipedia 92, 144, 155-56, 158, 244, 256
  Wiki Education Dashboard 159, 165
  Wikipedia Ambassadors 159
  Wikipedians 159
  Wikipedia Sandbox 161-62
Woodworking 10-11, 30, 236-37
Worcester Polytechnic Institute 231
Work 79

Work-study 36-37
Workshops 241
World Wide Web 92
Writing skills 47, 86, 155

X
XNTJ 216

Y
Yerkes-Dodson Curve 70, 71, 79, 82, 84, 99, 106, 122, 126, 129
YouTube 92, 129, 144, 229, 239, 244, 249

Z
Zeller-Townson, Riley 28
Zucke 38

www.ingramcontent.com/pod-product-compliance
Lightning Source LLC
Chambersburg PA
CBHW041956080526
44588CB00021B/2759